Artistic Circles

DESIGN & DECORATION IN THE AESTHETIC MOVEMENT

ARTISTIC CIRCLES

DESIGN & DECORATION IN THE AESTHETIC MOVEMENT

Charlotte Gere

V&A PUBLISHING

V&A Publishing acknowledge support from The Paul Mellon Centre for Studies in British Art with this publication

First published by
V&A Publishing, 2010

V&A Publishing
Victoria and Albert Museum
South Kensington
London SW7 2RL

Distributed in North America
by Harry N. Abrams, Inc., New York

ISBN 978 1 85177 602 3
Library of Congress Control Number
2009932299

10 9 8 7 6 5 4 3 2 1
2013 2012 2011 2010

Designer: Trevor Vincent
Editor: Johanna Stephenson

Printed in China

Front jacket:

Nellie (Ellen) Epps, *The 'Dutch'
Room in Townshend House* (detail),
oil painting, signed and dated 1873
(Private Collection)

Back jacket: (clockwise from top left):

Dish or charger in Iznik taste by J.-T. Deck,
formerly belonging to F. Leighton
(V&A: 226–1896)

Morris & Co., *Forest*, woven wool tapestry
designed by P. Webb and H. Dearle, 1887
(V&A: T.111–1926)

E. Burne-Jones, detail of the decorated
panel from an upright piano, 1860
(V&A: W.43–1926)

R. Norman Shaw, elevation of
studio-house for Marcus Stone, 1875
(Royal Academy of Arts)

E. Burne-Jones, *Chaucer Asleep*,
stained-glass panel, 1864
(V&A: 774–1864)

C.L. Dodgson, portrait photograph
of Dante Gabriel Rossetti, 1863
(V&A: 814–1928)

Decorator's specimen panel showing
dado, filling and frieze, about 1875
(V&A: E.656–1953)

P. Webb, panel of glass quarries,
possibly from Morris's Red House, 1859
(V&A: C.63–1979)

E. Burne-Jones, *The Garden of the
Hesperides*, gilded gesso panel, 1880–1
(V&A: Circ.525–1953)

J.W. Mackail, photograph of
William Morris aged 23, 1857

Frontispiece:

J.J.J. Tissot, *The Bunch of Lilacs*
(detail), oil painting, about 1875
(Private Collection)

Endpapers:

Morris, Marshall, Faulkner & Co.,
Pomegranate or *Fruit*, wallpaper designed by
William Morris, 1866. Woodblock printing
by Jeffrey & Co., from a contemporary
sample book (V&A: E.447-1919)

V&A

V&A Publishing
Victoria and Albert Museum
South Kensington
London SW7 2RL
www.vandabooks.com

Contents

Dante G. Rossetti, deceased.)

16, CHEYNE WALK, CHELSEA.

CATALOGUE OF THE

HOUSEHOLD & DECORATIVE FURNITURE

OF THE ABOVE WELL-KNOWN ARTIST AND ~~LITTERATEUR~~, *Poet*

Comprising—In addition to the Furniture of the usual description, A LARGE AND
RARE COLLECTION, among which will be found

A CARVED EBONY BEDSTEAD,

Reputed to have been the Property of Queen Mary;

A CARVED FOUR-POST BEDSTEAD,

Once the Property of the late Artist's Father, with Tapestry Hangings,

A LARGE VARIETY OF CABINETS IN CARVED OAK,

Also of the Painted Furniture Period and other styles;

COUCHES UPHOLSTERED IN GREEN STAMPED VELVET,

With Paintings in Panels by Dante G. Rossetti;

CHIPPENDALE CHAIRS & BOOKCASES,

A SMALL COLLECTION OF OIL PAINTINGS,

WATER-COLOR DRAWINGS & STUDIES OF CONSIDERABLE MERIT,

Old and Valuable Library of Books,

Many of particular interest to Artists, a portion being **Presentation Copies**;
Linen, China, Glass, Plated Goods, Ornamental Items, and Effects,

Which will be Sold by Auction, by Messrs.

T. G. WHARTON, MARTIN & CO.,

Upon the Premises,

16, CHEYNE WALK, CHELSEA,

On Wednesday, July 5th, 1882, and Two following Days,

At One o'clock punctually each day, (by direction of the Executor.)

There will be a Private View on the Saturday preceding the Sale, with admission by
Orders only, (which may be had of the Auctioneers.)   The Public View will be on the 3rd
and 4th July, and Catalogues, price One Shilling each, may be obtained on the Premises,
and of Messrs. T. G. WHARTON, MARTIN and Co., Auctioneers and Estate Agents,

1. BASINGHALL STREET, CITY, E.C.

Foreword

The money for the amazing houses that Victorian artists built for themselves came from pictures. Whether dark, garish or wispy in their great golden frames, those pictures can seem incomprehensible to schoolchildren visiting museums nowadays, and we can't blame them for laughing, since many critics and academics (who should know better) have grown up laughing at them too. The rest of us can enjoy them, just as my father Jeremy did, without shame – so much that he became fascinated by the artists, their models, mistresses, critics, patrons and the writers that provided their subjects, and felt compelled to discover them in their houses, to peer into their private lives and write about them, and even to emulate their lifestyles. The art of the period was the key, but the world it unlocked was his dream. Charlotte Gere's book explores this world with the privileged access of a well-informed chambermaid, for behind the public text of a painting, whether from Tennyson or Dickens, there is often a private story, one thoroughly human with passion, fear and frailty. It is impossible to look at Victorian pictures in the same way after reading about the lives of those who painted them.

Charlotte Gere has drawn in part on research and notes that my father made for a similar but never realised purpose. My mother and I are happy that his work has borne fruit in this rather different way, for this book is not only the back story to the pictures, it is the larger story of how a small coterie of artists and designers shaped the way in we which we all live today. It sets out the topography of artistic London, so we can see who were neighbours, in and out of each others' houses (or in Watts's case just 'in' – he went for dinner with the Prinseps at Little Holland House and stayed for twenty years). There is talent: the Pre-Raphaelites and the next generation of Aesthetic painters were uniquely skilled and original. There is beauty: the 'Three Graces', Greek 'stunners', the cousins Aglaia Coronio, Marie Zambaco and Marie Spartali. There is money, because Victorian artists commanded huge prices and paid their architect-designer friends lavishly to showcase them, and all this talent, beauty and money worked closely together in a hothouse dynamic. The houses of Victorian artists became the acme of taste throughout the world, and we are still living with their legacy.

Rupert Maas

1. Sale catalogue of the contents of Rossetti's house, T.G. Wharton, 5 July 1882, p.1

Preface and Acknowledgements

*In biographical and historical interest no pictures surpass views
of the interiors of artists' studios*

Frederic George Stephens, *Artists at Home* (London, 1884), p.1

The aim of this book is to track the influence of artists' houses and households on eclecticism in house decoration. The Art or Aesthetic Movement emerged as archaeologically correct Medievalism loosened its grip on art and design. Examining artists' houses and their eclectic contents forces us to stretch the conventional ideas that have grown up around the 'Aesthetic' concept, with its focus on chinamania and the rediscovered art of Japan. The revived Renaissance (a concept so alien to our notion of the progress of design and decoration towards modernism that it is largely ignored in design histories), with its panoply of carving and tapestry-covered walls, is much in evidence and the designs of Thomas Sheraton, meticulously reproduced, feature in many schemes. Many artists, even most, were in some sense collectors. Albert Moore had no interest in creating an elegant home, but he owned very fine ceramics and textiles, which he used as accessories in his paintings. Artists were pioneers in collecting antiques as a way of furnishing, as is shown in the sale catalogues following the deaths of many of the house-owners. Some were way in advance of their time in their knowledge and connoisseurship, as is demonstrated by the numbers of their possessions now in museums and art galleries around the country.

When delineating the elusive character of the Aesthetic Movement it is hard to avoid straying into the realms of Reformed Gothic on the one hand and the Arts and Crafts Movement on the other. The purpose-built artist's studio-house can be seen as a bridge between these linked developments, a distinct architectural type – red-brick, free-form and self-consciously historicist – which with its contents was hugely influential on the development of house-decoration and the rapidly expanding market in art-furniture and decorative artefacts. Artists' houses exemplify a central tenet of the Aesthetic Movement: the creation of a work of art in which every element is essential to the whole.

Using a social and cultural approach, the evidence reveals how such a specific architectural genre could shape the position in society of the occupants of the new houses and influence the development of domestic building for an emerging class, that of the educated middle-class professional. Elevated from their former artisan status, artists appeared to enjoy an exciting and notably free-spirited way of life. The highly visible studio-houses of eminent artists – owing to the ritual of 'Show Sunday' when members of the public were admitted to view the paintings destined for the annual Royal Academy exhibition – were part of the public presentation of the artist and a social site of some significance. The typically eclectic mix of antique and exotic items promoted the artist as possessor of taste and expertise. Journalistic coverage of artists' homes and lives is extraordinarily rich and informative. They were a gift to the newly proliferating illustrated periodicals. Frederic Leighton's studio-house and Lawrence Alma-Tadema's two North London houses were reported widely and in detail. In fact it is a moot point as to which of them had the greater coverage; in any event, it was remarkable for any class of professional person, particularly in the social climate of the age. Coming to the subject through evaluation of the surviving visual evidence throws up many new perspectives on the influence of this architectural genre on the Victorian public. Its legacy is still with us, in the picturesque development of London and its suburbs. In another sense, the freedom to use self-expression has left a beneficial mark on the decoration of houses ever since.

2. J.J.J. Tissot, *Hide and Seek*, oil painting, about 1877 (National Gallery of Art, Washington, DC)

9

The book has been a long time in the making and as a result many people to whom I am indebted will have no recollection of either the occasions or their insights that contributed to its evolution. My first thoughts on the subject were tentatively examined and abandoned more than ten years ago in conversations with the late Jeremy Maas, pioneer dealer in Victorian painting, who was himself thinking of a study on the same lines. He was a Victorian art scholar of such daunting stature that there could be no question of invading territory to which he had a prior claim, but when he heard of the imminent publication of Giles Walkley's *Artists' Houses in London, 1764–1914*, he reluctantly put the idea aside on the grounds that no publisher would want to bring out a book with such a similar topic. It was impossible to convince him that the two books would be quite dissimilar; while it was immediately apparent that Walkley had dealt exhaustively with his subject, a socio-economic study of the artist's house in its relation to the workings of the art world on Jeremy's lines had obvious possibilities and a broader scope. Through the generosity of his widow Antonia and his son Rupert I was privileged after his death to see the material he had collected, and the resulting book would have offered uniquely valuable insights into the artistic way of life and its finances. As the biographer of his predecessor Ernest Gambart, Jeremy understood intimately and from personal experience the role of those much-neglected catalysts, the dealers and gallery-owners, who have only a small role in the present work.

It is hard to be worthy of the guidance he unwittingly gave me in those conversations. Few people are equipped with the narrative flair and knowledge to tell the full story of Victorian art in the way that he was – his rapport with Victorian artists was quite uncanny; it seemed as if he must have known them personally – but through other projects I have gained some sort of perspective on the mid-Victorian world of design and interior decoration, and it is that aspect more than the financial side that this study explores. The formation of this world and its many coteries and social groupings was investigated in three ground-breaking books by William Gaunt, written during and just after the Second World War, a time when Victorian art had barely emerged from the disrepute into which it had fallen at the turn of the twentieth century. Much has come to light since then, particularly about the decoration and contents of the houses, disclosing a subject worthy of closer investigation, as Mark Girouard recognized in his pioneering articles for *Country Life* in 1972. Meanwhile, in her biography of George du Maurier published in 1969, Leonée Ormond placed the artist and his satires in context with a chapter on the Aesthetic Movement.

Also in 1969 Elizabeth Aslin published *The Aesthetic Movement: Prelude to Art Nouveau*, pinpointing the moment when design reform took a definite direction that would culminate in Art Nouveau and the Arts and Crafts Movement. The cultural homogeneity of the Aesthetic Movement was demonstrated by Mark Girouard in his survey of the 'Queen Anne' style in architecture, *Sweetness and Light*, published in 1977. As he remarked, the architects of the Movement saw themselves as artists, free to indulge their eclecticism. The personalities who created this world were vividly brought to life by Jeremy Maas in 1984 when he published his collection of artists' photographs, *The Victorian Art World in Photographs*. From 1980 the lives of many members of the Aesthetic circle were uncovered from their diaries and papers in a series of biographical studies by Virginia Surtees, among them G.P. Boyce, George Howard, Sir Coutts and Lady Lindsay and Ford Madox Brown. My debt to our conversations over the years is unquantifiable. In the 1990s the artist's position in Victorian culture was the subject of important contributions from Paula Gillett and Caroline Dakers. Much more recently, in 1996, Dianne Sachko Macleod included an illuminating examination of the Aesthetic Movement in relation to Victorian middle-class collecting. In 2006 Deborah Cohen's *Household Gods: The British and their Possessions* examined the important role of the Evangelical Movement on the attitudes of home-owners to their possessions

– and in a broader sense to consumerism – with its seep into instruction manuals on 'artistic' interior decoration and their relationship to the emerging consumer culture. Most recently, Judith Neiswander has looked at the political slant behind writings on domestic decoration in *The Cosmopolitan Interior, Liberalism and the Victorian Home, 1870–1914.*

For me, the world of A.W.N. Pugin, High Victorian Design and the counterbalancing movement for design reform began to unfold when I worked for the first time with the late Clive Wainwright in 1979, on an exhibition about Morris & Co. at the Fine Art Society. We were both to be involved in an exhibition organized by Marc Bascou (another valued mentor) in Paris, quirkily titled 'Gothic Revival, Architecture et arts décoratifs de l'Angleterre victorienne', held at the Musée d'Orsay in 1999. As a colleague Clive was generous to a fault in sharing his knowledge, and his pioneering work on the early collecting activities of the South Kensington Museum underpins my understanding of that institution. John Physick and Anthony Burton have both written on the history of the Victoria and Albert Museum, and I am indebted to their expertise in providing the basis on which to connect the development of the Museum, and its role as a high-profile showcase, within the emerging culture of the artist's house. For many years Frederic Leighton was involved with the South Kensington Museum in a number of capacities, both contributing to its decoration and as an advisor. Comparing his collection with that of the Museum as it existed when he and his architect George Aitchison were extending and equipping Leighton House sheds interesting light on the effect of the Museum's collecting policies in directing artistic taste. The significance of the Arab Hall as an artistic collaboration, and the way in which it uses a wide range of decorative materials, links it with experiments in decorating the South Kensington Museum. William Morris and Lawrence Alma-Tadema acted, like Leighton, as 'Art Referees' to the Museum.

In 1981 the Fine Art Society exhibition 'Architect-Designers, Pugin to Mackintosh' marked the start for me of a long collaboration with Michael Whiteway. That exhibition uncovered the intricately connected world of architecture and product design and was the starting point for our book on the same topic. Narrowing the focus to a single designer, Christopher Dresser, provided an opportunity to look at the relationship between domestic design and its producers and purveyors, as well as the chance to benefit from the expertise in this field of Harry Lyons, Stuart Durant, Judy Rudoe and David A. Taylor. Most recently, my discussions with Michael concerning the Aesthetic Movement have been of inestimable value in the context of the present book. Helen Dunstan of Haslam & Whiteway has been endlessly patient with queries, particularly about Morris & Co. wallpapers. David Taylor has been indefatigable in pursuing the comic history of the dado and most generous in sharing his findings.

In 1982 Jane Abdy involved me in the research towards her unusual project to look at the artistic milieu and lives of the late Victorian 'Souls' group, fellow travellers on the Aesthetic route, particularly in the matter of artistic dress. This resulted in an exhibition at her West End gallery and a book, published in 1984. An outcome of this focus on dress was an invitation from George Breeze and Sophia Wilson to contribute an essay on Victorian artists and Aesthetic dress to the catalogue of the exhibition on Pre-Raphaelite and artistic dress at the Cheltenham Art Gallery in 1996. Since then my other valued mentor on the subject has been Edwina Erhman (now at the V&A), with whom I had worked on the jewellery collection in the Museum of London.

The international importance of the Aesthetic Movement and its transatlantic development was revealed in 1986 with 'In Pursuit of Beauty: Americans and the Aesthetic Movement', the exhibition at the Metropolitan Museum in New York. The catalogue, with its succession of distinguished essays, put the subject on a new footing of grandeur and artistic ambition. The artistic roots of the Aesthetic interior, however, were still revealed to be unequivocally British. When in 1999 Dr

Caroline Dakers followed her groundbreaking 'biography of a house' (a minutely detailed account of the building of a key Souls house, 'Clouds' in Wiltshire) with her in-depth examination of the Holland Park Circle, she revealed a microcosm of one particular aspect of Victorian artistic social grouping. In the wake of that publication Dr Dakers floated a proposal to study George Aitchison and his patrons. To this I owe invaluable insights from a series of long meetings with her and Charles Hind of the RIBA Library (now at the V&A) and Martin Levy of Blairman's. In a long association with Leighton House Museum, I have had the benefit of unstinting help from Daniel Robbins, Reena Suleman and Alan Kirwan. Conversations with Louise Campbell of Warwick University greatly enhanced my understanding of Leighton's decorative intentions. Anne Anderson has generously shared her discoveries about Leighton's possessions, gleaned from the catalogue of the sale after his death. Leighton House provides a unique opportunity to examine in detail an important 'Aesthetic' architectural and decorative phenomenon. It was among the earliest of these artistic landmarks that determined the character of the developing suburb of Kensington, and also the picturesque style of late nineteenth-century Chelsea and Hampstead. The guidebooks to Leighton House and Linley Sambourne House are exemplary in the information they provide about the Victorian artist's domestic milieu. Shirley Nicholson, whose book about the Sambourne family, taken from Marion Sambourne's diaries, presents an artistic household in illuminating domestic detail, has been unfailingly generous with her knowledge.

In 1989 I was given an opportunity to pursue the history of nineteenth-century decoration and design on a more ample scale with a book on interior decoration. The research provided evidence of diversity and personal intervention in decorative choices that cannot be underestimated, a point that has obvious relevance to artists' houses. This publication inspired Charles Ryskamp, then Director of the Frick Collection in New York, to organize an exhibition of interior views in 1992. An historian by training, Charles was rigorous in requiring social background for the production of these works. A direct outcome of the Frick project was 'House Proud', an exhibition with accompanying publication celebrating the 2008 gift to the Cooper-Hewitt National Design Museum by Eugene Thaw of a collection of more than eighty watercolours of interiors.

My association with the Fine Art Society culminated in 2001 with an account of its 125-year history, a task that opened up a fruitful vista of the Victorian art world. Throughout my 30 years of working with the Society I have benefited probably much more than they have from talking to Andrew Mackintosh Patrick, Peyton Skipwith, Simon Edsor and Max Donnelly. I dragged Donato Esposito, then in the Department of Prints and Drawings at the British Museum, into looking at the print-dealing side of the FAS activities with me, and he has continued to send me interesting information and images related to artists' houses.

In 2000, centenary year of Oscar Wilde's death, David Dewing, Director of the Geffrye Museum, invited me to collaborate on an exhibition examining Wilde's relationship with the Aesthetic Movement. Both exhibition and accompanying book set Wilde's decorating activities in the context of artists' houses and artistic taste. This was followed in 2003 with the first of four exhibitions examining the way in which the domestic spaces of the urban middle-class are depicted in art, for which I was again guest-curator. While not directly concerned with the art world or the Aesthetic Movement, the pictures of several artists' rooms in the exhibitions represented a chance to think about their connection with urban development and middle-class values. Looking at the paintings from a socio-economic point of view had direct relevance for the angle taken by the present book; this new approach provoked intense discussions with the Geffrye Museum team, Christine Lalumia, Eleanor John and Judith Batalion, from which I gained revealing insights into the evolution of individual decorating modes and strategies.

For Victorian art in general I have had the most generous assistance from Julian Treuherz, former Keeper at the Walker Art Gallery in Liverpool, particularly on the subject of Alma-Tadema and his houses; from Judith Bronkhurst on William Holman Hunt; from Martin Beisly and Peter Brown at Christie's; from the late Christopher Wood on paintings of artists' studios; from John Christian, particularly on the subject of Edward Burne-Jones; from Barbara Bryant on G.F. Watts and particularly his Aesthetic portraits; from Richard and Leonée Ormond on Lord Leighton; from Donato Esposito on Edward Poynter and Luke Fildes; as well as unfailing encouragement from Rupert Maas. Clare Broomfield at the National Monuments Record helped far beyond the call of duty with my multiple enquiries about the London artists' houses. Jane Wainwright gave me useful information about the Victorian Society case records. The Local Studies and Reference departments at Kensington and Chelsea and Westminster libraries were endlessly patient with my questions. I am most grateful to Mary Butler, who was the first to express interest in this book, to my daughter Dr Cathy Gere, first reader of the manuscript and to the not-so-anonymous readers at the V&A, all of whose valuable suggestions I acted on.

At V&A Publishing Mark Eastment has been enthusiastic in his support of a book he inherited from his predecessor, Mary Butler; his suggestions for its improved usefulness have been incorporated to its advantage. Johanna Stephenson and Trevor Vincent have both far exceeded their briefs as editor and designer. Trevor and his wife Jacqui ask all the questions that the author, always too close to the subject, needs to address. Frances Ambler and Laura Potter had the difficult task of co-ordinating the illustrations, mediating between my high-flown and expensive ideas and the realities of a budget. We have found ways of working this out, without I hope compromising the end result.

Charlotte Gere

Sir J. E. Millais' House.   Drawn by F. G. Kitton.

3. F.G. KITTON, Sir J.E. Millais's House,
2 Palace Gate, *The Art Annual*, 1885

CHAPTER ONE

Princes of Bohemia

Artists are now brought forward entirely as fashionable objects; to respect them,
to get pleasure from their conversation, is simply not understood.

Prince Pückler-Muskau writing to his wife from Brighton in 1827[1]

4. Sir J.E. Millais, 1st Bt,
Self-portrait, photogravure,
frontispiece, *Life and Letters*, vol. I, 1899

5. G.F. Watts, *Portrait of Frederic Leighton*,
oil painting, 1871 (Leighton House Museum)

When Watts built his studio-house in
Melbury Road, he and Leighton became
close neighbours and saw one another
almost every day.

In 1876 a new feature appeared in London's artistic landscape. Early that year the large Neo-Renaissance palazzo built for John Everett Millais was unveiled in *The Builder* (15 April 1876, p.372), in – appropriately – Palace Gate (pl.3).[2] It was a suitably opulent residence for one of the most successful artists of the day, future baronet and President of the Royal Academy, the latter an intensely anticipated honour to come – but not yet. Millais, founding member of the Pre-Raphaelite Brotherhood and now a renowned portrait painter and Royal Academy favourite, had good reason to believe that he would need a house appropriate to a PRA. In the event it was Frederic Leighton, supreme Olympian, interpreter of the ancient world in aesthetic terms and ultimately a peer of the realm, who was elected President in 1878; he received the customary knighthood at the same time. At the Arts Club Millais congratulated the new President in a spontaneous and generous speech; Leighton, in spite of his privileged upbringing and Continental sophistication, lacked the mental agility to respond in a similar vein. He stuck to his prepared speech, which he had learned by heart and which sounded stilted by comparison. Millais was eventually elected President of the Royal Academy after Leighton's death in 1896, but the honour came too late, when he himself was already mortally ill.

It seems hardly coincidental that in 1876 the *Furniture Gazette* was moved to exclaim: 'There has assuredly never been since the world began an age in which people thought, talked, wrote and spent such inordinate sums of money and hours of time in cultivating and indulging their tastes'.[3] The Millais house was hugely significant, not just in artistic circles where it made a quantitative leap in the architectural ambitions of English artists, but also in re-drawing the social map of London. It pushed boundaries physically as well as socially. Millais had thrown down the gauntlet, challenging his new-rich and, in some cases, aristocratic neighbours with a grander house than had yet been achieved by either Leighton or the Dutch émigré classicist Lawrence Alma-Tadema (future knight and recipient of the Order of Merit, who specialized in the domestic life of the ancient world – Victorians in togas, as we now see it). With hindsight there is inevitability in this social shift, when artists were given titles and were able to break down barriers in Victorian society as a whole. Underpinning this story of the Victorian studios and their owners is a question: would they have been the same without this paradigm shift in the social status of art and its practitioners?

This is not a question for art history alone; it reaches into the heart of Victorian culture. It is about a network of people and their perception of themselves and an environment created from a shared sensibility which turned out to be appealing to the wider artistic milieu. This book is also about the domestic side of the artistic household, about adapting old houses as well as building new ones, about entertaining, shopping and decoration, wallpaper and dresses. By using contemporary images and concentrating on commentary of the time we can see the houses as the Victorians saw them, and try to understand their social and cultural messages. Many – even most – of the houses have been studied individually; what follows is an attempt to trace their mutual dependency and its wider impact on taste.

THE AESTHETIC MOVEMENT AND PUBLIC TASTE

It was more or less a foregone conclusion that the artistic community would have a crucial role to play in the evolution of the Art or Aesthetic Movement, since its raison d'être was the cult of beauty. The Aesthetic Movement, in which the artist's house as an architectural and design innovation played such a key role, was a product of the design reform movement which emerged in the 1840s and grew enormously in influence through the 1850s and 1860s. Coupled with greatly increased confidence in British design and designers, it was the first international design movement to originate in Britain. The Aesthetic Movement can best be understood in the context of debates taking place at a very high level on art and design education in the service of industry. Some of the prime movers in design and educational reform were the Radical Liberal politicians, such as William Ewart MP, whose brief included enabling the widest possible free access to libraries and museums.[4] The tenor of Aesthetic discourse is noticeably liberal – even Liberal in a political sense – with an emphasis on individuality and self-expression, very appealing to the middle-class homemaker struggling to escape outdated conventions. The Reformists' discussions were given urgent impetus by the revelation of serious design defects in the British goods on display at the Great Exhibition of 1851, the first to show the products of 'industry' (in the sense of 'making', a branch of manufacture) worldwide under one roof.[5] The discussions were driven by the need to match competition, particularly from the French with their superior design skills.

One outcome of these debates was the 'South Kensington system', a network of schools of design across the country; the other was the establishment of the first museum of design, the Museum of Ornamental Art (later the South Kensington Museum, known since 1899 as the Victoria and Albert Museum). The result of these initiatives was immediately apparent in the improvement of British submissions to subsequent World's Fairs and the enhanced reputation of British manufacturers abroad. By the time of the second International Exhibition in London in 1862, things had so visibly improved that attempts were already being made to replicate British design initiatives abroad.[6] In the wake of the South Kensington Museum similar institutions opened in Vienna (1864), Berlin (1867), Hamburg (1874), St Petersburg (1876) and so on across the Continent and the United States. The 1862 Exhibition marked a crucial point in the origins of the 'Art' Movement. Arguably, the artist's house with its eclectic decorative aesthetic was a logical conclusion of design reform, in which one of the most significant players was Sir Henry Cole, founding director of the South Kensington Museum. Cole's commercial design venture, 'Felix Summerly's Art-Manufactures', with its pioneering involvement of artist-designers, was the precursor of a network of 'art-furniture' companies – most famously Morris & Co. – supplying the components of an 'Aesthetic' style.

Several powerful forces joined a great assault on public taste, among them the historian Thomas Carlyle; the critic John Ruskin; Prince Albert, husband of the Queen; and Henry Cole, the Prince's immensely able lieutenant in his most ambitious undertaking, the Great Exhibition of 1851. The importance of their separate contributions can hardly be overstated: Carlyle and Ruskin were read with reverence and the Prince had the power and influence to get things done. Cole's relevance here can be judged from his mission to inspire designers and manufacturers and to improve public taste, a direct connection with the development of 'artistic' taste in home design and decoration.[7] The Art Movement – with its outcome, 'Aestheticism' – was a logical development of Reformed Gothic, blended with *japonisme* and a further eclectic range of sources from Ancient Egypt, Moorish Spain, Chinese, Indian and Persian art, and English eighteenth-century styles in various guises, a free style in architecture and domestic decoration.

Ruskin remarked, 'Remember the most beautiful things in the world are the most useless; peacocks and lilies for example'.[8] However, his own assessment of the Aesthetic Movement was wary, even hostile: the absence of moral or religious content, or of a conscious search for uplifting subject matter, he found unsatisfying. In the second volume of *Modern Painters*, written in 1882–3, he referred to the Movement as making art into 'at once the corruption, and the jest, of the vulgar world'. As Tim Hilton explains in his biography of Ruskin, 'The word "jest" is used because Ruskin's knowledge of the new social tendency was derived from reading of *Punch*, in whose cartoons of drawing rooms one discerns schematized paintings of the late Pre-Raphaelite sort. Their languid ladies are obviously drawn in mockery of Burne-Jones's paintings.'[9] The extent of Ruskin's influence on domestic design and decoration is one of the many ironies of the Victorian period. A brief look at his own domestic furnishing and decorating reveals a standard at odds with his impassioned critiques of public taste. When the time came to furnish his married home at 30 Herne Hill, his father, old Mr Ruskin, handed over £2,000 to an interior decorator to equip the house as he thought best. The job was carried out by an undistinguished London firm, Snell of Albemarle Street, which had furnished houses for the Ruskin family over many years. Ruskin was appalled by the modern and vulgar result but Snell's solidly long-lasting furniture was still in use at the end of his life. Arthur Severn, husband of Ruskin's cousin and companion Joan, wrote in a *Memoir* of the great critic:

> *The Professor never cared for the high art movement in furniture and china. He had no taste for such matters. He had never known anything but the heavy well-made mahogany kind of furniture … Anyone coming into his room would have said 'the person who owns this room likes comfort but has no eye for colour'. The Professor would notice a beautiful thing in a room and would certainly be struck if a room was large and stately and furnished with taste, but on the other hand, he wouldn't mind a room in execrable taste so long as there was a comfortable chair to sit in.*[10]

The focus of this volume is on the impact of artists' homes and gardens on the Aesthetic Movement, particularly those among them that attracted publicity in the press or featured in memoirs and letters of the time. Contemporary perceptions and opinion have shaped the selection; artists are included not because of the quality of their work or their place in the Victorian canon, but because their houses were interesting enough to merit recording. The story cuts across hierarchies established by posterity: some of these artists are household names; some belonged to the highest echelons of the establishment (no less than three of them were Presidents of the Royal Academy), as well as to all branches of artistic modernism; some are lesser known. It extends into the world of commercial art and caricature and to the more rarefied milieu of the aesthetic amateurs. The cast-list in full is long; the main protagonists, however, are few: those creative aesthetes and campaigners against the philistines who shaped the development of artistic homes in the 1870s and 1880s. Leaving aside people like shipping magnate Frederick Leyland, to be an Aesthetic patron did not necessarily equate with having aesthetic taste in decoration and furnishing. The Aesthetic Movement is not so much a style as a state of mind or trend, a means of personal expression – Victorian Post-Modernism, in effect, a movement that has itself borrowed extensively from Aestheticism. The notion that every aspect of an architectural scheme should be a work of art was a catalyst for innovation in building design and interior decoration, particularly relevant at a time when ardent design reformers were campaigning against the excesses of mid-nineteenth-century taste.

The artist-protagonists are representative in a wider sense than simply as the owners of houses that fit an 'Aesthetic' profile. They define to a greater or lesser degree the character of the Aesthetic Movement. George Frederic Watts, Millais, Leighton, the American James McNeill Whistler, Dante Gabriel Rossetti, Edward Burne-Jones, Alma-Tadema, Albert Moore, the French émigré James Tissot, and Edward Poynter: these are major players in a new approach to painting. William Morris was the Aesthetic decorator of choice; his legacy is probably the most long-

6. J.J.J. Tissot, 'Mr Frederic Leighton ARA',
Vanity Fair, 2 June 1872

7. G. Aitchison, presentation drawing
for Leighton House Arab Hall,
watercolour, 1879
(Royal Institute of British Architects)

The first design was submitted by
Aitchison on 19 July 1877.

lived at any time before or since. His firm, Morris, Marshall, Faulkner & Co., founded in 1861, provided a focus for the Movement, offering to supply all the elements of the Palace of Art, among them stained glass, painted tiles and mural decoration. It is no accident that the architects most closely identified with the new building style, Philip Webb, William Burges, George Aitchison, Richard Norman Shaw, Edward William Godwin, Robert Edis and Thomas Jeckyll, were all prominent in the Victorian 'Art' Movement. Walter Crane and Kate Greenaway might be said to have invented Aesthetic book illustration. Tissot nailed the essential Aesthete in Leighton for his *Vanity Fair* portrait of 1872, showing a languid figure leaning against a doorway in evening dress, with an over-large floral buttonhole (pl.6).

ARTISTS, STATUS AND VICTORIAN SOCIETY

The Victorian art world was a phenomenon; it expanded and flourished under intense public scrutiny. The story of artists' often ambivalent relations with London Society has a beginning, a middle and an end, from socially shunned outsiders to insiders at the heart of the establishment, and back to being – by choice – outsiders again. From quite unpromising beginnings their stock was raised socially and professionally, indeed it was transformed to an extent that has not since been equalled. The apotheosis came at the end of the nineteenth century, in 1896, when Sir Frederic Leighton, PRA, 1st Baronet, was raised to the peerage as Baron Leighton of Stretton on his deathbed. By an unlikely coincidence the social position of artists had been one of the topics addressed by a government select committee enquiring into the workings of the Royal Academy in 1863, shortly after Leighton had first settled in London. The committee questioned whether an artist was a 'gentlemen' or, because he made art with his own hands – as no gentleman would – an artisan or manual worker. The emergence of the artist as celebrity was not quite so straightforward; it was something more insidious in relation to the shifting structures of the Victorian class system. Bohemia was traded for the entrée into London Society, but it is a measure of how entrenched attitudes still were that this topic was on the agenda as late as 1863; the speed with which it became irrelevant is one of the issues examined here. However, Leighton's peerage in 1896, still a unique distinction for an artist, came as the whole edifice was about to crumble: insider status does not suit the artistic temperament and the opulent lifestyle of the patrician Royal Academicians died out, along with many of its trappings, not long after the turn of the last century. Now the art world has performed a full circle and art and artists are again top news. Even so, the houses built by Victorian Olympians have not been reclaimed; they are rarely owned by practising artists and those that survive are a reminder of a uniquely Victorian trend.

In 1877 Leighton, like Millais, was building: planning a spectacular 'Arab Hall' which would almost double the size of his already celebrated purpose-built studio-house in the Holland Park area of Kensington (pl.7). The scheme prepared by his architect George Aitchison heralds one of the most potent assemblages in the story of the Victorian artist's house, charting the heights of a successful career in terms of building a personal dream. Leighton's was one of the earliest and most unconventional of the purpose-built studio-houses. Begun in 1864, it celebrated his election as an Associate of the Royal Academy.[11] This marking of professional milestones is an important thread in the story of Victorian artists' status and, by extension, tracks the influence of their homes. Leighton's career brought him a house that was an internationally significant example of the genre in its architecture and its eclectic interior. It stands in an artists' quarter developed from scratch in the later nineteenth century, a neighbourhood of noteworthy houses for leading figures in the Victorian pantheon. Less than a hundred years later it was to be threatened with demolition, surviving only by the skin of its teeth, but that is another story, to be unravelled in a later chapter.

Watts, too, was building his first house in 1876, having lived hitherto with indulgent and generous friends; he chose the newly constructed Melbury Road, close to Leighton in Holland Park Road. Marcus Stone and Luke Fildes were also building houses in Melbury Road, designed by Richard Norman Shaw, following one another in quick succession in 1875–8. Norman Shaw's own house in Hampstead was completed in 1876. Also in 1876, Alma-Tadema's remarkable residence, Townshend House in Titchfield Terrace, Regent's Park, severely damaged in an explosion in 1874 on the nearby Regent's Canal, was again ready for occupation in greater glory than before. These splendid houses straddled apparently incompatible social worlds, London's High Society and artistic Bohemia, accommodating the social side of the studio, with the *haute monde* delightedly slumming and the bohemians tasting some of the pleasures of the London Season. They were frequented by patrons and collectors, artistically inclined members of the royal family and High Society as well as a more ramshackle coterie of friends and fellow artists. Apart from the social round, the houses also functioned in the professional lives of their owners, being visited by many hundreds on the informal 'open days' that preceded the opening of the Summer Exhibition at the Royal Academy. This was a genuinely different milieu, offering social benefits to both.

Although they were able to support the artistic ambitions of their prodigy son, the Millais family was not rich. Millais earned his wealth – at the height of his success he enjoyed an income of £30,000 per year – and he indulged himself with a rich man's house; he might have echoed Thomas Carlyle, who wonderingly remarked 'Has paint done all this, Mr Millais?'[12] He chose as architect his friend Philip Hardwick Jr, rather than one of the studio-house specialists such as Norman Shaw or Webb, rising stars in the new genre. Millais bought a large plot of land in an expensive part of the newly developed area of Kensington north of the museums. As one of the most successful English portrait painters of the age, and author of popular and lucrative historical and genre subjects, he had no need to stint on location. The shipping magnate and important collector F.R. Leyland and the aristocratic painter-Aesthete George Howard (later Earl of Carlisle) lived close by. Millais's neighbours were the wealthy professionals and members of the upper-class intelligentsia from among whom his patrons were drawn. The area round Queen's Gate, Prince's Gate and Palace Gate was developing a distinctive artistic character in which houses by Norman Shaw featured prominently.

Like Leighton, Millais eschewed the quaintness that characterized many artists' houses. The front door opened on to a 25-ft-square white marble and mosaic columned hall with a sweeping staircase leading up to a fountain topped by a black marble seal carved by Boehm, the general effect, according to *The Art Annual*, being 'that of a Genoese *palazzo*' (pl.8).[13] By April 1877 the vast 40-ft-long studio had already featured in *The Graphic*. It resembled a grand picture gallery in one of the private palaces of the old aristocracy in Mayfair, and could easily transform into a ballroom; indeed, the particulars of the 1897 sale after Millais's death described it as the 'Studio Picture Gallery or Ballroom'.[14] The studio was praised for its simplicity: 'there are no cunningly devised corners, or galleries, or inglenooks or window seats.'[15] Its likeness to an aristocratic townhouse might seem to challenge the still-wary upper classes who continued to regard artists as superior tradesmen, but Millais's critical and financial success had taken him beyond the confines of the artistic milieu.

When Millais was photographed in his studio by Rupert Potter, father of Beatrix, he was shown reading rather than preparing to paint.[16] Millais and Mr Potter were close friends and, indeed, collaborators, since the artist relied on landscape photographs taken in Scotland by Potter for his backgrounds. Rupert Potter also responded when child models proved too lively as sitters, photographing them in their poses for the artist. Beatrix Potter recorded in her journal an anecdote from her father:

The Hall.   Engraved by J. D. Cooper, from a Drawing by F. G. Kitton.

8. F.G. KITTON, The Hall,
2 Palace Gate, *The Art Annual*, 1885

Mr. Millais is going to paint the portrait of one of the Duchess of Edinburgh's children. The Duchess is staying with Princess Mary, Kensington Palace. Mr Millais went to see her yesterday, doubtless very shy. She offended him greatly. She enquired where his 'rooms' were, evidently doubtful whether a Princess might condescend to come to them. 'My <u>rooms</u> ma'am are in Palace Gate', and he told papa afterwards, with great indignation, he daresay they were much better than hers. He is right proud of his house.[17]

The act of reading could be construed as a mark of cultivated leisure, significant in the construction of a new artistic identity just as the photographs of Millais in Scotland show him in country clothes indulging in gentlemanly sporting activities. As a dedicated sportsman he had a considerable social advantage, allowing him to consort on equal terms with the countrymen among his patrons. Lillie Langtry remarked that 'he affected none of the eccentricity, either in dress or manner, usually ascribed to artists'.[18]

Millais is a contradictory presence in the Aesthetic Movement, in spite of the fact that he pioneered the 'subjectless' genre in painting with *Autumn Leaves* (1855–6; Manchester City Art Galleries), an intensely coloured meditation on transience, shown at the Royal Academy in 1856. It was a bold experiment, breaking the bounds of Pre-Raphaelitism while remaining true to its principles, and one of the first of the defining Aesthetic images, focusing on mood, beauty, atmosphere, referring only obliquely to the uplifting and spiritual qualities demanded by 'high art'. It has a sensual quality of vision, like the late style of Rossetti, an unequivocal Aesthete who entered the fray in 1859 with the sensational *Bocca Baciata* (Museum of Fine Arts, Boston), but the messages of death and decay are there nonetheless. Millais's great prosperity in his later career distanced him from the Pre-Raphaelite companions of his youth. In a photographic portrait by Mayall he seems deliberately dwarfed by the massive chimneypiece in his studio (pl.9). To the left of the fireplace is the great carved cabinet used in one of his most popular historical subjects, *Princess Elizabeth in Prison at St James's* (1879; Royal Holloway College). In a self-fulfilling prophecy, the cupboard itself is now in a grand Elizabethan mansion, Hatfield House in Hertfordshire. In contrast to Leighton's house, an embodiment of Aesthetic values, Millais's palatial mansion was the least typical of the purpose-built studio-houses which form the subject of this book; as one observer remarked it was a house 'into which the Aestheticism of the day does not enter'.[19] Many more studio-houses were to follow, not least Alma-Tadema's last residence, his 'Roman' villa in Grove End Road, St John's Wood. This 'imperial' residence equalled or even out-classed Millais's palazzo.

The alternative to the architect-designed studio-house was to impose the artistic way of life (and somehow to contrive a studio) on an elegant older house. This was the choice of Rossetti and Burne-Jones, just two who took this route. Morris built one of the first studio-houses; after he gave it up he could not afford to build again,

9. J.E. Millais in his studio, photogravure after J.J.E. Mayall for F.G. Stephens, *Artists at Home*, 1884

J.P. Mayall Photo.   London published by Sampson Low Marston Searle & Rivington 188 Fleet St   Park Lane Studio, London

and so lived in three old houses. Artistic taste, across a wide spectrum of apparently differing temperaments, was surprisingly consistent. The result was a distinctive architectural and decorative style, much admired and imitated in certain circles. By the 1870s the artist's studio-house was impossible to ignore; the role of their owners as tastemakers in matters of interior design can be traced forward to the present day and the rise of the professional decorator. The very different life-stories of members of the Pre-Raphaelite Brotherhood and their wider circle exemplify the possible choices and their consequences. As a founding member Millais was seen as an apostate, precipitating the demise of the Brotherhood when he was elected an Associate of the Royal Academy in 1853 and then marrying Ruskin's ex-wife in 1855. His large house in Palace Gate was furnished with an opulence which contrasts strikingly with the Aesthetic Morris-inspired schemes favoured by Rossetti and Burne-Jones and their many imitators. In a curious footnote to their former relationship, Millais acquired from Rossetti a pair of Chinese ebony and mother-of-pearl thrones which had belonged to the 'Giant Chang'.[20]

Images of artists, their houses and studios, fed an apparently insatiable curiosity about art and its practices. In the later nineteenth century artists' houses and their interiors figure conspicuously in the 'interior view' genre, in contrast with the earlier history of watercolours of rooms, principally a medium for recording royal and aristocratic residences. The advent of photography expanded the possibilities of this kind of recording; photographs and even postcards of artists at home were widely circulated, part of the mystique of 'Haunts of Famous Men' popular with the Victorians. The painted images were more private – their small size is often the clue – to be classed as memorials or intimate exchanges. All this invites speculation and interpretation, but the appetite among the general public for details about artists' homes is beyond doubt.

Sir Joshua Reynolds fired the first shot in the long battle to change public recognition of fine art and artists by including a bust of Michelangelo in his 1780 self-portrait (Royal Academy of Arts). As the founding President of the Royal Academy, his knighthood in 1768 had been a defining moment in public perception of the artist's position; but actual acceptance socially lagged far behind. However, by the end of the eighteenth century the position of artists in their relationship with polite society had begun the long process which culminated in the moment in 1896 when Leighton was awarded his barony. This slightly backhanded gesture arrived the evening before his death, with the certainty that he would have no heirs. Leighton's self-portrait, painted in 1880 for the Uffizi Gallery in Florence (almost exactly a century after Reynolds's self-portrait and with deliberate echoes of it), presents a figure of Renaissance magnificence (pl.10). Multiple references linking his position to the great artists of the past – the Parthenon frieze in the background, the Titianesque robe (in fact his doctoral gown from Oxford University) and the half-hidden Royal Academy gold medal – allied to a certain melancholy sensitivity suggest the burden of fame.

From Sir Edwin Landseer onwards Victorian artists benefited from the democratization of the British honours system. Millais was the first artist to be awarded a hereditary honour since Sir Godfrey Kneller in the seventeenth century: he was created a Baronet on the recommendation of Gladstone in 1885. His successor as President of the Royal Academy, Sir Edward Poynter, was awarded his baronetcy in 1902 (he had been knighted on his election as PRA). Leighton, knighted in 1878 when he became PRA, had been offered a baronetcy but declined, pressing the claims of Millais (whose loss of the RA Presidency in 1878 may have weighed somewhat on Leighton's mind) and George Frederic Watts (who also declined). Leighton's baronetcy came in the following year, but he had denied himself the distinction of being the first in Victorian times. Watts, whose life spanned the Victorian era (born in 1817, he died in 1904), twice turned down a baronetcy, settling instead for the Order of Merit, which, unlike Millais and Leighton, he lived to see instituted under Edward VII. Alma-Tadema was

10. FREDERIC LEIGHTON, *Self-portrait*,
oil painting, 1880
(Uffizi Gallery, Florence)

given the Order of Merit when a place became available after Watts's death in
1904. William Holman Hunt likewise was awarded the OM in 1905. In spite of
such conspicuous official endorsement, the often equivocal relationship between
Victorian artists and High Society lingered in certain circles for the greater part
of the nineteenth century.

REPORTING BOHEMIA

A burgeoning Victorian print culture fed the public appetite for stories and
pictures about celebrities and their homes and lives, which was further stimulated
by increasingly sophisticated illustrated periodicals; they in their turn craved fresh
material. A rich legacy survives from this coalition of interests. The extensive
visual record in all its variety and profusion – portraits, self-portraits, architectural
plans and schemes of decoration, interior views, photographs, illustrations and
engravings – is a measure of the importance of artists' houses in the new system
of home-making and consumerism in the nineteenth century.[21] The houses were
a product of a powerful alliance of commerce and art which brought riches and
recognition to those who were successful. If anything is needed to confirm the
importance of purpose-built studio-houses in defining the artist's position in
society, it is the attention paid to them in their own time. The moment, spread

over approximately two decades, when artistic taste headed the most forward-looking trends in architecture and decoration resulted from a major shift in status and prosperity for professional artists. An almost unprecedented situation arose, in which the taste of middle-class professionals who had so recently been regarded as inferior craftsmen or tradesmen, was subjected to minute critical appraisal and emulated by the upper classes. However, as Ruskin remarked, a vein of satire accompanied respectful reporting of the art world. The tension between admiration and mockery is intriguing, particularly since, over and above the crude jokes in papers like *Funny Folks*, quite savage caricature of artists and their world came from insiders. Neither George du Maurier nor Edward Linley Sambourne, the talented *Punch* cartoonists, can entirely escape the label of Aesthete. Alongside Du Maurier's alternative artistic world starring the ineffable Edwin and Angelina and the Cimabue Browns, Linley Sambourne mercilessly guyed artistic notions applied to fashion. His comic drawings, like the famous 'Grecian Bend' poking fun at Aesthetic classicism, were particularly clever in appearing at first glance to be conventional fashion plates.

Meanwhile, 1876 was something of a landmark in the narrative of artists' houses. A London decorator, H.J. Cooper, leading exponent of the Indian style of interior, jumped on to the bandwagon with his manual on *The Art of Furnishing on Rational and Aesthetic Principles*. In fact, 1876 saw the beginning of a spate of decorating advice, including the first of the Revd W.J. Loftie's popular series, 'Art at Home', for Macmillan. His own title was *A Plea for Art in the House*, equating beauty with godliness. Also in 1876 Du Maurier, whose 'chinamania' cartoons for *Punch* and his spoof decorating advice (the title of his imagined volume is 'The House and Home, or, Hints Towards a Grammar of Decorative Art', *Punch*, 21 August 1875, pp.68–9) were already giving the Aesthetic Movement its comic identity, posited a cultural checklist in his 'Intellectual Epicures': The caption reads:

> *Steeped in Aesthetic Culture, and surrounded by artistic wall-papers, blue china, Japanese fans, Mediaeval snuff-boxes, and his favourite periodicals of the eighteenth century, the dilettante De Tomkyns complacently boasts that he never reads a newspaper, and that events of the outer world possess no interest for him whatever.*[22]

As James Laver truly noted, such a forum was effective: 'The invaluable *Punch* … records like a seismograph every tremor in the social atmosphere'.[23] Any new social trend was grist to the satiric mill and through the 1870s and 1880s Du Maurier turned his attention to the Victorian artistic community, inventing a parallel artistic world which he chronicled in a series of comic drawings. He was reporting from the front line, so to speak, among his old comrades, who were now at the heart of artistic London. His victims seem to have taken his barbs with equanimity, even, like Oscar Wilde, revelling in the notoriety of being identified among the cast of characters.

The press played an important part in the aspirations of the Victorians, and it was here that many of the artists' studio-houses were first unveiled to public view. Newly introduced illustrated periodicals encouraged reporting of artists' homes and lives – gossip-mongering to a large extent.[24] Much of the popular new lifestyle journalism was taken up with descriptions of artists' houses and their social activities.[25] Long-running vignettes in the *Magazine of Art* ('Half-hours in the Studios') and the *Art Journal* ('The Round of the Studios') encouraged the idea that it was important to be up to date with artistic activities. In the early 1880s the popular authoress Mrs Haweis discovered a fruitful new direction for her journalism in describing artistic houses. In a series of articles for *The Queen* she depicted minutely and lyrically a succession of remarkable interiors conceived or commissioned by people in the arts. The articles were collected into *Beautiful Houses; Being a Description of Certain Well-Known Artistic Houses* (1882), a vellum-bound book with self-consciously anachronistic initial letters and old-style type employing the obsolete long 's'. The vellum binding suggests a precious old volume.

11. J.J. STEVENSON, The Red House, Bayswater, *Building News*, 18 September 1874

Stevenson's Red House was the precursor of many picturesque red-brick domestic buildings in late 19th-century London.

Her verbal portraits of the houses provided a shopping-list for the artistic style.

It is apparent that in terms of public curiosity the Palaces of Art created by the princes of the Victorian art world rivalled the houses of the aristocracy. Nearly half of the dozen houses described by Mrs Haweis belonged to practising artists.[26] Also featured was the London house of the distinguished patron-collector Alfred Morrison and those of two members of the Sassoon banking family. Reuben Sassoon was a prominent socialite, habitué of the Prince of Wales's 'Marlborough House Set' through their mutual interest in racing; he was known as the Prince's unofficial turf-accountant. J.J. Stevenson's striking example of the new style, Red House in Bayswater (now demolished), which had attracted much attention when it was built in 1870, was also included (pl.11). This distinctive townhouse set a precedent for the many so-called 'Queen Anne' houses for artists – and other 'artistic' clients – which followed in the 1870s.

At this same period the American ethical preacher and quondam journalist the Revd Moncure Daniel Conway flitted from salon to studio, picking up anecdotes for his audience at home, describing decoration and style and reporting on the social life of the intelligentsia. In the same year as the publication of *Beautiful Houses*, he included a great deal of material about artists' houses in articles on 'Decorative Art and Architecture in England' and 'Bedford Park', collected together in a volume entitled *Travels in South Kensington*. In 1883 Maurice B. Adams put together his accounts of 'Artists' Homes' which had appeared as articles in *Building News*; this was followed in 1884 by *Athenaeum* critic F.G. Stephens's defining publication *Artists at Home*, illustrated with portraits by the distinguished photographer J.J.E. Mayall. It shows artists as connoisseurs and men of taste, in studios filled with curious old furniture, Oriental artefacts and *objets d'art*. A series of special volumes dedicated to individual artists at work and at home was issued by *The Art Annual*: the volume for 1884–5 covers Leighton and Millais; in 1886 the subject was Alma-Tadema. The section on the Palace Gate house places great emphasis on its scale and splendour (pl.8). However, even in the seemingly 'real' an element of manipulation could be detected: Stephens was criticized by the *Art Journal* for the sleight-of-hand observable in his photographic portraits.

There is certain repetitiveness in the reporting of artist's houses, with much coverage of Leighton's house, American artist George Henry Boughton's Kensington house and Alma-Tadema's two St John's Wood residences. All three artists were chosen by Mrs Haweis for *Beautiful Houses*. Likewise, the George Howards – he spanned both camps as a landscape artist and patron of the Pre-Raphaelite painters as well as a fringe member of the upper-class intellectual and political coterie known as the 'Souls'– the millionaire Leyland (Whistler's patron who was the owner of the notorious 'Peacock Room') and Constantine Ionides all had houses of great architectural and decorative distinction. These attracted commentary in contemporary art magazines, feeding an appetite for playing the voyeur in the homes of the Aesthetic elite which seems to have been as great as that for actual instruction in decorating. Leyland, like a number of other collectors, admitted visitors to his house, 49 Princes Gate, at weekends when the London Season was over. As the general public gradually became conscious of artistic influence on many aspects of ordinary life, *Punch* started barracking the Aesthetes with Du Maurier's drawings of Aesthetic rooms appearing from 1875. Du Maurier's cartoons, collected into two volumes, significantly entitled 'Society Pictures', provide a running account of the middle-class accommodation of 'artistic' attitudes. The theme, a clash between pretentious artists, their Aesthete patrons and rich philistines, closely reflected the actual situation on the ground.[27]

Satire is an infallible indicator of celebrity. Du Maurier's Aesthetes live in Brompton ('Passionate Brompton'; the Cimabue Browns frequent 'one of the most artistic sets in Brompton and hold all things modern in contempt'[28]) and Kensington and take their attitudes from the artistic Chelsea set, collecting blue-and-white china and decorating with peacocks' feathers. The inhabitants of this

THE CIMABUE BROWNS.

1880.

12. G. DU MAURIER, 'The Cimabue Browns,
Train up the Child', *Punch Almanac*, 1880
(later published in *Society Pictures*,
London 1891, vol.II, p.222)

Antiquated Grandpapa (fresh from Ceylon)
'Now my Darlings, we're going to make a
regular day of it. First we'll go to the Zoo.
Then we'll have a jolly good blow-out at
the Langham Hotel. And then we'll go
and see the pantomime at Drury Lane!'

Master Cimabue
'Thanks awfully, Grandpapa! But we
prefer the National Gallery to the
Zoological Gardens!'

Miss Monna Givronda
'Yes, Grandpapa! – and we would
sooner hear Handel's *Judas Maccabeus*, or
Sebastian Bach's glorious "Passions-Musik",
than any Pantomime, thank you!'

Here Du Maurier has transposed a key
element of Victorian moral instruction
into an Aesthetic context.

largely fictional territory were marked by their 'intensity', their speech being punctuated by odd emphases – 'too utterly utter' was a catchphrase – and to be intense became a hallmark of Aesthetic sensibility. The Cimabue Browns (pl.12), Jellaby Postlethwaite the poet (identified, wrongly according to Du Maurier, with Oscar Wilde), Mr Grigsby, Maudle (another Wildean figure), Peter Pilcox the sculptor, et al., are vainglorious, or dupes, or both. Du Maurier was fascinated by the way the middle classes elected themselves critics of the arts, and much of the humour in his drawings revolves around mutual incomprehension. People adopting artistic dress and attitudes felt superior; their tastes are relentlessly mocked, the 'art' furniture in their rooms, the blue china, Japanese fans and Regency convex mirrors all recur regularly. The women dress 'artistically', their much-ridiculed style derived from late Pre-Raphaelitism and espoused by the Dress Reformers. After his arrival on the London social scene Wilde became a favourite butt; it is sometimes difficult to untangle the real man from the comic character, as Whistler appreciated:

> *Mr Du Maurier and Mr Wilde happening to meet in the rooms where Mr Whistler was holding his first exhibition of Venice etchings, the latter brought the two face to face, and taking each by the arm, inquired: 'I say, which one of you two invented the other, eh?'.*[29]

The young Beatrix Potter, however, detected something sly in Du Maurier's position: in her diary she reports hearing from Carrie Millais that Du Maurier had been spotted 'taking sketches' at a ball given by her father, the painter Millais, in 1884.[30]

SOCIAL AND DOMESTIC LIFE IN ARTISTIC HOUSEHOLDS

Not all successful artists hankered after a place in the upper reaches of the artistic establishment or in society as a whole: Rossetti, Millais's fellow Pre-Raphaelite Brother, revered by both Burne-Jones and Morris when they were young men, spurned honours and public life. In any case, the artistic community was not a single entity but a complex social structure in flux, with its own professional hierarchies. It can perhaps best be seen as a loosely constituted network of like-minded friends who rejected many of the rankings, inequalities and formalities of conventional society. The artists who achieved fame and noteworthy houses displayed markedly differing attitudes to these rewards and their obligations. Leighton, for example, who habitually wore a version of artistic costume, with an unstructured velvet jacket and a loose, flowing silk tie, his abundant hair worn long, nonetheless maintained a certain Olympian distance from Rossetti and his bohemian friends; although they must have met in that social melting pot Little Holland House, they did not frequent one another's houses. Their different social standing meant that although they interacted professionally, they might not connect socially.

The character of patronage broadened: taste reformers were addressing an audience who had never exercised aesthetic judgment before and the artistic milieu offered guidance in many areas such as decoration and dress. The artists' houses with their distinctive style were echoed in the decorative aspirations of the ever-rising middle class, Wilde's bourgeoisie. Among his memorable aphorisms he described artistic consumers as a 'strange mixture of romance and finance'. Victorians used terms like 'bourgeois' and 'bohemian' without defining them very clearly, but much was decided by wealth and access to culture or their lack. On the whole a consensus accepted the *Oxford English Dictionary* definition of the 'bohemian' as

> *a gipsy of society; one who either cuts himself off, or is by his habits cut off, from society for which he is otherwise fitted; especially an artist, literary man, or actor, who leads a free, vagabond, or irregular life, not being particular as to the society he frequents, and despising conventionalities generally.*

As an insider, Joseph Comyns Carr, director of the influential Grosvenor Gallery (pivotal rendezvous and centre of Aesthetic exhibiting), had a certain authority in demarcating these sensitive territorial boundaries. His anecdotal memoirs of the Victorian art world, *Coasting Bohemia* (1914), range across the spectrum of the admired artists of the day – he has little to say of the popular genre painters whose work filled the walls of the Academy every year.[31] Mark Girouard highlighted the distinction in his *Country Life* articles, denoting the Chelsea houses as 'bohemian'.[32]

The divisions in Bohemia resolved themselves into the very different society of Chelsea and the more stately gatherings in Holland Park. Rossetti and Whistler conducted their own versions of social life without reference to conventional expectations. They liked to frequent seedy taverns and dubious places of entertainment where the temptations included ratting and nude tableaux. Whistler was irresistibly drawn to Cremorne Pleasure Gardens on the Thames waterfront, by the time of his arrival in Chelsea a notorious haunt of prostitutes. For an entrance fee of a shilling visitors could dine in intimate supper-boxes before viewing firework displays and dancing and, as often as not, witnessing fights between the women. The gardens were plagued by drunkenness and brawling and other improprieties, but they inspired some of Whistler's most beautiful works. They were closed in 1877, ironically just as a great influx of artists was turning Chelsea into London's Latin Quarter.

Rossetti remained within the artistic coterie of his youth and kept faith with bohemian life. Burne-Jones and Morris evolved a socially evasive lifestyle that satisfied their artistic commitments and their dedication to the cult of beauty. However, Burne-Jones's intense class-consciousness comes across in Comyns

Carr's memoirs. An invitation Carr received reads: 'We shall meet on Sunday at lunch. Georgie is away, but Margaret [Burne-Jones's daughter] dispenses lower middle-class hospitality with a finish and calm which would not disgrace a higher social position'.[33] Burne-Jones spent anguished days trying to decide whether to accept his baronetcy in 1894 and ultimately did so only on behalf of his son. He felt unable to reveal his new status to the socialist Morris who, when he found out, could not believe it was true; he was shocked beyond measure. Morris himself went resolutely downwards from his prosperous middle-class background, embracing shop-keeping – the successful decorating firm of Morris & Co. – and socialism, and engaging personally in the manufacturing processes of his textile production. In his workman's smock and with his hands and arms indelibly stained blue from indigo dye he might be regarded as something of a social liability. But by various means, and often fighting a furious rearguard action, the Victorians adapted to this new social order. With traditional hierarchies of art laid aside, a motley crew emerges.

The general public harboured a number of preconceived ideas about artists and their world, nurtured to a large extent by fiction and satire. The chances in the 1840s of mixing socially with practising artists were still fairly remote, and so experience played little part in forming these ideas. Fictionally the artistic life was often a romantic fantasy: Henri Murger's *Scènes de la vie de Bohème* (1844, later to enjoy great success as an opera by Giacomo Puccini, *La Bohème*, first produced in Turin in 1896) was set in a Parisian garret, purveying a romantic view of a doomed struggle with adversity. W.M. Thackeray's *The Newcomes* (1853–4), with its picturesque artist hero Clive Newcome, was another influential example. Thackeray was writing at a time when artists were still barely on the fringes of society, and Newcome was amazed to discover in Paris that artists were regarded as equals in good society, and that Paul Delaroche and Horace Vernet dined with the French king.[34]

While gathering material for his *Notes sur l'Angleterre*, Hippolyte Taine, French man of letters, journalist and social historian, looked to the pages of *Punch* for evidence of the attitudes of the average Englishman; he found

> *At the opposite extreme* [to the John Bull type] *is to be found the artist-type.*
> *The superiority which French drawings* [by the caricaturist Gavarni] *give him,*
> *over the ordinary middle-class citizen, is well known: here, by a notable conjuncture,*
> *the opposite is the case. Musicians appear as performing monkeys introduced to*
> *the drawing-room to make their noises. Painters are depicted as bearded artisans,*
> *ill-paid, ill-clad, ill-bred, pretentious and only one step higher on the social scale*
> *than photographers ... Probably in the eyes of the gross John Bull I have just been*
> *describing, a painter is not a gentleman since he works with his hands while*
> *painting ... and artist's studios are said to be haunts of dissipation.*[35]

A clue to public fascination with the art world lies in that last sentence, but dissipation on its own would not have been enough. The Victorians admired – almost worshipped – success, and it was that to which they paid tribute.

The phenomenal global success of Du Maurier's novel of mid-nineteenth-century Bohemia, *Trilby*, published in 1894, is proof enough of the potency of the subject matter. Owing much to Murger's *Scènes de la vie de Bohème* (as Du Maurier acknowledged), *Trilby* was set in the Paris of his youth, and featured his friends, among them 'Jimmy' Whistler, Edward Poynter, Val Prinsep and Alecco Ionides, known collectively as the 'Paris Gang'.[36] Du Maurier's training in Paris, the setting for *Trilby*, reflects another aspect of the Victorian art world: its cosmopolitan character. Not only did a number of artists receive their artistic education on the Continent, in Paris, Rome, Florence and various German academies, but political upheavals brought a number of refugees to London.[37] Expansion in the Victorian art market presented them with opportunities to capitalize on Parisian chic and the superior technique learned in the *atelier* system, and they prospered here in ways that they might never have done on the Continent.[38] The growing power and visibility of the new intelligentsia, with its mixing of High Society and the cultivated middle-class with the previously untouchable worlds of studio, stage and concert hall, threatened an entrenched social order, whose members were quick to take up defensive positions of ridicule and wilful ignorance.

From a fictional and satirical standpoint the Victorian art world looks less of a powerful force for change than it really was. Were it not for the architectural legacy of the artists' houses, very much less might be understood about the Victorian social revolution in relation to the arts. Social attitudes had hardened with the rise of the professional and manufacturing classes. Artists and Aesthetes (a term used pejoratively in this context) threatened social and moral certainties with their unconventional lifestyles and eclectic tastes. Their advances into the stronghold of High Society were sometimes stealthy, with cautious forays into the fringe of the social whirl which constituted the London Season. Millais and his socially ambitious wife entertained on a grand scale. Not long after he had moved to Palace Gate, in November 1879 he gave a ball to celebrate his daughter Effie's marriage to Captain James. The ball was attended, according to *Vanity Fair*, by 'notable artists (with their wives in Grosvenor Gallery dresses)'; the *beau monde* was there as well, including its most recent star, Lillie Langtry, bearing a silver coffee-pot.

The author Vernon Lee, visiting Leighton's house in 1883, considered it 'quite the 8th wonder of the world', with the owner 'surrounded by fashionable women, a blend of Olympian Jove and a head waiter, a superb decorator and a superb piece of decoration'.[39] Leighton's house was among the most frequented by upper-class visitors in the later nineteenth century (pl.13). The house was like a carapace, any domestic functions being entirely subordinated to the precise needs of the artist-collector and to the entertainment of his patrons and friends. It has been subjected to intense scrutiny, both for the originality of its architecture and interior decoration and for its social significance.[40]

Leighton – inspiration for Disraeli's Gaston Phoebus in *Lothair* (1870) – was one of the unquestioned princes of the Victorian art world, a position of which he himself was surely aware. *Lothair* was published the year after Leighton's election as a full Academician. Disraeli saw him as a confident grandee: 'Mr Phoebus liked pomp and graceful ceremony, and was of the opinion that great artists should lead a princely life, so that in their manners and method of existence they might furnish models to mankind in general, and elevate the tone and taste of nations.'[41] Leighton would have taken his place in society whatever his chosen profession: his father and grandfather were eminent medical men and the young artist had a cosmopolitan education. Success had come to him very early, but as for any artist starting out, it was fluctuating, and Leighton could not have survived without an allowance from his father. He was a fluent linguist, socially adept, young and personable, and he was quickly drawn into the world of balls and receptions in the London houses of the aristocracy. This was the style of life to which many successful Victorian artists would eventually aspire, but it was still unusual in the 1850s. As a bachelor Leighton solved a number of problems around the social ambiguity of artists in which a wife was often seen as a liability. The artists' wives even more than the artists themselves occupied an ill-defined position, and it was an understood thing that these rising men could be entertained without their spouses except in circumstances of greatest intimacy. If Leighton had wanted to marry, and this remains an open question, he had put himself in an awkward position, consorting with people who would never have accepted him as a son-in-law. His admission to this world would lead him to matrimonial ambitions beyond the daughters of middle-class professional men who were his natural equals. Disraeli, in *Lothair*, marries Gaston Phoebus to someone who is recognizably a member of the cultivated Greek community in London, a plausible solution to the problem. The Ionides family, prominent in the Greek community and part of Leighton's social circle, were sufficiently exotic to live life outside the conventions of mid-Victorian society.

13. The Hall from the Arab Hall, Leighton House, photograph, 1895 (National Monuments Record)

The richly detailed interior of Leighton's house resembled a Venetian palazzo or an artist's house in the Italian Renaissance tradition.

14. L. DEUCHARS, *G.F. Watts in the Garden Arbour at Limnerslease,* oil painting, 1897, after a photograph by George Andrews (National Portrait Gallery)

It was the Ionides family who initiated the successful career of G.F. Watts. Watts had impossibly high aims for art, believing that it should communicate lofty ideas far beyond the merely visual. In a late portrait (1897) he is seated in a secluded part of the garden at Limnerslease in the Surrey countryside, dressed like a member of some ancient religious order (pl.14). The roundel of the Virgin and Child in the manner of Luca della Robbia, placed as if over an altar, suggests that his devotion to art is like a religious vocation. He attempted to convey notions of love and death, justice and faith in his paintings, and through them hoped to change the moral climate in the cause of women and the poor. He campaigned against heedless luxury and tight-lacing; the result, not surprisingly, was that he made a great deal less money than Millais, Leighton and Alma-Tadema. His high-mindedness did not deprive him of purpose-built residences and studios, but it did deny him a great fortune. His stated reasons for refusing the proffered baronetcies were financial, that he could not afford to sustain the honour, but there was a subtext: his marriage to Ellen Terry, contracted in 1864, was not ended by divorce until 1875, by which time she had two illegitimate children by another man, the architect E.W. Godwin. It was perfectly possible that one of them might have succeeded to the baronetcy, a prospect which Watts could hardly view with equanimity.

Edward Poynter, pillar of the artistic establishment who succeeded Millais as President of the Royal Academy, derived little pleasure from his baronetcy owing to his melancholic and undemonstrative temperament, barely concealed in a sympathetic portrait by his nephew, Philip Burne-Jones (pl.15). His wife remarked, 'I understand how miserable he must be'.[42] Poynter had been deflected from his original intention of following his father in a career as an architect when he met Leighton in Rome in 1852. He studied in Paris under the French Academician Charles Gleyre, and his membership of the so-called 'Paris Gang' (he shared lodgings with Whistler and Du Maurier) earned him immortality in Du Maurier's *Trilby*. His most significant patrons were the First Earl of Wharncliffe and the wealthy stockbroker and amateur artist John Postle Heseltine, both of the upper-class Aesthetic persuasion.

Poynter was photographed in 1884 by Mayall, surrounded by emblems of his successful career (pl.16). He was living at 28 Albert Gate in Knightsbridge at this date. His working studio was at the National Art Training School at South

15. P. Burne-Jones, *Sir Edward Poynter at his Easel*, oil painting, 1909 (National Portrait Gallery)

J.P. Mayall Photo.   *London published by Sampson Low Marston Searle & Rivington 188 Fleet St.*   Park Lane Studio. London.

16. E.J. Poynter in his studio, photogravure after J.J.E. Mayall for F.G. Stephens, *Artists at Home*, 1884

Kensington, of which he had become Principal in 1873, but he still defines himself by the tools of his trade. He is holding a drawing and is seated on a painter's 'donkey'. On the large easel behind him is a design for the decoration of the dome of St Paul's; the two other easels display reduced versions of *The Ides of March* (full-size version 1883; Manchester Art Gallery) and *The Meeting of Solomon and the Queen of Sheba* (full-size version 1890; Art Gallery of New South Wales). A collection of ceramics keeps company with antique furniture and Oriental rugs. Poynter's professional career took him to the heights of the Victorian art world, his directorship of the National Gallery being succeeded by the RA presidency which brought him a knighthood. His wife Agnes, like Georgiana Burne-Jones, one of the Macdonald sisters, died of cancer in 1906, leaving Poynter feeling guilty at his lack of consideration and sympathy as a husband and devastated that it was now too late.

Burne-Jones and Poynter were the leading figures in a remarkable matrimonial saga of the Victorian art world.[43] Their wives were two of the seven daughters of George Macdonald, an itinerant Methodist preacher, whose peripatetic and impoverished upbringing took place largely in the grim industrial towns of the North and Midlands. From these unpromising beginnings they rose with their successful husbands into the Victorian upper class. As well as Georgiana's marriage to Burne-Jones and Agnes's to Poynter, their eldest surviving sister, Alice, was married to the artist John Lockwood Kipling. As parents of Rudyard Kipling they obviously merit attention, but in this context, Lockwood is more interesting as a pioneer of Western-style art training in India, and as the designer of two royal 'Indian' interiors, the billiard room at Bagshot House for the Duke and Duchess of Connaught, and the Indian Room at Osborne House for Queen Victoria. Their younger sister, Louisa, married Alfred Baldwin; their son Stanley became a politician and eventually Prime Minister, and later Earl Baldwin of Bewdley. It is here that the social boundaries are effectively blurred: the Macdonald sisters were equal to the social and cultural demands of their husband's positions because irrespective of the lack of money and social status they were carefully educated by their father to fulfil intellectual and moral expectations.

As well as by worldly success, the public were attracted by the subversive and the anti-establishment, among them James McNeill Whistler, whose maverick activities and views were bandied about in bohemian circles. Then, too, there was the reclusive Burne-Jones, whose very elusiveness and reluctance to exhibit excited public interest. Published lives of artists, celebrations of genius and heavily angled autobiography – polite hagiography, in effect, and often unintentionally revealing – proliferated in the later years of the nineteenth century.[44] The class origins of some were simplified, often into something more humble and deprived, in order to emphasize the contrast with their later celebrity. The final wifely immolation would be as memorialist, with Mary Seton Watts and Georgiana Burne-Jones constructing the authorized version of their husbands' lives.

Much that reflected badly on the morality of these artists was covered up. Matters such as the marriage of 45-year-old Watts to Ellen Terry, who was barely 17, were dismissed in a sentence. When her childish antics embarrassed him, Watts sent her away. He had attempted to mould her into a suitable wife; she had been dazzled by the prospect of marriage to a great artist. He had taken her in default, it was said, of her sister Kate (who married the wealthy draper Arthur Lewis), or his great love Virginia Pattle, who preferred Lord Somers.[45] Life at Little Holland House, home of Sara Prinsep (née Pattle), Watts's hostess and protector for more than twenty years, hardly missed a beat, the whole affair being carried off with ineffable self-assurance by all concerned.

The unreconstructed bohemian milieu inhabited by Rossetti, whose wife had died of an overdose of laudanum, meant that he never troubled to conceal the fact that his ramshackle household included his model-mistress Fanny Cornforth, a former prostitute. His long affair with Jane Morris, wife of his once great friend, was no secret either. Tissot, who settled in London after the collapse of the Paris Commune, conducted a discreet liaison with a married woman. When the beautiful Mrs Newton died of consumption in 1882 he returned to Paris, abandoning his secluded villa and garden in St John's Wood where he had painted little but the story of himself and his mistress since their first meeting in 1875.[46]

Plain speaking about the true nature of Burne-Jones's harrowing and ultimately terrifying affair with his beautiful Anglo-Greek model and muse Mme Marie Zambaco, estranged wife of a Greek doctor living in Paris, had to await his twentieth-century biographer Penelope Fitzgerald.[47] This sort of drama drew women together; Georgie Burne-Jones was able to ride out the storm with the support of her friend Rosalind Howard, wife of George Howard (and later Countess of Carlisle). Georgie had much to forgive, not only in the Zambaco *débâcle* but also the succession of *amitiés amoureuses* conducted with well-born artistic ladies right up to Burne-Jones's death.[48] She could not, however, entirely conceal her own feelings for Morris; on their first encounter he struck her as 'very handsome … the statues of mediaeval kings often remind me of him', and references to him couched in the most flattering terms are scattered through the *Memorials*.[49]

Another submerged theme running through the domestic lives of these men was the idea of moulding a woman of a different age or class to be the ideal artist's wife. The precarious gentility of the rising artists made the manners of their marriage partners of urgent concern. Many had to suffer a humiliating period of education and instruction in deportment and etiquette, like Ellen Terry before

17. W. HOLMAN HUNT,
The Awakening Conscience,
oil painting, 1853
(Tate, London)

The model for Holman Hunt's modern-life
moralizing subject was Annie Miller.
His patron was so distressed by her
expression that the face had to be
re-painted.

18. J.J.J. TISSOT, *Rêverie*, etching, 1881
(V&A: E.275–1951)

The composition is taken from a photograph
of Kathleen Newton seated on the
conservatory steps at Grove End Road.

her marriage to Watts. The instructing of beautiful, but possibly illiterate and certainly socially unacceptable, working-class women happened often enough to be conspicuous by its absence from the pages of pious biographies. Drug-taking and bohemian disorder, too, were brushed under the carpet.

A tangle of motives is revealed here, not least the difficulty of marrying young women from the middle class, with all that implied in legitimate expectations on an uncertain income. Holman Hunt's relationship with the model Annie Miller is a classic example: well concealed by his widow, it was disinterred through the determination of his granddaughter.[50] Annie was raised in a Chelsea slum. She first modelled for Hunt when she was 15 years old; he began to think of her as a possible wife and had her educated for her future position. While he was away in the East she disobeyed his instructions not to sit for other painters. Hunt broke with her, because 'he could not get her to do what he wanted to make her a desirable wife to him, nor to wean herself from old objectionable habits'.[51] Annie was the model for Holman Hunt's most celebrated moralizing subject: *The Awakening Conscience* (pl.17) brought the narrative of objects to its highest degree of complexity and loaded meaning, in which the newness of the piano is as significant as the speaking countenance of the female protagonist. The scene-setting represents the antithesis of artistic taste. What now appears to be a template for the middle-class Victorian room startled the contemporary audience with the force of its meaning. In his fanatical concern for realism, Hunt hired a room in a *maison de convenance*, Woodbine Villa, 7 Alpha Place in St John's Wood, notoriously the location of households for 'kept women', and furnished it with 'common, modern, vulgar' contents.[52] Like the protagonist's profession, the piano was not concealed by 'tasteful' drapery, yet another indication of vulgarity. Hunt could not show a kept woman as anything but repentant. He was later ostracized in certain circles (and by his in-laws) when he committed the still illegal act of marrying his deceased wife's sister: he and Edith Waugh had to marry in Switzerland. Millais, too, found at first hand how unforgiving society could be: his wife Effie had been married to John Ruskin and had managed to obtain an annulment on the grounds of non-consummation of the marriage. She was forced to occupy a sort of half-world, invisible to certain sections of *haut monde*. Millais was forced to use his dying breath as a bargaining counter in his campaign to get Queen Victoria to receive her.

Morris, well-to-do, upper middle-class and a man of high principles, fell in love with and married Jane Burden, the working-class daughter of an Oxford stable hand, in 1859. Presented with such a good match, she had no choice but to accept him. He had painted her in 1858, soon after her emergence as a 'stunner', in the character of *La Belle Iseult* from Malory's *Morte d'Arthur*, ill with grief and attempting suicide at the rumour of Tristan's death (pl.19). King Mark has confined her in a tower, windowless but ornate with embroideries. Too much in this painting is prophetic for it to be entirely comfortable. The marriage was not happy, marred by Janey's long love affair with Rossetti and her chronic ill-health which confined her to a sofa. Morris's decision to build his 'Palace of Art', Red House, at Bexleyheath in the Kent countryside (p.158), a kind of King Mark's tower, may have been partly prompted by his wish to shield Janey from social obloquy. His first biographers, coupled with her own silence and reticence, did an excellent job of blurring Janey's origins. Modern biographers of the Victorians have uncovered these old scandals, probably far more commonly known about at the time than we can now appreciate, but very successfully covered up for the benefit of posterity.

Hints of these buried scandals and rumours were stimulating to the idea of artists as a breed apart. In the case of Tissot and Mrs Newton, the hints were positively blatant (pl.18). Although she is not identified by name, the implication of irregularity in some exhibition reviews is unambiguous, one remark in particular giving no room for doubt: the paintings featuring her were described as 'pictures of the "detached villa" kind'.[53] The lurid light playing over the art world did nothing to diminish its fascination.

A GOLDEN AGE

The nineteenth century has been called the 'Golden Age of the Living Painter' and the 'gentleman-artist'.[54] For a while at least, in the mid-century the conditions were perfect for art to flourish exceedingly, with the aims of artists exactly in tune with the expectations of their patrons. Works of art came under scrutiny as never before; exhibitions drew enormous, enthusiastic crowds. Year on year the annual Summer Exhibition at the Royal Academy caused previously unequalled levels of excitement: on several occasions the 'Picture of the Year' had to be railed off to protect it from the crowds pressing up to examine it. To modern eyes the level of reporting was astounding, with *The Times* sometimes running commentaries on the RA Summer Exhibition for as much as ten weeks. To be present at the exhibition opening was a social and fashionable necessity. In 1872 the *Spectator* ran an article on 'The Fascination of Money', stating 'Our millionaires are maniacs for collecting things'.[55] Reporting on 'The Picture Season in London' in 1877, Henry James remarked:

> *the taste for art in England is at bottom a fashion, a need for luxury ...*
> *But if art is a fashion in England, at least it is a great fashion. How these people*
> *have always needed, in a certain sort of way to be entertained; what handsome*
> *things they have collected about them ... on what a scale the consumption has*
> *always gone on![56]*

James believed that this mania was symptomatic of the age:

> *The great multiplicity of exhibitions is, I take it, a growth of our own day –*
> *a result of that democratization of all tastes and fashions which marks our*
> *glorious period. But the English have always bought pictures in quantities, and*
> *they certainly have often had the artistic intelligence to buy good ones.[57]*

Although Henry James believed that royal patronage played little part in the development of British public collections, the royal family was active in promoting the British School in painting and sculpture. Under the influence of Prince Albert, a highly educated and cultivated patron of the arts, Queen Victoria commissioned works and bought from exhibitions. In particular their seaside retreat, Osborne on the Isle of Wight, was a showcase for the arts, with its lavish use of painted decoration and collection of marble statues. The royal couple were generous lenders, and pictures from the collection featured in many important international exhibitions. Even if the Victorian royal collection seems to be punching a bit under its weight, it provides a wide panorama of painting by admired artists of the period, and while many of them are not among the Victorian giants as judged by history, they were successful and prosperous. A significant number owned architect-designed houses.

A diehard element in society inevitably survived through all these changes. George Smalley, London correspondent of the American *Tribune* newspaper and amusing commentator on London life, remembered the old Duchess of Cleveland's reaction to an unknown face at dinner in 'a very great house'; on being told it was Mr Leighton, a rising young painter she 'brooded a moment on this startling information' and remarked 'very gravely – "What strange people you do ask to meet us"'.[58] Leighton would not doubt have been piqued by this; as Du Maurier saw it he was 'very blasé and finikin, and quite spoilt – one of the world's little darlings, who won't make themselves agreeable to anything under a Duchess'.[59] Leighton was the acceptable face of art as far as High Society was concerned. Smalley, pandering to a taste in his audience for tales of the foibles of the aristocracy, was retelling in somewhat disingenuous terms anecdotes of a figure famously out of step with the altered aspects of English society. Daisy, Lady Warwick, heiress and one-time mistress of the Prince of Wales, remarked: 'As a class we did not like brains. We acknowledged that pictures should be painted, books written, the law

19. W. MORRIS, *La Belle Iseult*, oil painting, 1858 (Tate, London)

Morris made this one attempt at a romantic historical subject in the Pre-Raphaelite manner, using his future wife as his model. The accessories, notably the embroideries and missal, are revealing of Morris's early collecting tastes.

administered; we even acknowledged that there was a certain stratum whose job it might be to do these things.' Lady Warwick did not impose artists on her sporting friends and, indeed, as she pointed out, anyone bold enough to stray from the norms of High Society would certainly be ostracized.[60] She met the grander members of the artistic establishment – Leighton, Burne-Jones, Millais, Watts, Poynter and Whistler – through Lord Wharncliffe, a noted patron and collector.

Lady St Helier, writing somewhat patronizingly of London at this time, remarked:

> *Before long, however, the world began to realize the enormous crowd of brilliant men and women who had hitherto lived unrecognized and unappreciated at their very gates; and those to whose houses they were welcomed found their rooms filled with distinguished guests, and the beau monde flocking in numbers to make their acquaintance.*[61]

Her own background as a member of the Scottish nobility, and through a first marriage to a younger son of the Stanleys of Alderley a sister-in-law to Rosalind Howard, gave her a perspective on the shifting fortunes of the aristocratic fringe. As Mrs Jeune (her second husband, a member of the legal profession, was ennobled as Lord St Helier) she was a successful society hostess, combining journalism with a slightly bohemian social circle. She was known to favour writers and musicians and was an early sponsor of Oscar Wilde – who treated her disgracefully – in his dazzling rise to social prominence.

A bohemian world, where social distinctions were of no account, was a refuge from the rigid etiquette of the London Season, which had become increasingly cumbersome and impersonal, exclusive but not select. In the huge houses of the aristocracy a mob of hundreds would be entertained, often including numbers of guests unknown to the hostess. The 'Smart Set' remained relentlessly focused on gambling, hunting and racing. Artistic soirées were more enjoyable, mixing carefully chosen people from the worlds of art, theatre and music with the more adventurous members of London society. They fulfilled a pressing need, to provide a social structure for the newly wealthy professional and mercantile elite, whose background or occupation still barred them from High Society. This alliance between the contemporary art world and the new rich had wide-reaching social consequences. Britain's escalating industrial and mercantile wealth ensured that possessions and other outward signs of status ultimately came to mean as much as – or more than – lineage and land-ownership, both of which were fatally eroded by the agricultural depression of the 1880s. The cultural authority of the upper classes had also been seriously questioned by Matthew Arnold in 1869, with his withering designations of 'barbarians' and 'philistines'.[62]

The social transformation of the art world was greatly eased by the rise in status and prosperity of the industrial and mercantile classes, intent on the rewards of mixing in artistic circles with their implications of knowledge, taste and discrimination. Professional men and businessmen, bankers, lawyers, surgeons, stockbrokers, wine merchants and shop proprietors – all occupations followed by prominent collectors – were among the most active supporters of the art of their time, outdoing the old aristocracy, whose patronage of living artists remained cautious and traditional (much portraiture and sporting art).[63] It is no accident that several of the great public art galleries have their origins in nineteenth-century middle-class collections. The provincial manufacturing and commercial elite had risen to heights of wealth and status which allowed them to exercise their patronage on a grand scale.

Volunteer military training and good works further consolidated artists' social position. Again Leighton is the exemplar: he rose to be Lieutenant-Colonel of the Volunteer Artists' Rifles and he was one of the moving spirits in the initiatives to bring art to the underprivileged at the South London Art Gallery and Whitechapel.[64] The Artists' Rifles were a serious response to the perceived threat from the French under Napoleon III, and eventually attracted a good turn-out of recruits. Leighton, with his German upbringing, brought valuable habits of punctuality and thoroughness to his role. His notebooks are peppered with lists reminding him of the many requirements of the annual camp, an excellent excuse for some manly antics in the outdoors. However, his legendary urbanity must have been sorely tried on occasion: Rossetti, an unlikely recruit, wished to be given the precise reason for every order and would often argue the point. Morris seemed to be quite unable to turn in the right direction and on the order 'right turn' he would invariably turn left. The barracks were initially at the back of Burlington House, but the building was needed when the Royal Academy moved there in 1869, and the recently founded Arts Club in Hanover Square became the Regimental Headquarters thereafter.

'High art' at the top of the many-layered structure was the prerogative of the few, but the endless proliferation of decorative painting, illustration work and reproductive tasks provided a massive workforce with some kind of a living, even respectable security. With photography still in its infancy there was a great deal for artists to do at a strictly commercial level, for example in book-illustration, topographical drawing and news reporting for illustrated periodicals. These periodicals consumed masses of black-and-white drawings, rendered for reproduction into highly skilled engravings. *Punch*, issued from 1841, was in a class of its own; the artists employed were among the most talented illustrators of the day. The high reputations once enjoyed by skilled black-and-white illustrators for papers like the *Illustrated London News* and the *Graphic* are now forgotten, but they brought prosperity and, in some cases, handsome houses. Luke Fildes made his name initially as a *Graphic* illustrator. Reporting on current events demanded speed and facility: William Simpson was the first war artist, covering the Crimean Campaign with such immediacy that the readers of his reports felt that they too had been present. The sale of copyrights and prints augmented the earning power of the most successful. Reproductive print-making was big business. The accomplished Victorian engraver Samuel Cousins was the first to be accorded appropriate recognition – and to command decent fees for his work – as well as the first to be elected to the Royal Academy in 1855. He lived in a rather severe but substantial house in North Terrace, Camden Town, his walls hung with the finest examples of his own remarkable technique.

Watercolour painting, regarded as a particularly English speciality, offered a profitable career. A technical revolution in the 1840s, involving the use of opaque mediums and gum, produced results close to the rich effects obtainable with oil-paints. Two societies of painters in watercolours provided exhibiting space and an audience.[65] Although traditionalists might deplore the loss of the essential characteristic of the medium – transparency – watercolour 'paintings' commanded good prices. The vastly increased prestige of watercolour painting is evidenced in the numbers of watercolours included in the popular loan exhibitions mounted all around the country and attended by the public in their thousands. A number of the most successful practitioners owned purpose-built studio-houses. Edward Henry Corbould, a favourite of Queen Victoria and instructor of the royal children, occupied the handsome Eldon Lodge on the corner of Eldon Road and Victoria Road in Kensington. Corbould took over the red-brick house from his cousin, the artist A.H. Corbould, and altered it extensively to accommodate a large studio. This was described in 1868 as 'something between a baronial hall and a refectory in a rich monastery'.[66] As W.S. Clarke, author of *The Suburban Homes of London*, remarked in 1881, 'Victoria-road, with its surroundings, is noted for being inhabited by artists of high standing, and its villas are certainly beautiful miniatures in themselves'.[67]

The armed services produced competent watercolourists, whose talents were honed by map-making. Even now, red-brick artists' studios built for such near-forgotten figures as the soldier-painter Edward Conyngham Sterling

(38 Sheffield Terrace, by Alfred Waterhouse) and war artist-reporter James Prinsep Beadle (17b Eldon Road, next door to Corbould's house) rear up in the terraces of Kensington, breaking the uniformity of an earlier urban pattern. Paul Naftel and his family (four of them painters and, with the exception of his daughter Maude, now almost unknown) owned a substantial studio-house in Chelsea, built by John Pollard Seddon in 1883. The red-brick studio complex, with its vast north-facing windows, forms part of picturesque group of artists' houses at 74 to 78 Elm Park Road, the striking asymmetrical mass heavily trimmed with white and embellished with terracotta panels of sunflowers. They contrast with the gaunt yellow-brick terraced character of the street and the adjoining area. Another soldier-artist, Lt Col. Henry Pilleau, occupied number 74 and Pownoll Toker Williams number 78; both were landscape watercolourists and minor Royal Academy exhibitors.

The fortunes of artists were also intimately bound up with the expansion of the print-publishing and picture-dealing professions. The picture trade was dominated by several influential figures, leader among them in the mid-nineteenth century being Ernest Gambart – 'that vampire Gambart' as he was called by one disaffected artist.[68] Gambart had a large house, 62 Avenue Road in St John's Wood, then a fast-developing artists' quarter, with Alma-Tadema, George Dunlop Leslie and Tissot living nearby.

SHIFTING BOHEMIA

The Victorian art world was by no means a single entity. Young artists congregated around an admired mentor. Clubs and cliques were formed, flourished and dispersed. These groups drifted in eddies and rivulets around London, reforming where the action was, or fetching up in some still rural location before it became fashionable and built up. In the mid-century the artists' quarter shifted from its long-time centre, the old 'Latin Quarter', a long swathe stretching from Newman Street, north of Oxford Street, through Soho and Charing Cross down to the Thames at Blackfriars Bridge. The artists' colourmen and suppliers who had clustered in Berner's Street and Rathbone Place outstayed the departure of the artists from Soho and Fitzrovia. James Sant, who in 1871 succeeded Sir George Hayter as Queen Victoria's Principal Painter-in-Ordinary, had a successful career as a portrait painter. In a self-portrait aged about 20, he presents a youthful and ambitious version of himself which adheres closely to the fictional model of a romantic bohemian (pl.21). In his untidy, makeshift studio in Soho Square, the very antithesis of a fashionable destination, he struggles with a canvas of vast dimensions. Typical props of the artist's working environment litter the space, unframed works hung anyhow on the walls, sketches tumbling from an open portfolio, the mirror reflecting the image in progress, plaster casts, bits of armour, even a globe. The simplest contrivance for making a studio in a conventional dwelling house was the enlargement of a north-facing window, cutting the opening up into the cornice as Sant has done here. The window is partly draped with a blanket to regulate the light. When Sant was photographed in old age for a record of Members and Associates of the Royal Academy, he presented a respectable figure in jacket, waistcoat and striped trousers, his palette and brush striking a note of irrelevance.

Artists' studios remained deeply fascinating to the public, the ambience, the decoration, the accumulation of objects, artistic or curious, suggesting an aesthetic voyage. Many artists conformed to the romantic fictional image by wearing velvet jackets and soft collars with silk ties, even when other unconventional habits were abandoned in favour of middle-class propriety. The artist at home was a popular nineteenth-century genre because it was seen as revealing the subject's originality and taste. The reality was often more mundane. Essentially, the studio was a down-to-earth working environment: most of the hundreds of artists' studios in London were strictly utilitarian, dusty and chill, with cold light pouring in from the high north-facing window. Keene's attic studio from 1845 to 1857 on the Strand at

20. C. KEENE, *Self-portrait in the Artist's Studio*, inscribed 'A foggy day Painter cleaning his skylight', drawing, about 1850 (British Museum)

Charing Cross was filled with props, old armour and costumes; here he cooked primitive meals and smoked pipes of murderously strong tobacco (pl.20).[69] It bore little resemblance to the popular idea of a site invested with mysterious life and romance. Keene moved a number of times, coming to rest in Chelsea in 1873, finally in 1879 alighting at 239 King's Road where he stayed until his death in 1891.

Before he settled on Chelsea, Rossetti lived in a number of different apartments, more or less adapted to use as a studio, around Bloomsbury and down towards the Thames near Blackfriars Bridge. In the mid-1850s he was at Red Lion Square in Bloomsbury, in a set of dilapidated rooms later occupied by Morris and Burne-Jones. His brief marriage to the beautiful red-haired model and artist Lizzie Siddal was lived out in rooms at Chatham Place in the last house by Blackfriars Bridge, eventually to be demolished to make way for the Thames Embankment. Here Rossetti spent his time dreaming up wallpaper designs and nurturing a seemingly impossible ambition to live in a beautiful seventeenth-century house on the river at Cheyne Walk in Chelsea. A drawing of Lizzie at Chatham Place shows her silhouetted against the window overlooking their view of the river and Blackfriars Bridge.[70] Another of Rossetti's Chatham Place drawings, this time of the model

21. J. SANT, RA, *Self-portrait*, oil painting, about 1854 (National Portrait Gallery)

Sant presents himself as a romantic young artist surrounded by the conventional props of the studio, an interesting contrast with the posed photographic portraits used by F.G. Stephens for *Artists at Home* in 1884.

22. D.G. ROSSETTI, *George Price Boyce
with Fanny Cornforth at Rossetti's Studio,
Chatham Place*, pen-and-ink drawing, 1858
(Tullie House Art Gallery, Carlisle)

23. J.R. SPENCER STANHOPE,
Thoughts of the Past, oil painting, 1858–9
(Tate, London)

The model is Fanny Cornforth in the role
of a repentant prostitute. The geraniums
in their pots beneath the window are
struggling up towards the light.

Fanny Cornforth with his friend George Price Boyce, records an occasion when Boyce visited December 1858 (pl.22).[71] Fanny was sitting to Roddam Spencer Stanhope in the studio below for his painting *Thoughts of the Past* (pl.23), and the company afterwards went upstairs to Rossetti's rooms.[72] The image of intimacy between unmarried friends of widely differing social class is provocative. Boyce had been shocked at the suggestion that an artist friend had gone so far as to kiss his sister while having no serious matrimonial intentions towards her, but the same rules did not apply to relations with golden-haired Fanny, Rossetti's long-time mistress with whom Boyce was also intimate. In fact, the woman in *Thoughts of the Past* is a repentant prostitute; the subject would have had a double meaning of corruption for the Victorian public since it was painted during the period of the Great Stink, when the Thames gave off noxious fumes from the untreated sewage which drained into it. Boyce was still living at the Adelphi, but he was a frequent visitor to Chatham Place and he became the occupant of the rambling quarters after Rossetti's removal to Chelsea. On the wall behind the figures there hangs a drawing of another favourite model, the actress Louisa Ruth Herbert. Burne-Jones, visiting for the first time, remembered the floor of this room being covered with designs for pictures and books.[73] Rossetti had already made some imaginative alterations to the decoration, putting Dutch tiles round the fireplace, amassing old willow pattern china and even designing a bold and unusual wallpaper to replace the one shown here, which he described in a letter to William Allingham:

> *We have got our rooms quite jolly now. Our drawing-room is a beauty I assure
> you, already, and on the first country trip we make we shall have it newly papered
> from a design of mine which I have an opportunity of getting made by a paper-
> manufacturer, some-what as below* [*a bold sketch of the pattern is included
> at this point in the letter*]. *I shall have it printed on common brown packing-
> paper and on blue grocer's-paper, to try which is best.*[74]

The design of trees was to reach the whole height of the room. The pattern was quite unlike any wallpaper then available. With its colourways of black and Venetian red, Rossetti predicted that the effect would be 'rather sombre, but I think rich also'. The wallpaper experiment seems not to have been repeated. This is not to say that Rossetti lost interest in the subject: he corresponded about suitable wallpapers as backgrounds to his paintings with at least two of his patrons. In 1875 he wrote to Frederick Leyland:

I ought to keep you informed that I got from Queen Square [premises of Morris & Co.] two further variations of the paper, much inferior however to the first. On comparing the first with my own pattern, I think it may be made to do if a lighter fibre is introduced in the leaves of the dark branch – that part of the pattern being rather cutting, though much less so than in the later versions.[75]

His letters are a mine of information on decorating and furnishing. The subject crops up throughout his occupation of Tudor House in Chelsea (see p.173) and at Kelmscott Manor (p.168).

THE ARTISTIC ESTABLISHMENT

The Private View of the annual Summer Exhibition at the Royal Academy marked the start of the London season. The RA had moved premises in 1869 from the National Gallery in Trafalgar Square to Burlington House in Piccadilly and, after a somewhat moribund period, was soon to enjoy huge prestige under the presidency of Leighton (pl.24). Even before his arrival in 1878 the Academy, by virtue of its exclusive position, enjoyed an unprecedented influence with the public. The Summer Exhibition regularly attracted well over 300,000 visitors, reflecting the enormous cultural value placed on contemporary art. The purpose of the Royal Academy was to establish and promote a British school of art, an aim entirely in tune with the tastes of the Victorian art public. Many middle-class collectors concentrated

24. G. Greville Manton, *The Royal Academy Conversazione*, watercolour, 1891 (National Portrait Gallery)

Sir Frederic Leighton is receiving guests including Alma-Tadema, Millais, Burne-Jones, W.P. Frith, James Sant, Marcus Stone and Ellen Terry.

NTENDED FACADE OF THE GROSVENOR GALLERY, NEW BOND STREET.—MR. WILLIAM THOMAS SAMS, ARCHITECT.
DRAWING BY PALLADIO.

25. The Grosvenor Gallery in
New Bond Street, exterior view,
Illustrated London News, 1877

The gallery opened in what was fast
becoming the centre of picture-dealing
and 'Art' decoration outlets.

on purchases from the RA, and those collections that eventually formed the basis of public art galleries offer an interesting view of mainstream Victorian taste.[76] Competition for admired works pushed up prices, contributing to the prosperity of successful artists – to the despair of the overlooked and neglected among them.

In the winter months loan exhibitions of Old Masters swelled numbers at the RA still further. Although the attendance at these events was by no means as great as at the Private View of the Summer Exhibition, they were notable social gatherings nonetheless (pl.26). The Duchess of Rutland, herself an artist of considerable talent, is in the foreground of a huge group portrait which contains numerous other members of the circle. Henry Jamyn Brooks was inspired by Frith's comic rendering of the same scene (see pl.69) to paint the private viewing at the Royal Academy of the exhibition of Old Masters in 1889.

The greatest challenge to the Academy's disputed primacy was Sir Coutts Lindsay's Grosvenor Gallery, which opened at 135 New Bond Street in May 1877 (pl.25).[77] The Italianate palazzo was inaugurated with a great fanfare of publicity. Sir Coutts Lindsay, who was a cousin by marriage to Princess Louise and married to a Rothschild heiress, conceived the Grosvenor Gallery as an alternative for artists dissatisfied with the Royal Academy. It was clever to choose these dissidents, since their work had not recently been shown in public and curiosity fuelled an impressive response to the opening of the first exhibition. The chosen exhibitors, Watts, Whistler, Albert Moore and Burne-Jones among them, gave a distinctive 'Aesthetic' flavour to the gallery. Watts showed portraits of beautiful women, among them the Hon. Mrs Percy Wyndham and Blanche Lindsay herself, in Renaissance-style robes ('Grosvenor Gallery dresses', perhaps), offering an epitome of Aesthetic mood and dress.[78] Several Royal Academy stalwarts showed as well, among them Alma-Tadema, Millais, Leighton, Tissot and Holman Hunt. Sir Coutts wanted to ensure that the gallery avoided a reputation as an anti-Academy venture, like the *Salon des refusés* in Paris, and he had secured the co-operation of the President, Sir Francis Grant, who showed four works in the inaugural exhibition. The Lindsays had hoped to attract Rossetti, but he declined, writing meanwhile 'your scheme must succeed were it but for one name associated with it – that of Burne-Jones – a name representing the loveliest art we have'.

In the years between 1870, the date at which he resigned from the Old Watercolour Society, and 1877 Burne-Jones hardly exhibited his work in public. As with Rossetti, critical differences of opinion had led him to sever his connections with the official art world. He relied on a few private patrons and his work for Morris & Co. as a means to live and continue painting. It is hard now to imagine his total obscurity in the eyes of the general public, and the interest his participation generated – at least that section of it that prided itself on a cultivated knowledge of modern art which comes from annual attendance at the Royal Academy. His involvement with the Grosvenor Gallery was to transform Burne-Jones into one of the leading figures in the English art world. It brought him a greatly enlarged circle of wealthy and aristocratic patrons. It is probably also true to say that without his participation interest in the venture would have been very much cooler.

For Coutts Lindsay, an old habitué of Little Holland House, these artists were his friends. Henry James was an early visitor, reporting that:

this has been a good year from the sightseer's point of view inasmuch as it has witnessed the inception (I believe that is the proper word in such cases) of an artistic enterprise of an unusually brilliant sort. I suppose it is correct to speak of the Grosvenor Gallery as primarily an artistic enterprise; for it has had its origin, on the part of its distinguished proprietor (Sir Coutts Lindsay), rather in the love of pictures than in the love of money … In so far as his beautiful rooms in Bond Street are a commercial speculation, this side of their character has been gilded over, and dissimulated in the most graceful manner.[79]

26. H. Jamyn Brooks, *Private View of the Old Masters Exhibition at the Royal Academy*, oil painting, 1889 (National Portrait Gallery)

The occasion is the 1888 Winter Exhibition of Old Masters at Burlington House. This panorama of the art world, the establishment and artistic members of the aristocracy, includes many of the studio-visiting public. Millais, with Philip Burne-Jones behind him, dominates the group to the left; George Richmond in a skull cap is to their right. Frith can just be seen behind Alma-Tadema in his trademark pince-nez. Holman Hunt is talking to Ruskin, and Poynter is shaking hands with Laura Alma-Tadema. Leighton, as a leading instigator in the series of loan exhibitions at the RA, is at the centre of the composition, holding a catalogue. Gladstone forms part of the right-hand group, with Margot Asquith (née Tennant), Marcus Stone and G.F. Watts.

The inauguration of the Grosvenor was a social as much as a cultural event. Not to receive an invitation was regarded as social annihilation. With the intention of bringing his gallery artists into contact with their patrons Sir Coutts drew up a list including several members of the royal family and High Society, as well as many of the exhibitors. Louise Jopling, herself a Grosvenor Gallery artist, wrote: 'The glamour of fashion was over it, and the great help that Lady Lindsay was able to give by holding Sunday receptions there made it one of the most fashionable resorts of the London seasons.' Whistler enlivened the proceedings by making deliberate *faux pas* to embarrass Lady Lindsay, whom he suspected of keeping the bohemian world at a distance.

The Grosvenor Gallery, while being imposing, shared its aesthetic with the grander studio-houses. It was conceived in the spirit of an Italian palazzo, bridging the gap between the artist's house and the more splendid mansions of Aesthetic patrons, who were expected to be the Grosvenor patrons. The Palladian entrance came from a demolished church, Santa Lucia in Venice; the approach to the first-floor gallery was through a lobby lined with dark green Genoa marble columns. The blue coved ceiling, which showed the phases of the moon and was sprinkled with gold stars, was Whistler's work; above a dado covered in green velvet, deep crimson silk damask panels were divided by 16 Ionic pilasters, fluted and gilt, rescued from the Italian Opera House in Paris.[80] The silk came from Lyons and

FRUSTRATED SOCIAL AMBITION   1881.

27. G. DU MAURIER, 'Frustrated Social
Ambition, Mrs Cimabue Brown with
Maudle and Postlethwaite', from *Punch*,
included in the collection of cartoons
published as *Society Pictures*
(n.d., about 1888), vol.II, p.241

cost £1,000, but the rich colour proved unpopular with most of the artists since
it overwhelmed the delicate tones of the pictures; it was replaced with greeny-
gold, the origin of the famous 'greenery-yallery Grosvenor Gallery' in Gilbert
and Sullivan's *Patience*. The only dissenting voice in the removal of the crimson
silk was that of Watts; he knew that his rich-toned paintings looked well on the
crimson ground. The huge space was filled with palms, velvet sofas, marble and gilt
tables and blue-and-white flowerpots.

Inevitably the Grosvenor supplied material for *Punch's* satirical roundabout: Du
Maurier's cartoons dwell frequently on the absurdities of the Grosvenor's artistic
fashions, the object of relentless mockery in comic drawings. The Cimabue Browns
(pl.27) were thought to be based on real people, among them Alice Comyns Carr,
wife of Joe Comyns Carr, who was proud to be singled out for notice: like Wilde,
she detected a certain advantage in such notoriety. As she remarked,

*I had long been accustomed to supporting a certain amount of ridicule in the matter
of clothes, because in the days when bustles and skin-tight dresses were the fashion,
and a twenty-inch waist the aim of every self-respecting woman, my frocks followed
the simple, straight line as waistless as those of today.*

Over a period of four years *Punch* printed illustrated guides parodying the
Grosvenor Gallery pictures. Whistler, with his instantly recognizable appearance,
was an obvious butt. The first Grosvenor exhibition was to have disastrous
consequences for him: Ruskin reviewed the exhibition and his remarks about
Whistler's 'Nocturnes' so enraged the artist that he sued for libel in a notorious
case that bankrupted him. As a result he lost his White House in Chelsea, designed
for him by Godwin.

One of the reasons for the Grosvenor's success was, as Mrs Jopling remarked,
'That man of genius, Burne-Jones exhibited there, and his pictures became the
rage. Fashion, always ready to adopt anything new, set all the town wild to copy
the dress and attitudes of his wonderful nymphs'.[81] Despite the publicity and its
social réclame, the Grosvenor closed its doors in 1890.[82] Coutts Lindsay was an
aristocrat and an artist; his fellow directors, C.E. Hallé, portrait painter son of the
famous conductor, and the critic and theatrical impresario Joe Comyns Carr, were
not businessmen either. In a disastrous move, Sir Coutts separated from his wife,
whose funds had provided for the building and running of the gallery. When she
withdrew her support it stumbled on for a few more years but was bound to end
sooner or later. The Grosvenor foundered on personalities as well. Following a
difference of opinion with Coutts Lindsay over business policy, Hallé and Comyns
Carr left to start up their own New Gallery. Disaffected artists left too, and socially
it was no longer a novelty.

At the Grosvenor the Lindsays were immensely valuable social catalysts, but the
social traffic was by no means all one way. The art world, having created its own
distinctive social milieu, was not dependant on the approval of High Society. Several
artists belonged to the Athenaeum, stronghold of Church and Establishment, and
delicate matters (concerning, for example, the elections at the Royal Academy)
were informally decided in those august precincts. Artists had their own clubs – a
lot of clubs – some short-lived, like the Hogarth Club, and others long forgotten.
A telling example of the communal spirit, the Hogarth Club (1858–61) was an
exhibiting society, one of the earliest among the informal network of gathering
places that was eventually to encompass the Cosmopolitan Club, the Garrick, the
Arts Club, and the Artists' Rifles (p.40).[83] The Hogarth wielded influence quite out
of proportion to its three short years of existence: exhibitions of Pre-Raphaelite
art and design put it at the cutting edge. With hindsight the members can be
seen as the advance guard in the Victorian art world, many of them not obviously
'clubbable' individuals. Certainly they were the fount of a distinctive trend in
progressive architectural development.

For Webb, leading exponent of the 'artistic' dwelling, his Hogarth Club membership ensured access to many – if not most – of his Aesthetic patrons, among them Watts and his aristocratic pupil Spencer Stanhope, Morris, Rossetti, Boyce and Prinsep. Other artist-architect members, valuable as associates and influences, included Ruskin, Leighton, Ford Madox Brown, the artist-architect William Burges (whose own studio-house had claims to be the most outlandish of them all), George Edmund Street (Webb's employer with whom Morris spent his brief architectural pupilage) and George Frederick Bodley, first patron of Morris and Webb's great venture, the artistic decorating business of Morris, Marshall, Faulkner & Co.[84] All seven founding partners of the 'Firm', as it came to be called, were Hogarth Club members.

Of the hundred members of the Hogarth Club, fifty were to be artists; the others were writers and amateurs interested in the arts. A member important to Leighton and his architect Aitchison was the banker Stewart Hodgson, owner of Aesthetic houses in London and Surrey and a distinguished patron. Of significance to Webb and Morris was Col. W.J. Gillum, retired soldier and philanthropist, whose initiatives for training poor boys for useful employment included the industrial Home for Destitute Boys in Euston Road, where much of the early Webb/Morris-designed furniture was made. Gillum was an amateur artist who took lessons from Madox Brown, so his Church Hill House at New Barnet, designed by Webb in 1868, might be numbered amongst the roll-call of artists' houses. It certainly shares many decorative features with Webb's other studio-houses.

The Arts Club (founded 1863) and the Chelsea Arts Club (founded 1891) are still in existence.[85] They fulfilled a valuable function as meeting-places for artists. Young men who trained in Paris and Rome had been accustomed to an informal café society where artists gathered to discuss their work; this amenity simply did not exist in London. The prosperous silk-mercer and enthusiastic amateur painter Arthur Lewis was one of the leading promoters of the Arts Club in Hanover Square, which was near his home in Jermyn Street and even nearer to the premises of Lewis & Allenby, at the corner of Conduit Street and Regent Street. Lewis was very shortly to move to Moray Lodge, a large house on Campden Hill in Kensington (site of his Saturday evening bachelor parties featuring the 'Moray Minstrels', who would sing part-songs, glees and madrigals before feasting on oysters), and the Arts Club became a refuge in the centre of Town. This was even more to the point as artists moved to what was still suburban London, Chelsea, Kensington, Hampstead and Chiswick.

Initially the Arts Club had a strong literary bent. The first chairman was Thomas Hughes, author of *Tom Brown's Schooldays*; Wilkie Collins and Charles Dickens were among the first members. Gradually it became almost exclusively artistic: Leighton was chairman in the 1870s; Whistler belonged, of course, along with nearly every other artist, architect or designer of note. With interiors designed by Robert Edis, the Arts Club was open from 6 o'clock in the morning; all meals were served, from breakfast to late-night supper after the theatre. The tone was boisterous and rowdy, with much glee-singing and billiards. More seriously, it acted as an unofficial forum for the discussion of all kinds of artistic business, not least the question of election to the Royal Academy. Some members graduated to the Athenaeum, even more a fount of patronage and political influence.

The Chelsea Arts Club was founded by a group of young artists at a time when there were hundreds of studios in the area, most of them strictly utilitarian and not suitable for entertaining. Whistler joined, but it was – and is still – rather different in character to the Arts Club, which was by that date in the premises in Dover Street where it remains to this day.

Artistic social events had a character all their own, the settings, the utensils (blue-and-white porcelain, eighteenth-century silver plate) the clothes (particularly the clothes), even the food, all ignored the conventions of the Victorian bourgeoisie. Rossetti's ramshackle establishment in Chelsea was from 1862 a gathering place for artists and collectors of blue-and-white Oriental porcelain (pl.28). In this,

28. Chinese blue-and-white porcelain
from the Whistler and Rossetti collections
(V&A: C.770–1910, C.836&A–1910,
C.935–1910, C.769–1910)

Rossetti's great enthusiasm for many years, he and Whistler were rivals. Du Maurier, who was to make comic capital out of 'chinamania' in his cartoons for *Punch*, was fascinated by this rivalry. He was present at a dinner given by Whistler, which was served on fine blue-and-white porcelain, 'about sixty pounds' worth, and his anxiety about it during dinner was great fun'.[86] Collecting and connoisseurship brought common ground with wealthy patrons and a distinctive strand of sociability developed outside the confines of London society.[87] As well as Whistler and Rossetti, Norman Shaw, creator of so many artists' houses, shared a passion for blue-and-white porcelain with Leyland and the surgeon Sir Henry Thompson. Thompson's dinners – or 'Octaves' – at which eight guests who were fellow 'chinamaniacs' would gather for an eight-course dinner served on fine examples of Oriental porcelain, were treasured and privileged occasions.

Whistler's 'Sunday breakfasts' were notorious: in spite of the unreliable behaviour of the host – guests who had been summoned for midday often did not see him in their midst until 2 o'clock – they were eagerly attended by cultivated members of society, who found Whistler's rudeness and cruel wit entertaining. Louise Jopling, diligent recorder of this aspect of London social life, remembered:

> *One met all the best Society there – the people with brains, and those who had enough to appreciate them. Whistler was an inimitable host. He loved to be the Sun around whom we lesser lights revolved. He ignored no one. All came under his influence, and in consequence no one was bored, no one was dull. Indeed, who could be when anywhere near that brilliant personality?* [88]

When she first visited Whistler some time earlier she was much struck with the decoration:

> *We were shown into a nearly empty drawing-room, with only a large sofa, one or two occasional chairs, and a small Chippendale table. The floor was covered with fine, pale, straw-coloured matting. Some priceless blue china was distributed about the room, which had a wonderful air of refined simplicity.*[89]

Mrs Jopling is being disingenuous; she tended to romanticize artistic circles. Members of 'Society' who frequented occasions like Whistler's breakfasts were deliberately flouting convention. Whistler could, in fact, be very difficult indeed, and many found his voice with its strange accent and disconcerting emphasis on unrelated points maddening. What was exciting to rebels from the stuffy world of society entertaining was the possibility of meeting the excluded, dropped for 'living in sin' or accepting payment for what should have been an elegant pastime. It is almost impossible now to navigate the intricate social distinctions among the upper-class intelligentsia, but George Eliot, for example, shunned for living openly with a married man, attended Leighton's musical soirées. The close-knit world of

29

30

31

29–31. D.W. Wynfield, (from top)
William Holman Hunt, Frederic Leighton
and J.E. Millais in historic fancy dress,
photographs from *Collection of
Photographic Portraits of Living Artists*,
1864 (V&A: PH.132–1945, PH.133–1945,
PH.125–1945)

artists, patrons and their friends occupied a special niche in nineteenth-century social hierarchies. A rough and ready social climate prevailed in the more ad hoc households: 'A few blokes and coves – not to say worse – are coming at 8 or so on Friday evening to participate in oysters and obloquy.' Thus wrote Rossetti, hoping to tempt Madox Brown to a gathering of artist friends in 1861.[90] Rossetti's letters, with Boyce's and Madox Brown's diaries, all of them published, chronicle the daily activities of artists and their friends, particularly the Pre-Raphaelite circle.[91] They were in and out of one another's houses all the time but, owing to their generally impecunious state, the provision of food and drink was on a modest scale. One consideration prevailed – the good use of daylight – and invitations were only extended or accepted after dusk.

Convivial gatherings in studios, at sketching clubs and on riotous country outings were gradually transformed into a more complex structure, where art and culture could meet High Society. They wielded an influence on fashion and the social scene out of all proportion to their numbers. Studio parties were memorable entertainments, for example at the Tademas, whose parties were legendary, a mixture of high Aestheticism, eccentric costumes, practical jokes and simple fun. The sight of Alma-Tadema himself in a Roman toga, but still wearing his steel-rimmed glasses, must have been exquisitely amusing. Fancy-dress balls were all the rage, with artists no less than with society hostesses – in fact probably rather more, through their ready access to the costumes. An intriguing oddity, David Wilkie Wynfield's *Collection of Photographic Portraits of Living Artists* (1864), in which the sitters appear in different historic guises inspired by painting from the past, contributes to the idea of the artist-eccentric (pls 29–31).[92] The photographs were published in 1864 and the choice of character is often revealing. Millais has chosen to represent Dante, adopting a pose in profile to suggest the sharp silhouette effect of early Italian portraiture, while Watts posed as a Venetian grandee in a costume inspired by Titian.

Music, the defining ingredient of cultivated entertaining, was much in evidence at studio parties. The intimate and informal social gatherings of artists and their friends featured very fine musical entertainment, provided by leading professional musicians, at some cost, as is revealed in Leighton's banking details. Leighton's first musical party took place in the spring of 1867: it was to become an annual event. Maurice Baring was taken as a child to an afternoon party at Leighton's house, an occasion where the finest musicians played, in 'a large Moorish room full of flowers' while the audience of about thirty guests sat in groups round the piano. It looked, wrote Baring 'like a Du Maurier illustration'.[93] Alma-Tadema's musical soirées were a celebrated feature of the London social scene, and some of the most accomplished musicians of the day were persuaded to play at them. They were dreaded by Alma-Tadema's brother-in-law, Edmund Gosse, who hated music, but most of the guests were delighted. One, Lady Monkswell, attended a particularly memorable evening:

> I went to a party at Alma Tadema's which suited me exactly. I sat on a comfortable sofa & heard Brühl, a new man, play a most wonderful what I took to be a fantasia of Liszt's. Then dear Joachim played a Bach suite, & afterwards these two great swells played the 2nd part of the Kreutzer Sonata together ... I afterwards examined Tadema's picture for Sir H Thompson – a Roman inner court planted quite full with great red poppies & sunflowers.[94]

Of course this was a civilized way of showing off the pictures in the name of wider culture. Alma-Tadema's reputation as a serious music-lover may have prompted his only commission to design an interior scheme, a sumptuous Music Room for the mining and railroad millionaire Henry Gurdon Marquand (see p.208).[95]

Alma-Tadema himself was very musical, but his penchant for bad jokes masked his serious appreciation. Joe Comyns Carr recalled a celebration of the host's

32. G. DU MAURIER, *The Height of Aesthetic Exclusiveness*, pen-and-ink drawing for the cartoon published in *Punch*, 1 November 1879 (V&A: E.396–1948)

This drawing was given by Du Maurier to Edmund Gosse, Alma-Tadema's brother-in-law, who endured Aesthetic musical events with as much stoicism as he could muster.

birthday where a ferocious clockwork tiger formed the main attraction. The artist found it quite irresistible, and the party was punctuated by the sound of the animal skittering across the polished black floorboards.[96] Maurice Baring was acute in comparing the artistic scene to a Du Maurier illustration. In *Punch* Du Maurier is particularly savage on the subject of musical soirées, possibly because he felt he had endured enough of them on the art world circuit. He presented his drawing *The Height of Aesthetic Exclusiveness* (pl.32) to Gosse in 1883, recognizing what Gosse had to endure in pursuit of the Aesthetic ideal.[97]

In fact, the question of exactly how to negotiate the new social order continued to perplex many people. However, artistic social circles resembled High Society in one important respect: soirées, receptions and musical evenings, even balls, offered opportunities for girls to meet their future partners. The Millais children married well. Other examples spring to mind: for example, Alma-Tadema met his second wife at the home of Madox Brown. Laura Epps was the daughter of a distinguished homeopathic doctor who was also the heir to a commercial fortune as a member of the Epps cocoa dynasty. Violet Hunt met Oscar Wilde at William Bell Scott's house in Chelsea, and in old age she would point out to visitors the chair in which he sat when he proposed to her, in spite of the fact that nothing came of it. Val Prinsep, artist son of Thoby and Sara Prinsep (whose tenancy of Little Holland House was the focus of an artistic coterie as well as being home to Watts for 25 years), married Leyland's daughter. One of the Thornycroft daughters, the painter Theresa, married into the Sassoon banking dynasty (memorably described as 'the Rothschilds of the East'). The connection between the families began when Theresa's mother, Mary Thornycroft, was sculpting Alfred's parents; it developed when her brother, Hamo, was engaged in making a statue of Alfred Sassoon's sister, Rachel. In spite of the prominent position of the Thornycrofts, as recipients of much royal patronage, the match was not welcome to the Sassoons. More to the point, that a marriage should result from an artist-patron relationship would have been unthinkable in earlier social hierarchies.[98]

By the late years of the century reporting on artists' houses almost saturated the art press, and a certain enervating cynicism began to take over. To regard featuring in a publication in itself as a mark of success is the subject of R.L. Stevenson's pointed parody:

> *The door of No. 7 bore a brass plate inscribed with the legend 'W.D. Pitman, Artist.' It was not a particularly clean brass plate, nor was No. 7 itself a particularly inviting place of residence. Yet it had a character of its own, such as may well quicken the pulse of the reader's curiosity. For here was the home of an artist — and a distinguished artist too, highly distinguished by his ill-success — which had never been made the subject of an article in the illustrated magazines. No wood-engraver had ever reproduced 'a corner in the back drawing-room' or 'the studio mantelpiece' of No. 7; no young lady author had ever commented on 'the unaffected simplicity' with which Mr Pitman received her in the midst of his 'treasures.' It is an omission I would gladly supply; but our business is only with the backward parts and 'abject rear' of this aesthetic dwelling.*[99]

Although to all intents and purposes the pact between Society and Bohemia was working, with artists appearing to secure for themselves a pretty good foothold in Society with a capital 'S', it was deceptive: the royals and the aristocracy were amusing themselves with the unconventional attitudes of their bohemian counterparts. The social position achieved by successful artists in the Victorian age was uncongenial to the bohemians of the early twentieth century, and the ground won at such hard cost was cheerfully abandoned. The passing of the romantic bohemian artistic type was marked by Lewis Hind in the *Windsor Magazine* in 1896. In 'How Famous Painters Work. Peeps into their studios' he remarks on how ordinary they have become:

> *Nowadays there is not much to distinguish the average eminent painter from any other average eminent man. If you were to meet Sir John Millais in a first-class carriage on the Underground railway you would probably take him for a country squire. Mr Alma-Tadema might be a Dutch tulip-grower; Mr Luke Fildes a French merchant; Mr Seymour Lucas a man with a keen eye for a horse; Mr Marcus Stone a lord; Mr Herkomer an actor; and Mr Dicksee a fashionable young doctor with a pretty taste in furniture and pottery.*
>
> *As a matter of fact the painting of pictures only too often develops into a business, much as the selling of dry goods or the manufacture of chemicals.*[100]

There had been numerous irregular ménages among Victorian artists, but the new bohemians in the early twentieth century lived in open defiance of middle-class morality. Writers and artists of the Bloomsbury Group challenged Victorian taboos with unconventional sexual relationships and their indifference to social and domestic propriety. London's bohemian life in the 1930s, with its deliberately déclassé tone and drunken partying, was appealing in the way that the studio life of the Aesthetes had appealed as an alternative to the conventions and restrictions of Victorian polite society.

The 'show studio' seemed completely implausible and looks increasingly unlikely to return in our own time, in the opening years of the new millennium. None but family and close friends are welcome in the working studio of Lucian Freud, with its elegant early nineteenth-century architectural bones almost completely obscured by encrusted paint. The equally paint-spattered studio of Francis Bacon, the workshop of sculptor Eduardo Paolozzi and the vast spaces of old warehouses filled with industrial fittings, a stark contrast to the princely splendours of Leighton House and Palace Gate or the modernist purity of Whistler's White House, have become the artistic icons of the twentieth century.

CHAPTER TWO

The Victorian Artist's House

There is one prime duty to leave artists alone – you can easily spoil them, you can't make them. One of the great blessings of living in England is that in the main artists are left quite alone, and if ever they are successful it is a great peril for them. Abroad they look out for them, watch and coddle them, and that is very tiresome and does no good, though it is pretty and graceful on the part of people. Here it is different and I am glad of it. While they are let quite alone and never noticed there is delirious hope.[1]

These sentiments, expressed by the determinedly reclusive Edward Burne-Jones, were not widely shared. Houses of Victorian artists were designed to impress, a far cry from the romantic notion of the artist's lonely struggle, lived out in the Spartan conditions of a freezing garret, propounded in Murger's *Scènes de la vie de Bohème* (1844). In fact, masses of people saw inside these houses; they were, in effect 'show' houses, part of newly constructed social rituals peculiar to the art world, which emerged as a result of intense interest in art and artists at the time. The open studio formed a key element in the programme of exhibiting and contact with potential patrons. While the starving artist in a garret still had wide currency in fiction, this was not in keeping with the increasingly prosperous Victorian art world.[2] With the development of studio visiting as a social pastime, as well as the reception of sitters to consider, the romantic idea of the bohemian artist able to ignore polite social protocols became increasingly untenable.

In any case, this is the carefully crafted 'secret' Burne-Jones: he is being disingenuous. He led a pretty active social life, as references in contemporary memoirs demonstrate, and many people were welcomed in his own houses. The impact of his idiosyncratic personal decorating style was unforgettable, and his visitors' reports verge on the lyrical. However, in one way he was adamant in his coy elusiveness: in spite of the fact that he was lured into accepting election to the Royal Academy by Leighton, he would have nothing to do with the most public of these rituals, 'Show Sunday', when visitors were admitted to artists' studios to view works about to be sent to the Royal Academy Summer Exhibition. Numbers recorded for these events, often in the high hundreds, give an idea of a widespread voyeuristic interest in the artistic milieu, enabling all kinds of people to view and adapt to their own purposes the decorative ideas of the artistic elite. They came to see the studios and their owners quite as much as their art. This sort of curiosity was repugnant to Burne-Jones.

Burne-Jones ultimately enjoyed the rewards of success in the Victorian art world, inhabiting an architecturally distinguished eighteenth-century house with a large working studio in the garden and pretty rooms full of 'artistic' things. It is true that he did not build on a scale with a number of his contemporaries, but he was in a weak position when it came to disdaining the fruits of his success. As the prolific art critic and writer Alfred Lys Baldry remarked of the great period of artistic building in the 1860s and 1870s,

Housebuilding became a fashion that scarcely any rising artist with a balance at the bank could resist. He felt he must surround himself with visible evidences of the appreciation in which he was held or there would be a danger that the public, always too ready to judge by externals, would pass him by as a failure, and prefer to him some of his more demonstrative competitors.[3]

33. J. ATKINSON GRIMSHAW,
The Chorale (detail), oil painting, 1878
(Private Collection)

This room in the artist's house is deliberately tricked out with many elements of the artistic interior.

THE EVOLUTION OF THE ARTIST'S HOUSE AND GARDEN

Millais boasted to Holman Hunt in 1877, 'My new home shall be a Palace such as Italian painters commonly used, but an eye-opener to the public, as an attic is still associated with our craft'.[4] His image of the Old Masters in their grandeur was timely. Interest in the Italian painters of the Renaissance had been stimulated by the translation of Giorgio Vasari's *Lives of the Most Eminent Painters, Sculptors and Architects*, published in London in 1851. Noting Vasari's interest in, for example, Mantegna's house, Raphael's Roman palazzo and Giulio Romano's frescoed house in Mantua, it is not difficult to make the connection between worldly success as an artist and the possession of a splendid house.

For artists associated with the Aesthetic Movement it was a theme of the period. J.F. Lewis exhibited an imaginary watercolour portrait of Murillo in his studio at the Manchester 'Art Treasures' exhibition in 1857. In about 1861 Simeon Solomon made two watercolour versions of a Renaissance artist in his studio (Whitworth Art Gallery, Manchester, and British Museum), a subject reaffirming the importance and seriousness of his own art and of art in general. Rossetti had made several studies of this kind in the early 1850s, the closest being *Giorgione Painting* (about 1853; Birmingham Museum and Art Gallery). Solomon's painting is much more specific in its detail of the painter's studio and its furniture. The big sleeves of the dresses are a preview of artistic women's costume. Like Lewis's *Murillo*, Rossetti's *Giorgione* exploits the 'great artist' genre, in itself a stimulus to public interest in the artist-heroes of the Italian Renaissance. Interest in Giorgione was probably provoked by Ruskin's lyrical account of the artist's boyhood in the final volume of *Modern Painters*, which appeared in 1860.

In 1867 Jacob Burckhardt included artists' houses as a distinctive genre in *Architecture of the Italian Renaissance*, demonstrating the diversity of talents of the Old Masters, who practised as architects and sculptors as well as painters. The idea of an architecturally distinguished studio-house was adopted with enthusiasm in France, where successful artists built palatial homes, exotically decorated. Widely publicized, they inspired grandiose artists' residences in many other countries. They contributed to the perception of the great artist as master of all the arts. Leighton, for example, exemplified this Renaissance ideal, being painter, sculptor, amateur architect and accomplished decorative artist with ambitious mural programmes to his credit. These publications were the prelude to a flood of writings on artists' homes and studios.

Inevitably this development was largely a London phenomenon; most artists felt the need to be at the hub, where things happened and patrons congregated. On the whole urban architecture, in this as in many other aspects, forged ahead of rural development. Particularly revealing are the auction catalogues of artists' houses, some posthumous or in the wake of financial disaster as in the case of Whistler, with their lists of accumulated curiosities and examples of artistic furniture (see pl.1). Considered together, the houses reveal interesting architectural, decorative (as in the ubiquitous Morris wallpapers, blue-and-white china, decorative tiles and Oriental rugs) and style associations, as well as social patterns and connections. As in fine art, the Aesthetic interior subsumed moral messages in richness of texture and colour; interior design was freed from didacticism and realism and even, to a certain extent, domestic propriety. The artistic community was close-knit, a web of friendships and professional relations between artist and patron. It brought together people from very diverse social backgrounds in a loose confederacy, presaging a new social order, almost a class of its own, whose identity consolidated in artistic London in the twentieth century. Public interest in artists' lives and their environment ensured wide exposure in the press, embracing a large cast of characters, but at its core a smaller, tightly knit group of artists, architects and designers wielded influence way outside the artistic community. They attracted attention because they were interesting, often larger than life like Leighton and William Morris, or, like Rossetti and Whistler, scornful of conventional expectations.

The trajectory of the purpose-built artist's house and its garden as it entered fashionable consciousness is fascinating to follow. A distinctive house-type, which wrapped the external envelope around the interior spaces, contrasted with the conventional urban plan. Aligned to suit individual needs for light and access, it derived ultimately from the architecture of A.W.N. Pugin and the Gothic Revival. From its origins in practicality and convenience, the artist's house with its contents forms an essential component of the Aesthetic Movement. The immediate outcome was a spread of 'hands-on' interior decoration as home owners created their own artistic style. In the long term it led to a key place in International Art Nouveau, with every element in the room considered in relation to the whole. Artists as homeowners and decorators span both sides of the Movement, as its creators and as consumers. With hindsight, the Aesthetic Movement has acquired such a strong visual identity that it is hard to know just how it seemed at the time. The style of life that evolved from the Victorian artistic milieu was the first in which middle-class taste had a serious impact on fashions in decorating, and a visible effect on the cultivated upper classes; it has a direct bearing on the way we live now. One of the more beguiling aspects of 'artistic' home-making was that, demonstrably, a beautiful environment was not necessarily linked to wealth.

With much of the building taking place on spacious plots in suburban London, gardens assumed a considerable importance to these artists' residences. The idea that distinguished the urban garden from its rural counterpart was that it should form an additional living space or 'room' as an adjunct to the house. The space could be backed with ornamental trelliswork, and furnished with balustrade and steps set with stone urns and large terracotta pots overflowing with plants. A shift in fashion to the architectural Italianate style of garden also favoured small spaces, as an impression of grandeur and lavish expenditure could be achieved within a

34. M. STONE, RA, *Two's Company, Three's None*, oil painting, 1892 (Blackburn Museum and Art Gallery)

A sentimental Regency scene set in the garden of Stone's Melbury Road studio-house, showing the huge urn on a pedestal and vernacular 'Old English' furniture.

relatively tiny compass. While access to the aristocratic masterpieces of formal Italianate planning at estates like Trentham, Alton Towers and Holkham Hall could be difficult, the fashionable Italian gardens in such public places as Regent's Park and Hyde Park were open to all. The Italian and Dutch gardens at Holland House, much admired by artists, inspired many similar experiments.

From 1861 until about 1880 the public could visit the Horticultural Society's garden with its enormous conservatory, built on land at South Kensington which had been purchased with profits from the 1851 Great Exhibition. The garden was laid out with geometric flower borders in a Florentine scroll pattern, monogram beds in box and gravel 'embroidery', gravel walks, basins and cascades. It was welcomed as a model for future urban gardeners. There was a terrace with two bandstands, balustraded and furnished with great urns filled with flowers. The vast conservatory was crammed with exotics, conspicuous among them the large-leaved banana trees. The tessellated floor by Messrs Minton was a showpiece for their tile mosaic work. This intensive gardening style was suited to the formal London garden. Both Tissot and Marcus Stone made good use of their carefully designed town gardens in their popular romantic subject matter (pl.34). Through its development, from intense formality with geometric bedding to a more unstructured, but still controlled, 'French' style, Tissot's St John's Wood garden perfectly exemplifies the lessons taught at South Kensington.

THE INFLUENCE OF THE SOUTH KENSINGTON MUSEUM

Meanwhile, many aspects of the rapidly developing South Kensington Museum offer a mirror to the parallel development of the artists' houses. Both promoted the home as a work of art. Many of the artists whose lives and houses are examined in this book were involved in some capacity with the museum and its collections. The museum was responsible for creating public interest in the wider artistic milieu. Its purpose, to provide inspiration to designers and manufacturers and to improve public taste, has a direct relevance to 'artistic' taste in home design and decoration.[5] Founding director Sir Henry Cole was not afraid to be didactic, and one of his earliest assaults on public taste, or lack of it, was the display in 1852 of 87 examples of 'False Principles in Decoration' designed to illustrate where British manufacturers were in error. The chief fault in Cole's eyes was the 'direct imitation of nature', illustrated by a furnishing chintz printed with roses and blue ribbons on a white ground. This project caused a good deal of outrage, since many of the exhibits were the cherished choices of up-and-coming middle-class households.

The Museum building itself was conceived as a display of modern construction methods and materials, both inside and out, its mission being to use 'the highest art available'. Cole saw the opportunity to advertise the virtues of a whole range of new building materials, including cast iron, terracotta, tiles and sculptural ceramics, mosaics, tessellated flooring and durable wall-coverings. The use of colour and the unusual use of ceramic material, both for walls and floors, were hugely influential. Leighton's house is just one example: the mosaic-tiled floors in the hallway are strongly reminiscent of those laid from about 1864 in the South Kensington Museum's ground-level galleries. These were made by students of the South Kensington Mosaic Class, formed in 1862.

Not least amongst the Museum's functions was publicizing artistic interior decoration through William Morris's 'Green Dining Room' (1866) and the Japanesque blue-and-white 'Grill Room' decorated by Edward Poynter (1868). With its carefully designed Japanese-style details (particularly the elegant iron and brass grill), the Grill Room was a practical demonstration of the application of an Aesthetic work of art to a domestic situation (pl.35). And the deal worked both ways: it is a measure of the South Kensington influence that during the 1870s Morris was developing a large range of wallpapers and textiles inspired by artefacts in the Museum collections.[6]

35. E.J. POYNTER, cartoon for tile panel, 'October', in the Grill Room, South Kensington Museum, watercolour, 1870 (V&A: 7916.10)

A key example of the Museum's patronage of the Art Movement was the very big commission for painted tiles – including those for the Grill Room – from the Kensington Gore Art Pottery Studio, which was actually on the premises. The artists employed in decorating the Museum uncannily echo the identities of the owners of distinctive houses. As well as Morris and Poynter, Leighton was commissioned in 1869 to make vast mural lunettes in the South Court, illustrating the place of the industrial arts in peace and war. He worked on them throughout the 1870s and 1880s.[7] The Renaissance-style scheme for the South Court was specifically designed to highlight the possibilities of various techniques and materials, including mosaic and polychromed iron. It was a success with the visitors, who regarded the frescoes as examples of elegance and beauty. Photographs of the lunettes were sent to provincial art schools and a number of copies were made, ensuring familiarity with a wide public.

Philip Webb, Burne-Jones and Morris were all involved in the design and execution of the Green Dining Room, an important legacy of the London International Exhibition of 1862 (pl.36), at which the decorating firm Morris, Marshall, Faulkner & Co. made its debut. This brave venture involving, in some capacity or other, most of the participants in the artistic revolution, signalled important changes in domestic design and decoration. Morris had a radical concept in mind that would put the domestic arts on a level with the Fine Arts. Well in advance of new decorating taste, the dining room looks forward in structure and treatment to the wall-divisions and painted woodwork of the artistic style. The

36. P. WEBB, scheme for the Green Dining Room at the South Kensington Museum, watercolour, 1866
(V&A: E.5096–1960)

37. E. Burne-Jones for Morris, Marshall, Faulkner & Co., 'Chaucer Asleep', 1864, stained-glass panel from the series of Chaucer's *Legend of Goode Women* (V&A: 774–1864)

A duplicate of one of the stained-glass panels used in Myles Birket Foster's house, The Hill, Witley in Surrey.

painted wainscoting inspired Godwin, among others, and led to the fashion for the 'dado', one of those curious crazes which the Victorians adopted with merry abandon while also mocking it tirelessly.

The Museum's patronage of Morris's firm came at a crucial moment in its development. It was closely followed by another commission of enormous prestige, the decoration of the 'Armoury' and 'Tapestry Room' at St James's Palace for Queen Victoria. The Morris enterprise was given a further boost by the 1864 'Exhibition of Stained Glass, Mosaics Etc.', held at the South Kensington Museum, from which the Museum acquired a number of stained-glass panels (pl.37).

THE AESTHETIC MOVEMENT AND THE CULT OF BEAUTY

In spite of the prescriptive stance taken, in their different ways, by both Cole and Morris, personal preferences played a large part in the decoration of the 'artistic' house. The Art Movement offered a real and viable alternative to following the herd. Rules on decorating and furnishing could be adapted or even ignored (as by the artists themselves), and this was explicitly sanctioned by a new breed of advice manual on house decoration.[8] A particularly modern trait, the cult of individuality, was endorsed by Mrs Haweis, who exhorted her readers to assert their own taste and develop a personal style. As she remarked in *The Art of Beauty* (1878), 'we naturally turn to artists to tell us what to do'. Artistic taste was seen as an antidote to materialistic Victorian middle-class values, with the pursuit of beauty given precedence over the philistine pursuit of wealth. It is worth remembering that beauty to the Victorians was not just a sensory experience: in 1890 Mrs Panton sententiously remarked that 'when people care for their homes, they are much better in every way, mentally and morally, than those who only regard them as places to eat and sleep in … while if a house is made beautiful, those who dwell in it will … cultivate home virtue'.[9] As an artist's daughter (her father was W.P. Frith), Jane Ellen Panton, columnist for the *Ladies Pictorial*, was in a key position to exploit interest in the new concept of 'interior decoration'; her books were very successful, going into many editions and remaining in print for years. Frith's own taste in house decoration was of the solidly prosperous middle-class variety.

The artist's studio-house had unfolded as an architectural type with a set of newly written rules seeking originality and artistic distinction both externally and internally.[10] Because it did not ape aristocratic taste, followers of Aestheticism felt in control of their middle-class identity. In a sense the Aesthetic interior, primarily motivated by an abstract concept of 'beauty' rather than fashion or cost, allowed anyone and everyone to be an artist, through the medium of a consciously artistic milieu. Ironically, of course, it could not be achieved by the layman without a measure of vulgar wealth: in contrast to the artists themselves, their patrons who followed their decorating ideas were economically well-endowed, often by inheritance.[11] Not everyone found the eclectic ensemble enticing; it obliterated certain well-established conventions in gender-typing of rooms – the feminine rococo-revival drawing room, the Renaissance dining room and the masculine Gothic-style library – and it is noticeable that these orderly conventions were largely perpetuated in the 'Aesthetic' mansions of wealthy amateurs and collectors, who furnished in recognizable historic and exotic styles attached to particular rooms (Moorish smoking rooms and Japanese and Indian boudoirs were popular over a long period).

F.R. Leyland's externally unassuming stuccoed terrace house at 49 Prince's Gate had, in addition to the 'Peacock Room' created by Whistler, an Italianate entrance hall, a Renaissance triple reception room on the first floor, and a panelled 'Tapestry' room used as a morning room.[12] These conventions extended to colours and textiles, with light-coloured chintzes in the female domain and rich, dark velvet and plush in the male quarters. However, Aestheticism largely overcame the heavily gendered perception of separate spheres in collecting, where women are characterized as the curators of 'old china', fans, lace, embroideries and bric-à-brac in general, and men as connoisseurs of the fine arts of painting and sculpture. The old hierarchies of display, with paintings covering the walls of a designated picture gallery, gave way to the crowded assemblage of fine and applied arts together. Du Maurier offers a contemporary slant on the blurring of gendered roles in his 'Chinamania' satires, alternating men and women as chinamaniacs and showing couples collaborating as collectors. The two cartoons featured in the *Punch Almanack* for 1875, 'Acute Chinamania' (a woman laments her broken vase) and 'Acute Chinamania (Incurable)' (a man boasts of the rarity of his broken dish), make exactly this alternation. 'Pet and Hobby (showing that Chinamaniacs have their Affections like other People)' extends the story to include a precocious child (pl.38): the legend reads

> *Dorothy 'Oh, Mother! I love you better than Silver, and better than Gold.'*
> *Mother 'And better than Blue China, Dorothy?'*
> *Dorothy (after slight hesitation) 'Yes, Mother! Better than Blue China!'*
> *Mother (much moved), 'D – d – d – darling.'* [13]

Nonetheless, men clung to their decision-making role, as is particularly apparent in the decorating decisions taken by Linley Sambourne and Oscar Wilde. While editor of *Women's World* Wilde in fact paid lip-service to the idea of the woman as decorator and home-maker, but in practice he tightly controlled the style of house in Tite Street he shared with his wife, Constance.

38. G. DU MAURIER, *Pet and Hobby*, pen-and-ink drawing, 1876 (V&A: E.399–1948)

The cartoon appeared in *Punch* on 26 August 1876. Du Maurier's drawings have a subtlety and satiric edge that is inevitably lost in reproduction. The Madonna and Child imagery, with an Oriental dish as halo, would not have been lost on *Punch* readers.

As the Art Movement developed it blended with *japonisme* and a further eclectic range of sources from Ancient Egypt, Moorish Spain, Chinese, Indian and Persian art, and English eighteenth-century styles in various guises, expressed in a free style in architecture and domestic decoration. The stars of architecture and design that emerged from the 1862 International Exhibition were set to transform domestic arts; as well as Norman Shaw and Burges, these included John Pollard Seddon and G.E. Street; and Street's pupils Webb and Morris with their artist associates in the Morris decorating firm, Madox Brown, Rossetti and Burne-Jones. Street's office was the training ground for the elite of this generation, providing the principal players in the formation of the new genre.

In place of Pugin, who had died ten years earlier, Burges organized the 1862 Medieval Court for the Ecclesiological Society, and his commitment to colour permeated the whole display. The painted furniture constituted a miniature picture gallery of advanced taste, with contributions from Rossetti, Madox Brown and Burne-Jones, Poynter, Simeon Solomon, Albert Moore and Henry Stacy Marks, all important to Aestheticism in painting. Aestheticism had high-profile advocates in Whistler and Wilde, both – not coincidentally – aspiring to a 'House Beautiful', in Wilde's case a collaboration between the two of them. For a while advanced taste would be defined by the eclecticism of the Aesthetic Movement, but alongside the claims of Japan, 'Queen Anne' and the French Renaissance style preferred by the very rich, a Reformed Gothic legacy survived. Burges's schemes for the millionaire Marquess of Bute at Cardiff Castle and Castell Coch, and his own personal 'palace of art', Tower House in Kensington (see p.155), perpetuated the handmade interior. Architect-designers working for the furniture trade met the more practical requirements of the intellectual and artistic middle class.

Clearly, architectural and design patronage by artists and their middle-class patrons rather than the aristocracy and the wealthy upper-middle class was likely to have interesting results. The taste that emerged brought into being a whole troupe of companies supplying 'Art Furniture', 'Art Wallpaper', 'Art Pottery' and all the accessories of the fashionable interior. The term 'Art Furniture' was coined by Charles L. Eastlake in *Hints on Household Taste* (1868) specifically for products designed by architects or artists and made by craftsmen. Significantly, workshops where they were created were often 'studios'. Eastlake's seminal publication was the stimulus of much that occurred in artistic home decoration, including the discriminating choice of wallpapers and textiles. Although Morris's patterns are overwhelmingly evident in the schemes surveyed here, wallpapers and textiles as defining elements in the Aesthetic interior attracted many leading designers, among them Godwin, Bruce Talbert, Christopher Dresser and Walter Crane.

Commercially, 'artistic' style drew on a number of sources, including the modern Gothic, Islamic art, *japonisme* and the Moorish wood-carving admired by artist-collectors. William Watt's Artistic Furniture Warehouse was making up Godwin's designs as early as 1867 (pl.39). Dresser's ground-breaking Art Furnishers' Alliance (1880–3) in New Bond Street, founded to supply 'whatever is necessary to the complete artistic furnishing of a house', was described as selling 'aesthetic' furnishings; Thomas Goode, the elegant Queen Anne-style emporium in South Audley Street, had an 'Aesthetic Room'. Other 'art-furnishers' were quick to spot the trend. Reports in the press express high hopes for Dresser's emporium, the *Daily News* opining that the Art Furnishers' Alliance would introduce the public to a new style of decoration, 'making all things as beautiful as their nature will admit of'.[14] *Funny Folks* was not so respectful, as usual finding something inherently comical in all attempts at artistic styling: 'The latest branching out of the aesthetes is in the form of an Art-Furnishers' Alliance in New Bond-street, under the art-advisorship of Dr Dresser. Clearly he is expected to be the re-Dresser of our Philistine enormities.'[15]

Design Reform proselytizing and the succession of World's Fairs had opened the eyes of the general public to choices and to the wide range of design products

39. E.W. Godwin, design for a
display of Anglo-Japanese furniture,
watercolour, about 1875
(V&A: E.482–1963)

available – the illustrated exhibition catalogues offered visions of shopping opportunities – and public enthusiasm developed that modern phenomenon, recreational shopping. Initially 'Art' manufactures were expensive and exclusive, but the notion quickly took hold in the middle-class marketplace and the term was indiscriminately applied to mass-manufactured goods that were a far cry from anything actually in the artists' houses. Early on, Mrs Haweis had announced in *The Queen* that 'a blue pot and a fat sunflower … are all that is needed to be fashionably aesthetic'. The middle-class artistic house is a celebration of shopping on a grand scale; it contributed to the rise of specialist decorating firms (notably Morris & Co., the direct outcome of building and decorating a 'palace of art') and such artistic emporia as Liberty's of Regent Street. Like Morris & Co., Liberty was a great survivor, managing to make commercial sense out of the 'Art' furnishing movement. Morris had shown how it was possible to retail the artistic look, and the new department stores made it fatally easy. Arthur Lasenby Liberty took up where Godwin and Dresser left off and created his eponymous 'look'.

While the Art Movement was driven by designers and manufacturers, the Aesthetic Movement was largely created by its consumers, the collectors and patrons who made a distinctive milieu of their homes and the contents. Whistler and Godwin, consummate Aesthetes both, bridged the gap, acting as creators of Aesthetic art and design, consumers of art manufactures, and at the same time pioneer collectors of Japanese art. Antique collecting as a middle-class pastime was part of the mix. The eclectic combination of antiques found by chance in unlikely places with specially created furniture and architectural details now relied on yet another resource, through merchants importing from India and Japan in bulk. It is obviously something of a misconception to imagine that 'artistic' taste can be pinpointed and slipped into a neat category in Victorian culture. Artistic taste exhibited an unprecedented capacity for crossing class barriers.[16]

The broad reach of the artist's house aesthetic and the Art Movement in general was also in part due to the aristocratic amateurs, who demonstrated a sincere commitment to mainstream professional careers as artists. Among them was George Howard, who even when he succeeded as Earl of Carlisle managed to combine his heavy duties as a landowner with exhibiting his work. Upper-class patrons combined old-fashioned patronage and collecting with using the newly developed Art Movement supply chain. George Howard commissioned a much-admired purpose-built studio-house by Philip Webb with decoration by the Morris firm and murals by Burne-Jones and Walter Crane (a far cry from the modest shopper for 'Art' wallpapers and fabrics). There was access to serious money, too, in the industrial and mercantile fortunes whose possessors often chose to demonstrate their cultural credentials through art patronage; they built and decorated houses to accommodate their collections that betray a very clear debt to the artists' studio-houses. The American architectural critic Clarence Cook, author of an influential decorating manual *The House Beautiful* (1878), certainly believed so: in his suggestions for the decoration of the 'living-room' (a very modern concept) he extols the supply of furnishing fabrics:

> *As for the coverings of cushions, we need not be at a loss, for there has not been in the last fifty years such a supply of materials for this purpose as there is to-day: the stuffs themselves of first-rate make, and the designs as good as ever were produced at any time.*

And now we reach the nub of the matter:

> *We have serges nowadays, in colors whose delightfulness we all recognize in the pictures that Alma Tadema, and Morris, and Burne-Jones and Rossetti paint, colors that have been turning all the plain girls to beauties of late, and making the beauties more dangerous than ever – the mistletoe-green, the blue-green, the duck's-egg, the rose-amber, the pomegranate-flower, and so forth, and so on, – colors which we owe to the English poet-artists who are oddly lumped together as the Pre-Raphaelites, and who make the new rainbow to confound the scientific decorators who were so sure of what colors would go together, and what colors wouldn't.*[17]

40. G. DU MAURIER, 'The Mutual Admirationists', 1880, from *Society Pictures*, vol.II, p.232

THE MUTUAL ADMIRATIONISTS.

1880.

(Fragments overheard by Grigsby and the Colonel at one of Prigsby's Afternoon Teas.)

Young Maudle (to Mrs. Lyon Hunter and her Daughters). " IN THE SUPREMEST POETRY, *SHAKSPEARE'S* FOR INSTANCE, OR *POSTLE-THWAITE'S*, OR *SHELLEY'S*, ONE ALWAYS FEELS THAT, &C., &C., &C."

Young Postlethwaite (to the three Miss Bilderbogies). " THE *GREATEST* PAINTERS OF *ALL*, SUCH AS *VELASQUEZ*, OR *MAUDLE*, OR EVEN *TITIAN*, INVARIABLY SUGGEST TO ONE, &C., &C., &C."

41. Decorator's specimen panel of wallpaper showing dado, filling and frieze, possibly designed by B.J. Talbert, about 1875 (V&A: E.656–1953)

It was not only the textiles, but the entire decorative scheme that was influenced by the artistic colours detailed above.

The term 'Aesthetic' was bandied about in the 1870s and 1880s, and while it failed to produce a coherent label that could be attached to art and design products – it was more often used to describe colours and styles of dress – it gained wide currency as an idea. An 'Aesthete' had certain unhealthy characteristics, defined in popular culture largely through mockery and satire. Particularly, too great an interest in the decoration and beautification of the home was regarded as effeminate; this was in spite of the fact that although lip-service was increasingly paid to women's choices in this area, men still largely controlled the expenditure and the decisions. The attitude of the general public was summed up by Du Maurier in 'The Mutual Admirationists', set very obviously in an artist's studio, the bohemians being indicated by their unconventional dress (pl.40). Du Maurier's cast of 'Aesthetic' characters featured over a span of about ten years, fixing an image of the artistic milieu, albeit exaggerated but with some undeniable 'hits', in the public mind.

The hallmark of an Aesthetic interior was the 'dado', a low wainscoting painted in a complementary or contrasting colour to the wall above (pl.41). Following the example of the Green Dining Room at the South Kensington Museum, it was Eastlake who was responsible for promoting the tripartite treatment of walls. Broken up into dado, filling and frieze, panels were conveniently supplied in one piece by the enterprising firm of Jeffrey & Co., but most often in artistic households it was devised from unusual materials such as Japanese matting or leather paper. Dresser, in his *Principles of Decorative Design* (1873), wrote about the treatment of the patterned dado with an explanatory illustration (pl.42). The following is an extract from a much longer passage:

> *I like the formation of a dado, for it affords an opportunity of giving apparent stability to the wall by making its lower portion dark; and furniture is invariably much improved by being seen against a dark background. The occupants of a room always look better when viewed in conjunction with a dark background, and ladies' dresses certainly do.*
>
> *The dark dado gives the desired background without rendering it necessary that the entire wall be dark. If the furniture be mahogany, it will be wonderfully improved by being placed against a chocolate wall.*[18]

Dresser recommended a blue dado:

> *A citrine wall comes well with a deep blue, or blue and white ceiling, if blue prevails in the cornice, and this wall may have a dark blue (ultramarine and black with a little white) dado, or a rich maroon dado (brown lake). If the blue dado is employed the skirting should be indigo, which, when varnished and seen in conjunction with the blue, will appear black as jet.*

This is decorating advice at its most specific and explains the success of what might be termed the 'Dresser project', a combination of designs, publications and lectures on artistic decoration. However, the passage of time inevitably eroded the fashionable appeal of what was no longer a novelty. A sure sign was that, by the early 1880s, the 'artistic' treatment of walls had fallen victim to a barrage of satire.[19] *Punch* started in on the dado as early as 1875 (23 October), with some spoof decorating advice from Leonardo Della Robbia de Tudor Westpond Tumpkyns. 'Expense should be no object. My aim is to create a National taste in internal and external House Decoration', he announced. The piece runs to two columns and is too long to quote, but it starts with a cod definition of the dado and goes on to recommend flock wallpaper, a tiled hall floor and a novelty door-knocker. As with all satire, this is close to the truth. The comic paper *Judy* has an undeniably cruel piece on 'The Sage-green Sickness' in 1880 (pl.43) illustrated with an 'Aesthetic' set-piece of Japanese fans and sunflower dado.

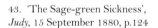

42. C. Dresser, scheme for wall-decoration with dado, *Principles of Decorative Design*, 1873, colour plate opposite p.84

43. 'The Sage-green Sickness', *Judy*, 15 September 1880, p.124

This is just one of many examples in a campaign of mockery waged in comic papers in Britain and America from the mid-1870s.

THE SAGE-GREEN SICKNESS.

In quick succession in 1881 two theatrical productions opened in London, mercilessly satirizing artistic dress, manners and interior decoration. First to open, at the Prince of Wales Theatre in February, was *The Colonel* by Frank Burnand, editor of *Punch*, and only weeks later, in April, Gilbert and Sullivan's *Patience*. *The Colonel* has been quite overshadowed by *Patience*, but it attracted a good deal of attention in the press, particular notice being taken of the 'Aesthetic' scene-setting. Particularly revealing about attitudes to the Aesthetic Movement, the reviewer in *The Stage*, signing simply 'DA', wrote:

> *It would have been strange indeed if the modern craze for art furniture and art costume had not been sooner or later caricatured upon the stage. The theatre itself has had a great deal to do with encouraging the subject of the caricature, and the appointments of the pieces produced by Messrs. Bancroft and Hare have helped to extend the prevalent fashion for subdued form and colour within doors. It by no means follows, however, that because a fashion affords an opportunity for burlesque that it is*

on that account to be deprecated. Black, angular furniture and flowing draperies of sage green and peacock blue are very much better than the Rococo Spanish mahogany monstrosities and garish dress patterns which satisfied our parents. Prior to the Great Exhibition of 1851 the furniture of middle-class English homes and the dresses worn by middle-class English women may fairly be described as triumphs of bad taste. We have improved since then, and it may even be admitted that there is a tendency just now to carry the love of the beautiful a trifle too far. It does not, however, follow that a fondness for elegant forms and harmonious colouring must necessarily be accompanied by a ridiculous affectation of manners, or that we cannot emulate Athenian culture without being a nation of milksops.[20]

The following extract from a review in *The Observer* takes the story further:

The second act has for its scene a room decorated in such Philistine fashion as to contrast in the most forcible manner possible with the æsthetic apartment, in which lilies and sunflowers run impossible riot. We are not sure, however, whether Mrs. Blyth's studiously common-place parlour would not please the really æsthetic eye more than the grotesque drawing-room supposed to be fitted up in accordance with the taste of the cult. Whatever the excesses of Mr. Burne Jones's indiscreet followers may have been, their influence has as yet been decidedly beneficial so far as the upholstery and dress of the period are concerned. So it would be hard, indeed, if, except in a joke, such a fireplace as Mrs. Forrester's and such a coiffure as Lady Tompkins's were laid to their charge.[21]

Burnand had appealed to Du Maurier in July 1880 for advice on the design of the stage set, and he suggested the following:

Try & have a room papered with Morris' green Daisy, with a dado six feet high of green-blue serge in folds – and a matting with rugs for floor (Indian red matting if possible) – spider-legged black tables & sideboard – black rush-bottomed chairs & arm chairs; blue china plates on the wall with plenty of space between – here & there a blue china vase with an enormous hawthorn or almond blossom sprig ... also on mantel piece pots with lilies & peacock feathers – plain dull yellow curtains lined with dull blue for windows if wanted. Japanese sixpenny fans now & then on the walls in this picturesque unexpectedness.[22]

On 29 July Godwin, resenting the fact that one of the stage settings bore a marked similarity to his own ideas on decoration, responded with a minutely detailed appraisal of the sets:

There are but two scenes in the comedy, both interiors, one supposed to be founded on aestheticism, the other on common sense. Looking round the last, we find it very much upholstered with yards on yards of curtain stuff of a staring, loud pattern: an entirely vulgar uninteresting, unpleasant apartment. But it is <u>this</u> the moral of the piece indicates as right. Turning to the other room that is presented to us as wrong, we find it furnished with artistic and simple things: a charming cabinet in walnut designed by Mr Padgett for the green room; some simple inexpensive black Sussex chairs, like those sold by Wm. Morris and Co.; a black coffee table, after the well-known example originally designed in 1867 by the writer of these notes; a quite simple writing table, matting on the floor, a green and yellow paper on the walls, a sunflower frieze, and a Japanese treatment of the ceiling (storks), and a red sun such as we see in Japanese books and on hand-screens, make up a scene which, if found wanting in certain details and forced in sunflowers, is certainly an interesting room, with individuality about it, and, what is most important, harmonious and pleasing.[23]

In 1881 Du Maurier announced the death of the Movement, composing a lament for his world of Aesthetes, 'The Downfall of the Dado'. In the verses a group of Aesthetes give up their sage-green clothes, break their blue-and-white china and tear up the lilies and sunflowers.[24] They all seize hatchets, pokers and chisels and proceed to demolish the dado. It goes without saying that this obituary for artistic taste and interior style was wildly premature. However, the following year Walter Hamilton published *The Aesthetic Movement in England*, a survey of what in his mind seemed almost to have become history. Of course the movement had not died; it lingered in commerce and popular taste for many years, but the initiative was passing to the Arts and Crafts experiments, which were just beginning to gather momentum.

The Aesthetes were easy targets and, therefore, heaven-sent fodder for *Punch* and other satirical publications, where a sneering tone was commonly used in items on the subject. On 31 March 1883 *Punch* ran a spoof advertisement:

> *To be sold, the whole of the Stock-in-Trade, Appliances and Inventions of a Successful Aesthete, who is retiring from business. This will include a large stock of faded lilies, dilapidated Sunflowers, and shabby Peacock's Feathers, several long-haired Wigs, a collection of incomprehensible Poems, entitled Instructions to Aesthetes, continuing a list of aesthetic catchwords, drawings of aesthetic attitudes, and many choice secrets of the craft. Also, a number of well-used Dadoes, sad-coloured Draperies, blue and white China, and brass fenders … no reasonable offer refused.*

In fact the dado saga continued with a squib in *Funny Folks* (31 March 1883) illustrated with a room clearly furnished by Godwin. The caption reads: 'Those dreadful holidays. Awkward position of the Montresor Dado family on Easter Monday. Servants out for a holiday, every shop shut, and nothing in the house but a philistine Hot Cross bun. If sunflowers had only been in season!' *Funny Folks*, describing itself as 'A weekly budget of funny pictures, funny notes, etc.', was published in London from 1874 to 1894. In January 1882 it jumped on the obituary bandwagon with a final shaft: the cartoon is titled 'Exodus of the Aesthetes' and shows Oscar Wilde on his way to America, leading the main constituents of the Aesthetic tendency with him, including a book of 'designs for dados'.

DEVISING THE ARTIST'S HOUSE AND STUDIO

Artistic design promoted dream houses; the plans for many artists' houses started out as idealistic communal ventures, embodying common aims and achievements. The best-known example is Morris's Red House, but several of the houses were shared. Rossetti's original scheme for Tudor House was a communal household with his brother William Michael, the poet Algernon Swinburne, and the writer George Meredith. Others were passed from hand to hand: 1 Tor Villa on Campden Hill was occupied successively by a number of different artists. In 1857 Holman Hunt took it from the landscape and genre painter James Clark Hook, and lived there with Robert Braithwaite Martineau and Michael Halliday, both genre painters with a strong Pre-Raphaelite bent. Hunt and his friends were succeeded by a landscape watercolourist with a confusingly similar name, Alfred William Hunt. In nearby Kensington Square, Poynter took over from Burne-Jones. Traces of artistic decoration left by the successive tenants formed a palimpsest of reformed taste.

The innovative character of purpose-built studio-houses attracted comment and criticism, not all of it favourable, as witness the repeated complaints from the Metropolitan Board of Works at any sign of originality or innovation. The Board's advisers evinced a liking for the sort of conventional – and often historically incorrect – ornament that was quite incompatible with the studio-house aesthetic. With some rare exceptions – for example Whistler's strikingly modern White House in Chelsea, designed for him by Godwin – the preferred architectural type was derived from seventeenth-century English and Dutch precedents, under the generic label 'Queen Anne'. Even as late as 1889 the style, much in evidence in Tite Street, Chelsea, a miniature artists' quarter of its own, was not always popular:

Alongside this artistic squalor [the surrounding streets of old Chelsea] *we have the curious contrast of artistic splendour in a blazing, brand-new quarter, of which the sacred centre is Tite Street. Here amid much that is good and genuine in our modern manner, there is an aggressive affectation of antiquity shown by the little houses and studios obtruding on the street … all in raging red brick, and in the so-called Queen Anne style.*[25]

Architecturally the legacy of the purpose-built studio-house was widespread and long-lived, particularly apparent in the use of traditional building materials (the red brick buildings contrasted strongly with the pale stucco of the mid-nineteenth-century urban landscape) and from the 1870s onwards in the use of ornament (terracotta modelled panels, tile inserts and stained glass) for domestic buildings. Following this lead, the subsequent architectural development of districts where artists' houses proliferated was often quaint and picturesque, notably in Melbury Road in the Holland Park area of Kensington, in Hampstead, particularly the length of Frognal from the end of Church Row to Oak Hill Park, and along the river Thames in Chelsea. Bedford Park was a direct outcome, built for 'artistic people of moderate incomes'.

An American perspective on this 'artistic' urban house style was provided by the cultivated and cosmopolitan American visitor Mrs Henry Adams, who lived in London for a period in 1879. Writing to her father in Boston, she remarked:

The red brick houses à la Queen Anne, with red-tiled roofs and carved brick ornament and wrought-iron balconies, are delicious; and the London smoke and soot softens them at once, so that they look as if they had grown on the spot from seed. They are far less gimcracky than Mrs Fiske's corner of Clarendon and Commonwealth Avenue [in Boston], *and have no savour of affectation, here at least.*[26]

The more easily copied of artistic decorating fashions cast a shadow very widely, with the popular Morris & Co. wallpapers and simple 'Sussex' chairs, the collections of Oriental porcelain and embroideries lingering in artistic suburban houses well into the twentieth century. Bedford Park, the first 'garden suburb', retains its artistic character even today. In fact, it survived the 1960s by the skin of its teeth, through the efforts of the fledgling Victorian Society. All these areas retain examples of their Victorian artistic heritage, but most of the artists have now departed to more affordable neighbourhoods. Houses in the Aesthetic taste for wealthy connoisseurs and collectors in the Brompton area and parts of Bayswater followed in the footsteps of successful artists who had either built for themselves or taken on earlier houses displaying many of the same architectural characteristics.

In the literature on artists' houses Leighton's studio-house and the one next door, designed by Webb for Val Prinsep, contend for the distinction of being first in London. Maurice B. Adams, writing in the *Building News* in 1880, called Prinsep's 'the first artist's house of its kind erected in London', and Henry-Russell Hitchcock singled it out as the first English studio-house.[27] In fact, not only was Prinsep's house Webb's third studio-house, but by 1864 several artists owned purpose-built London houses with integral studios: John Linnell in Bayswater, Sir Edwin Landseer in St John's Wood, Richard Redgrave and Charles West Cope in Knightsbridge (a pair of attached houses, 27–28 Hyde Park Gate; 1841) and James Rannie Swinton in Pimlico (a large corner house at 33 Warwick Square; 1858–60). A successful Scottish society portrait painter with an aristocratic clientele – by appointment, it might be remarked, to a succession of fashionable beauties – Swinton commissioned his studio-house from the architect George Morgan as a place to live and work, and to receive and impress his patrons. The house, first to be built privately, still stands at an axis to the street, a feature that would distinguish artists' houses from their neighbours and already announcing an extravagant disregard for the symmetry of contemporary urban development. Swinton's house was planned on grand lines, with a magnificent entrance hall and imposing *escalier d'arrivé* with a domed roof, a ballroom on the first floor and a huge glass conservatory. In its ostentation it was almost a blueprint for Millais's Kensington palazzo, built some twelve years later. In 1865 Swinton married Blanche Fitzgerald De Ros, daughter of the Irish peer Baron De Ros.

Contemporary with Swinton's house is the Kensington terraced development, 1–7 Cromwell Place (1858–9), by the speculative builder Sir Charles Freake. These 'gentlemen's studios' were occupied by Sir Coutts Lindsay, artist-founder of the Grosvenor Gallery; Lord Somers, amateur artist-photographer; and Millais. However, they all conform to conventional urban architectural styles of their time rather than breaking new ground like the later houses. Outside London, the railway-fuelled exodus had already produced a little cluster of home-counties studio-houses: William Morris's Red House at Bexleyheath in Kent (1858–9), John Roddam Spencer Stanhope's Fairmile at Cobham in Surrey in 1860 (both by Webb) and The Hill at Witley in Surrey for Myles Birket Foster, to name just a few.

Morris's Red House, the first modern domestic house discussed by Hermann Muthesius in his important study *The English House* (*Das Englische Haus*, originally published in Berlin in 1904), provides a pertinent departure point. Commissioned by the privately wealthy Morris when he was only 25 years old and designed by his friend Webb, the house, a landmark in domestic architecture and certainly the first middle-class 'Palace of Art', was completed in 1859 (pl.44). Muthesius, who offers a Continental view of all that was singular in English domestic buildings from 1860, called it – with pardonable exaggeration – 'the first private house of the new artistic culture'; it also embodied the spirit of community, with the women and men of the household banding together to achieve their high aims for its beautification. Rossetti, one of the collaborators in its decoration, called it 'more a poem than a house … but admirable to live in too'; had it been finished to Morris's plans it would have achieved that ideal in reality as well as in conception.[28] Muthesius understood the importance of the Red House experiment, stressing that

> *The interior is a whole, the essence of which lies, in fact in its totality, in its quality in space. In conceiving the interior as a work of art, therefore, the artist must first think of it as a space, that is, as the over-all form and the interrelationships of the space-enclosing surfaces.*[29]

He goes on to trace a line from the romantic vernacular revival – a key element in Aesthetic taste – to the beginnings of modernism, moving from 'Red House' to Bedford Park and Hampstead Garden Suburb and through to Charles Rennie Mackintosh's Mains Street flat in Glasgow (pl.45).[30]

Mackintosh just makes it into the Victorian period as an 'artistic' architect. The Mains Street flat dates from 1900; his most ambitious undertaking, Windyhill, Kilmalcolm, near Glasgow, designed in the same year for a friend, William Davidson, a wealthy Glasgow provision merchant, was one of only three complete homes created by him. It survives intact (or nearly so: some of the furniture was donated to the Glasgow School of Art in 1937), and as a dwelling house it poses all the challenges that arise when trying to lead a domestic life within a work of art. In 1900 Mackintosh had complete control of the house and its contents, designing furniture, fireplaces, panelling, stained glass, light-fittings and built-in cupboards. Although it is an extreme example of the fully integrated total work of art, it has proved very liveable, remaining in private ownership for more than a hundred years, during which time it changed hands only four times. The steep hillside garden is still as it was in Mackintosh's day.

The architectural historian Nikolaus Pevsner positioned Mackintosh firmly as a pioneer of the Modern Movement: William Morris and E.W. Godwin are identified similarly as proto-modernists (not without fairly impassioned debate on the legitimacy of these propositions), begging the question as to whether the eclectic artist's house as an architectural genre is more than just a pointer towards a modern way of living.[31] Perhaps it actually heralded the fully developed modern

RED HOUSE, UPTON.

44. F. Griggs, *Red House, Upton (Bexleyheath),*
illustration from J.W. Mackail's biography
of William Morris, 1899

45. C.R. Mackintosh, interior
in his Mains Street flat, Glasgow,
photograph, 1899
(Annan Collection, Glasgow)

lifestyle that arrived over decades of redefinition in the last quarter of the twentieth century. The real innovation arrived with the notion, promoted by Norman Shaw and Webb, that an artist's house should embody a distinctive architectural character (see pls 50–53). An essential feature was that the external elevation was dictated by the peculiar requirements of the artist's household. The orientation of the house was decided by the need for its integral studio to face north, introducing a welcome asymmetry into the traditional urban street pattern. Another key element was the fastidious choice of building materials, using warm red brick, stone dressings and terracotta ornament. In the large windows, the close grid of glazing bars or even latticed panes contrasted with the widespread use of large panes of plate-glass for the Italianate stuccoed terraced houses favoured by urban developers.

The architect-designed artist's house with its 'show studio' was an asset of considerable value, a mark of worldly and professional success. Almost mythic significance attached to the studio-houses rising in the mid-1870s in Melbury Road (part of the Holland Estate in Kensington) as their ownership appeared to herald enormous esteem and financial gain for their occupants. However, one inhabitant of this charmed quarter who had no truck with the society side of studio life was Albert Moore: he resisted all bourgeois aspirations. He lived in a purpose-built studio designed by himself on the corner of Holland Lane, close to Leighton, but he had no respect for his creation, and it was exactly that: a working studio. Walford Graham Robertson, elegant and well-to-do young dilettante, writer, collector, theatre designer and Whistlerian painter, who 'knew everybody', was Moore's pupil while still a schoolboy. He found Moore 'a strange and interesting figure in the world of art. Few people knew him well, for he seldom took the trouble to make

46. A. MOORE, *Pomegranates*,
oil painting, 1866
(Guildhall Art Gallery)

Moore's extensive accumulation of ceramics and textiles was not an art collection in the sense of Leighton's, deliberately pursued by a connoisseur, but its constituents conformed to Aesthetic taste.

friends, yet he was the most gentle and affectionate of friends'.[32] Moore's dwelling and workplace consisted of 'two huge studios, a sitting-room with nothing to sit on in it, a bedroom and … a kitchen'.[33] It was overrun with cats and spiders, the pipes leaked and the rooms were covered in dust. The studios were never decorated, dusted or mended, and when the roof dripped, jugs were set to catch the water. It is ironic that Moore shunned interior decor and the Aesthetic lifestyle since his paintings offer the most refined colour harmonies and elegant upholstery, inspiring to the artistic decorator (pl.46). His studio housed an extensive collection of exotic furniture, beautiful pots and vases, silks and lace, which he deployed in endless studies of classically draped women which made his reputation.

Robertson was the ultimate in *fin-de-siècle* dandyism. His early flirtation with painting gave way later to a passion for the theatre and he took up designing and play-writing; but his apprenticeship was very much within the orbit of the Aesthetic Movement. He haunted Burne-Jones's studio and tagged after Whistler, becoming his friend in the 1890s; he attended soirées and cultivated celebrities. His work is more like Whistler's than his teacher Moore's, revealing muted colours with a predominance of grey and the fluid brushwork which was Whistler's trademark. He is now best known for his memoir, *Time Was*, published in 1931, a fount of studio gossip and charming anecdotes of all the prominent figures in the arts. He inhabited two artists' houses, his own in Melbury Road and Sandhills in Surrey, previously home of the watercolourist Helen Allingham.

ARTISTS AND THEIR ARCHITECTS

Artists were exacting clients, and they usually chose architects with considerable 'edge': it took stamina to employ Webb or Godwin. Norman Shaw's pleasing character was a quality very much on display in his houses, and it is probably no coincidence that he had a number of patrons from the wealthy artistic upper and middle class. What it took to employ Burges was money – a great deal of it – with the net result that his only artist client was himself.

Webb's Red House for Morris provided the template for the domestic 'Palace of Art'; he went on to design 1 Palace Green for George Howard (1867–8) and George Price Boyce's vernacular-style red-brick house in Chelsea (1868–9). An austere character, Webb's architectural career was his whole existence; examining the detail of his design and building work and his relations with clients from within the Pre-Raphaelite circle of artists, collectors and patrons reveals much about him as a person. His succession of clients throws a fascinating light on one of the many close-knit networks which snaked their way through the intricacies of Victorian society. A perfectionist, he was unable to work for people who did not share his views on good architecture and building practice. Some sharp exchanges resulted even from his relationships with sympathetic employers. Owing to his insistence on designing every detail of every building, he was not prolific. He was fanatically scrupulous about money and often worked without a fee or refused money owing to him if any dispute arose about his professional competence. The result was an impoverished, but not unhappy, old age.

Leighton's relationship with his architect, George Aitchison, also embodies a fascinating story of artistic collaboration. It was the only domestic architectural commission undertaken by Aitchison and carried through every stage to its final form. Their partnership lasted from the first discussion of the plan in 1864 until the last refinement of the Arabian fantasy in 1896, the year of Leighton's death. Payments to Aitchison are recorded for each of those 32 years.[34] Leighton rejected the cosily picturesque 'Olde English' style which had become the accepted architectural language for 'artistic' dwellings. The rather austere, plain exterior of his house gives way to a rich and colourful interior, glowing with tiles and glossy black wood incised with gold. With its mixed classical references and forward-looking use of iron and glass, as well as the exotic Arab Hall added in 1878,

47. Leighton House, the Italianate exterior with Grecian detailing showing the Arab Hall extension and the ziggurats on the parapet (Leighton House Museum)

48. Carved wood canopy from the interior of Lululaund, home of the painter Sir Hubert von Herkomer, Bushey, Hertfordshire (V&A: W.21–1980)

The house was partly demolished in 1938; this highly ornate arched vaulted canopy with floral scroll motifs and lancet trefoil arches gives a flavour of the richly decorated interior.

49. J. CALLCOTT HORSLEY, RA, *A Pleasant Corner*, oil painting, signed and dated 1865 (Royal Academy of Arts)

This shows an early example of the inglenook, which became popular with admirers of the Olde English style.

Leighton's house remains unique (pl.47). Aitchison went on to design Watts's picture gallery and to advise Alma-Tadema on his St John's Wood house. He was the creator of some of the most exquisite interiors of the 'Art Movement' for his wealthy Aesthete patrons.

Remarking on the rise of artistic interior decoration in the 1870s, the American journalist Moncure Conway summed up the position: artistically decorated houses were bound to be the prerogative of either 'millionaires or artists'. The artists, he remarked, 'could do much of the work themselves, and the millionaires could command special labors'.[35] He went on to cite the many elements in Alma-Tadema's house designed by the artist. The exceptional versatility of Victorian artists, who could turn their hands to painting, sculpture, architecture – both Leighton and Alma-Tadema received the Gold Medal of the Royal Institute of British Architects for their architectural exactitude in subject matter – mural painting, print-making, decorative design, even stage design and costume, obviously included a high degree of skill in interior decoration. Whistler in particular was renowned for his decorating ideas, and his advice was eagerly sought.[36] The subtle chromatics of grey and gold in his own rooms are known from portraits and the Japanese subjects painted in his studio.

Lululaund, the wonderful fantasy built and elaborately embellished by Hubert von Herkomer at Bushey, on the outskirts of London, is an example of Conway's theory (pl.48). The house was built over a long period, 1886–94, with the proceeds of an exceedingly successful artistic career. In a complicated bargain involving a portrait in exchange for house plans, Herkomer managed to persuade the American architect Henry Hobson Richardson to provide the design, the only example of his architecture in Britain. The house was basically Romanesque in character, a curious addition to the landscape of the Home Counties. Although Richardson did not admire Burges's Tower House (which he had seen on a trip to London in 1882), Lululaund has more than a touch of its 'medieval' romanticism. The interior was fitted out like a Northern Renaissance palace, reminiscent of Herkomer's Bavarian origins. Herkomer himself, with his father, a skilled wood-carver, provided many of the interior architectural fittings, including a massive fireplace and throne-like stalls for seating, and a profusion of carved wood panelling; he established a flourishing art school on the premises. Significantly, Lys Baldry made his comment about the artistic appetite for house-building (quoted on p.56) in his study of Herkomer.

The spending power of the now lesser-known Victorian academicians should not be underrated. The connection between Victorian prosperity and property is evident in the number of second-ranking artists who were able to afford architect-designed houses. Norman Shaw, for example, was drawn into his specialization in artists' houses by a curious route, through the history and genre painter John Callcott Horsley, academician and teacher, and brother-in-law of the great engineer Isambard Kingdom Brunel. Horsley chose a romantic tile-hung exercise in the vernacular, Willesley, near Cranbrook in Kent, begun in 1864. Horsley's Diploma Work, exhibited at the RA in 1866 (pl.49), shows the dining room inglenook in the house at Willesley.[37] He was an exact contemporary of G.F. Watts, born in the same year and dying only a year before him. An unusual addition to the Aesthetic advance guard who usually made up Norman Shaw's artist-clients, Horsley was born into a highly cultivated artistic family with other artist members – his great-uncle was Augustus Wall Callcott, marine and landscape painter, and Surveyor of Pictures to the Royal Collection. He was almost by right a member of Victorian art-world establishment, director of the life-classes at the Government School of Design at South Kensington and the most successful member of the group known as the Cranbrook Colony, which included F.D. Hardy, Thomas Webster, G.B. O'Neill and A.E. Mulready. The subject matter of the group is usually rural low-life, and the the rustic buildings in which their scenes were set inspired a strand of nostalgia in artistic decoration.

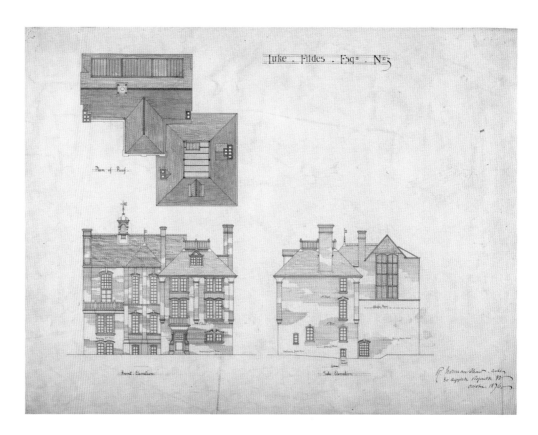

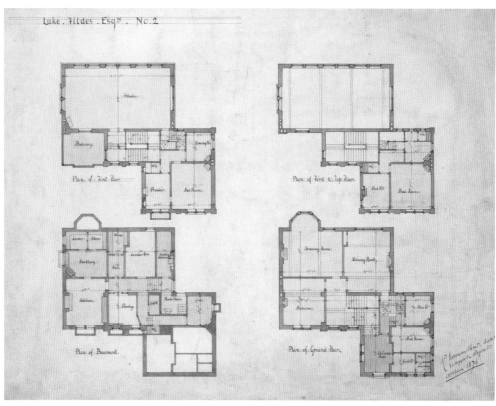

50, 51. R. NORMAN SHAW, elevation and plan,
11 Melbury Road, Kensington, for Luke Fildes,
pen-and-ink and watercolour,
signed and dated October 1876
(Royal Academy of Arts)

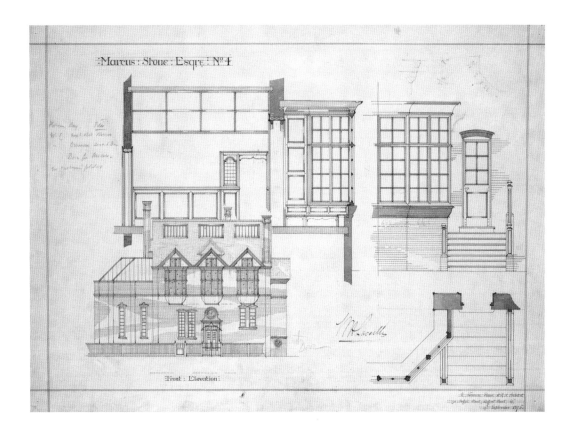

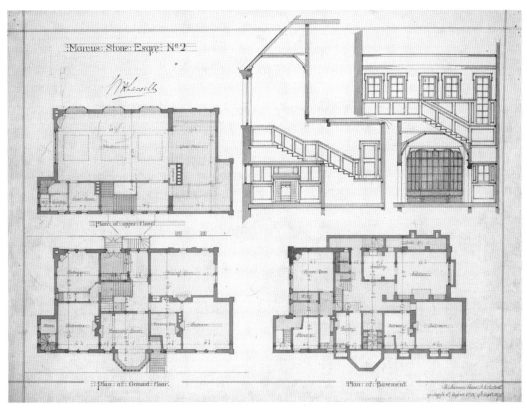

52, 53. R. NORMAN SHAW, elevation and plan,
studio-house for Marcus Stone, Melbury Road,
Kensington, pen-and-ink and watercolour,
signed and dated 9 September 1875
(Royal Academy of Arts)

In fact, Horsley himself was really based in London, in the family house in Kensington; Willesley was his country retreat. His patronage of Norman Shaw was a key to bringing the architect to the attention of house-builders in artistic circles. Willesley was Shaw's first significant domestic commission. Horsley's painting shows the architect-designed house of a prosperous artist, but still exhibits the nostalgia for traditional rural architectural features of the rustic genre, the small-paned windows and high-backed bench, adapted to artistic taste (pl.49). This is an early example of the modern 'inglenook' which was one of the most distinctive features of the 'Olde English' style and an almost essential mark of artistic taste in interior design.[38] It was one of the first of what was to become almost a cliché of the Arts and Crafts style of architecture.

These early exercises, which were sophisticated alterations rather than full-blown architectural projects, led to commissions from marine painter Edward William Cooke RA (Glen Andred, Groombridge, Kent, 1866–8) and Orientalist Frederick Goodall (Grim's Dyke, Harrow Weald, 1870–2, later the home of W.S. Gilbert). Shaw designed a large number of artists' houses in the course of his career, including two of the Melbury Road mansions, for Marcus Stone and Luke Fildes (pls 50–53), the Kensington house of George Henry Boughton and the Hampstead residences of Edwin Long, Frank Holl and Kate Greenaway (see p.211), as well as one for his own use. Shaw's success was assured: he was a supremely talented architectural draughtsman, exhibiting annually at the Royal Academy, where elevations of these houses were seen by the public.

The home of another illustrator, Harrison Weir (Charles Darwin's friend who was an animal specialist working for illustrated periodicals – he was the longest-serving artist on *The Illustrated London News*), a large, romantic, nine-bedroomed tile-hung red-brick house named Weirleigh, survives at Brenchley in Kent.[39] Described by the local auctioneers as 'artistic', it was bought in the 1880s by the parents of the poet Siegfried Sassoon, and features nostalgically in his volumes of childhood reminiscence.[40] Weir had acquired a cottage adjoining his garden to use as a studio. When Sassoon's parents arrived, a studio designed by an old family friend, the architect John Belcher, was added to the house for Siegfried's artist mother, Theresa Sassoon (née Thornycroft). The large garden with its trees and flowering shrubs, ferneries and sloping lawns, was an added amenity and under Theresa's care it became a notable showplace. Although Mrs Sassoon was rather disparaging about Weirleigh, it has many features in common with the Kensington artists' houses, including that belonging to her own family. Moreton House, the Thornycroft family's artistic powerhouse, a red-brick studio house also by Belcher, had been built in Melbury Road in 1877. The Sassoon family belonged at the very centre of the 'artistic' house movement: both Siegfried's grandfather and great uncle were the owners of houses selected by Mrs Haweis for inclusion in her *Beautiful Houses*.

THE NARRATIVE OF THE STUDIO

The idea of 'the studio' as a site of creativity and cultural importance manifested itself as a romanticized subject in contemporary art. The Orientalist and artist-traveller John Frederick Lewis moved to 21 St John's Wood Road, not far from his friend Landseer, in 1827, the year in which he was elected as an Associate of the Old Watercolour Society. Lewis's image of *A Studio* (pl.54), possibly an imaginary view of his own studio, shows a romanticized interior, linking it to a traditional idea of Olde England and to the great artists of the past. There is a resemblance to the romantic genre of popular watercolour scene, showing artists of 'olden times' enacting some dramatic episode from their lives, which developed in parallel with the artist's house as an architectural genre.

Lewis went on to paint Orientalist subjects, many of them based on his studio in Cairo (pl.56). He was in the Middle East from 1840 until 1851, and the careful

54. J.F. LEWIS, *A Studio,*
watercolour, about 1830
(V&A: 620–1870)

studies of his house and studio which he made there served him for the rest of career when painting immensely popular scenes of harem life (pl.55). In Lewis's Eastern subjects, Orientalism and Aestheticism meet. A taste for the exotic had been fostered by other artist-travellers of the mid-nineteenth century, notably Leighton, and lesser known artists like Frank Dillon and Carl Haag, both of whom had exotic studios.

Rooms as autobiography reinforce the idea of a cultivated and socially sophisticated character as well as a commitment to work. Such images appear not to be merely documentary, snapshots of the creative process, but convey complex messages about fame versus integrity.

The anecdotal approach to depicting artists' rooms and studios, which developed in more intimate detail throughout the Victorian period, was a considerable innovation compared with the conventions of the eighteenth-century artist's studio portrait. The biographical particulars that distinguish artists' portraits from the early Victorian period are a distinct contrast with the reticence and unspecific framework of the 'conversation piece', a formula which had been worked out in the 1740s. In the earlier portraits a few stock props identify the man with his profession – brushes and a palette being the obvious accessories – and convey messages about

55. J.F. LEWIS, *Life in the Harem*,
Cairo, watercolour,
signed and dated 1858
(V&A: 679–1893)

Lewis's immensely successful Harem
subjects served to popularize the
Cairene style, of carved screens
and divans heaped with silk cushions,
in artistic houses.

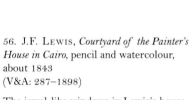

56. J.F. LEWIS, *Courtyard of the Painter's
House in Cairo*, pencil and watercolour,
about 1843
(V&A: 287–1898)

The jewel-like windows in Lewis's house
inspired the stained glass for Owen Jones's
1863 Oriental Courts at the South Kensington
Museum. These intensely patterned galleries
were almost exactly contemporary with the
Webb-Morris Green Dining room (pl.36)
which survives, unlike almost all of Jones's
decorative work, making his impact on the
Aesthetic Movement hard to evaluate.

culture and high aspirations. These cultural ambitions persisted in the nineteenth century, but now conveyed with literary realism.

It must be significant that a number of the interior views were made either when leaving a house (for example, watercolours showing rooms in Alma-Tadema's Townshend House, pp.198–9) or at a death (the views by T.M. Rooke of G.F. Watts's studio, p.142, and Burne-Jones's The Grange, p.190, and by Ambrose Poynter of Burne-Jones's studio, p.194). The posthumous portrait of Rossetti (p.177) in his Chelsea sitting room, painted from memory soon after his death by his assistant, Henry Treffry Dunn, is a defining image of Victorian artistic taste. Treffry Dunn described the house and its exotica, with its garden full of Rossetti's collections of animals, as 'a sort of miniature South Kensington Museum and Zoo Gardens combined'.[41] It is tempting to see a pattern in the fact that these posthumous records portray artists who were famously wary of the public and reluctant to exhibit their work. Neither Rossetti nor Burne-Jones had any truck

with the 'show-studio' merry-go-round; Watts built an additional studio solely
for the purpose of showing his paintings to visitors without his being obliged to
meet them. His London house was designed without a spare room, as being 'more
convenient'.

Alma-Tadema's studios were a succession of three-dimensional works of art
(pl.57). The creative milieu could be revealing. Wilfred Meynell said of Alma-
Tadema: 'The artist lives his whole life under his own roof, and every room bears
witness to his presence ... Townshend House is the entire scene of Mr Alma-
Tadema's toil, happiness and triumph, and is an epitome of his history.'[42] Leighton's
studio-house attracted – and still attracts – a great deal of interest because it so
uniquely serves its purpose. After his death Leighton's sisters wrote to the *Times*
(26 January 1899) outlining his motivation: 'He built his house as it now stands for
his own artistic delight. Every stone of it had been the object of his loving care. It
was a joy to him until the moment when he lay down to die.' It was carefully stage-
managed and photographed in 1895 (pl.13), shortly before he died, and completely
recorded after his death.

Probably more by coincidence than design, Frederick Evans's two sessions of
photography at Kelmscott Manor, Cotswold home of William Morris, happened
just before and immediately after Morris's death, in 1896 and 1897. Ambrose
Poynter, son of the President of the Royal Academy, was admitted to Burne-
Jones's studio on the day after his death in order to make a record of it. These
memorials belong with the Victorian death-bed genre, alongside death masks and
macabre deathbed portraits.

57. L. Alma-Tadema in his studio
at Townshend House, Regent's Park,
photogravure after J.J.E. Mayall
for F.G. Stephens, *Artists at Home*, 1884

58. Leighton photographed in his studio, 1880s (Leighton House Museum)

THE EVOLUTION OF THE 'HOUSE BEAUTIFUL' AND THE ART OF THE INTERIOR

The genesis of 'artistic' taste coincided with the rise of the professional decorator and an explosion of publishing on style and decoration. 'Most people are now alive to the importance of beauty as a refining influence. The appetite for artistic instruction is even ravenous'. Mrs Haweis made this comment as she was about to cash in once again on the public's hunger for 'artistic' decorating advice.[43] The artist in his uniquely exquisite surroundings is implicit in this vision of cultivated refinement. Manuals on the art of decoration rely heavily on the example of the artist-decorator and collector rather than on the conventional upper-class home. There must be a connection between the fact that many of the successful authors of Victorian decorating manuals had artistic allegiances and relationships and the widespread acceptance of the idea that the 'artistic' style was synonymous with the 'Art of Decoration'.[44] Morris believed that his mission as an artist was 'to revive a sense of beauty in household decoration … to restore the dignity of art to ordinary household decoration'.[45] The popularity of 'artistic' decorating advice suggests that the kind of eclectic installation found in artists' homes and studios had become a benchmark of cultivated taste. This anti-high-Victorian style became fashionable with the wealthy middle class, who assumed that their tastes and dislikes created some kind of absolute standard against which philistine lapses could be measured. In fact, many of Morris's best clients (as opposed to the customers in the shop) were drawn from the mercantile new rich.

Walter Crane was one of the artists closely involved in the creation of the 'Palace of Art', designing, among other things, the mosaic frieze above the tile panels for Leighton's Arab Hall. He was deeply embedded in the Morris–Burne-Jones circle as well as being part of the Leighton–Aitchison nexus. He made decorative

schemes for a number of artistic patrons as well as for his own eighteenth-century home, The Old House, Holland Street in Kensington (pl.59): his wallpaper, 'Lily and Rose', is visible in the dining room.[46] Crane believed that his illustrated books had a measurable influence on fashion and decoration, providing original and colourful ideas in accessible form. It was his children's books with their elaborate 'artistic' settings that fed the home decorating mania. In his *Reminiscences* Crane recalled that he was in 'the habit of putting in all sorts of subsidiary detail that interested me and [I] often made them the vehicle for my ideas in furniture and decoration'.[47]

Crane's simple elegance epitomized a fashionable decorating style, which he summarized in his frontispiece for *The House Beautiful* (1878) by the American Clarence Cook, one of the most successful decorating advice manuals of the period (pl.61). The imagined room revisits the style of Crane's 1871 portrait of his wife

59. W. CRANE, the dining room at 13 Holland Street, photograph, 1890s (Royal Borough of Kensington and Chelsea)

60. G.A. Storey and his wife Emily, photogravure after J.J.E. Mayall for F.G. Stephens, *Artists at Home*, 1884

"MY LADY'S CHAMBER."

61. W. CRANE, frontispiece to Clarence Cook, *The House Beautiful*, 1878

62. F. HOLLYER, *Mary Frances,
Mrs Walter Crane*, platinotype, 1886
(V&A: 7811–1938)

63. W. CRANE, *At Home, a Portrait*,
oil painting, 1871
(Leeds City Art Gallery)

Mary Frances Crane is standing by the tiled
fireplace in the artist's house in Rome.

(pl.63). Painted during the Cranes' extended honeymoon in Italy, a simple but distinctive scheme has been achieved with tiles, rugs and blue-and-white china. The embroidered hanging was worked in Rome, where Mrs Crane (née Frances Mary Andrews) discovered a circle of English art-embroidery enthusiasts. The subject is Diana the Huntress (i.e. Mrs Crane, pl.62) pursuing a crane. Photographs of Emily Storey (pl.60), wife of the artist G.A. Storey and member of the St John's Wood Clique, show her wearing a dress like that in Crane's frontispiece to *The House Beautiful*, its long body, fitting over the hips, a fourteenth-century style that was fashionable as well as artistic. Boughton's paintings – and possibly his wife's unusual style of dress – played a considerable part in the fashion for historical nostalgia; but he remarked to an interviewer from the *Tailor and Cutter* magazine, 'So-called artistic costumes generally appear more or less singular and ridiculous'.[48] But contemporary dress fashion was worse: as Millais remarked, 'Artists have to wrestle to-day with the horrible antagonism of modern dress; no wonder, therefore, that few recent portraits look really dignified'.[49]

The most intensive flurry of artistic house-building came at a moment of maximum fashionable nostalgia for the past, in architecture, design, dress, decoration, book illustration and even gardening. It embraced 'Queen Anne' (very broadly interpreted) and 'Olde English' for architecture and furniture, Georgian and Regency fashions in dress and informal gardening styles. Artists' houses and their art were often inextricably entwined, through the use of both house and garden as settings for subjects. In search of nostalgic atmosphere, both Stone and Fildes rendered their huge studio windows almost useless by insisting on leaded lights which severely reduced the daylight. G.H. Boughton was to make the same error at West House. These houses were not cheap and it is a puzzle to work out how they were afforded on the strength of still largely untried talents.

Another source of inspiration, popular publications on olden-day houses were very influential. Joseph Nash's three-volume study of *The Mansions of England in Olden Times* (issued in parts, 1839–49), illustrated with fanciful scenes of the domestic life of the past looking remarkably like Victorian family life, had a wide circulation.[50] Crane himself had pored over these volumes as a child. Nash was patronized by the royal family and much imitated. A watercolour by the little-known woman artist Ellen Clacy, of around 1880, shows the china cabinet at Knole, the great Tudor house in Kent belonging to the Sackville family (pl.64). The porcelain collection was formed in the eighteenth century by Lady Betty Germaine, friend of Horace Walpole. Lady Betty's china closet and bedroom survive still at Knole, with some of her possessions: a little four-poster bed lined with cream quilting and topped with ostrich plumes at each corner, a spinning-wheel and a ring box, along with a portrait of her wearing a blue brocade dress. The pot-pourri at Knole was always made to her recipe. The idea of the 'china closet' inspired many imitations in late nineteenth-century artistic houses, notably in the form of the ubiquitous overmantel with its shelves and niches forming a personal museum in miniature. It is surely no coincidence that the dress in this picture closely resembles that in Crane's illustration to *The House Beautiful*.

The architect Robert W. Edis, friend of Godwin, showed how it was done. In a series of six 'plain practical lectures in furniture and decoration' delivered to the Royal Society of Arts he talked about cleanliness and fitness for purpose, with advice on cost. The lectures became a book, his 1881 instruction manual *The Decoration and Furnishing of Town Houses*. He used his rooms in Upper Berkeley Street as illustrations (pl.65). The wallpaper is by Morris, the popular 'Fruit', choice of so many artist decorators. The frieze showing a rustic scene with a peacock was painted by Henry Stacy Marks, member of the St John's Wood Clique (p.195) and collaborator with Godwin and Burges. The chair is a fashionable model, designed by Godwin; the cabinet may also be Godwin's design. The bric-à-brac is a typical choice of the fashionable aesthete-collector. The drawings were made from photographs taken around 1880, and they are accurate down to last detail.

64. E. CLACY, *The China Cabinet at Knole*, watercolour, about 1880 (V&A: E.1908–1990)

Many artistic home decorators created their own nostalgic china cabinet in a nest of little shelves forming an overmantel.

Frontispiece.

A·Drawing·Room·Corner· R.W.EDIS, F.S.A. ARCHT

65. R.W. EDIS, drawing room in his house, frontispiece from *The Decoration and Furnishing of Town Houses*, 1881

The wallpaper is Morris's 'Fruit' or 'Pomegranate'; the frieze is by Henry Stacy Marks.

MODEL WIVES: A WOMAN'S TOUCH

A feature of the new decorating scene was the involvement of middle-class women, both as arbiters of taste (and authors of the above-mentioned decorating manuals) and as practitioners of interior design in either a professional or amateur capacity. As middle-class women became involved in the decision-making process, and were to a greater extent in control of domestic expenditure, this gave particular scope to artists' wives, whose own artistic ambitions were circumscribed by marriage and motherhood. The involvement of women also redefined the place taken in home decoration by the decorative arts, identified as being domestic and painstaking, and regarded as suitable to the talents and refined sensibilities of women. The home, remade as a modest but richly evocative personal Palace of Art, offered a platform for their gifts. Artistic sensibilities were sharpened by reporting in illustrated periodicals and the proliferation of manuals of instruction aimed largely at women. This had an impact on the way taste travelled, reversing the route by which ideas filtered from top to bottom of the class structure which had remained unquestioned until this point. Artists' wives bore a heavy burden of creating the perfect ambience for their husbands' professional advancement, as well as sometimes forging more or less successful artistic careers of their own.

The artist's household is something of a throwback, tracing its character to the time before the separation of business and domestic life which occurred in the eighteenth century. Life in the artist's family was conducted under one roof and revolved round the studio. In fact, an almost eighteenth-century pattern prevailed, with the entire household, including the wife, domestics and assistants (like the apprentices of earlier times) all engaged in the enterprise. The constant demand on them to act as models was a considerable strain on the wives, who also, unlike most middle-class wives at a similar economic level, worked alongside the few domestic servants. Red Lion Mary (Mary Nicholson), who looked after Morris and Burne-Jones at Red Lion Square, acted as a model on one occasion but embroidering hangings was her main contribution to the Morris enterprise.[51] The staffing of Morris's Red House was exiguous, cook, housemaid and coachman-groom, with a nursemaid after the arrival of the daughters: Webb, a committed socialist, had provided very nice servant's quarters.[52] Rossetti's bachelor establishment at Tudor House was served by a cook and housemaid, erratically supervised by Fanny Cornforth and Rossetti himself. Later there were manservants, prone to extravagance and wastefulness.[53] In Leighton's perfectly regulated household the domestics lived in the basement and the two rooms above the artist's austere, cell-like bedroom. There were three in all, butler, cook-housekeeper and housemaid; the coachman lived in a nearby mews with his wife and five children.[54] The Linley Sambournes' tall, awkward terraced house and its myriad contents were cared for by four female servants, probably inadequate to the couple's social aspirations. The turnover of staff was rapid, some not lasting the probationary month.[55] The constant presence of the head of the house and the sacrosanct workplace – the studio – were causes of considerable tension.

Most artists had a terror of their studios being cleaned. The annual spring-clean of Leighton's studio was carried out at the end of September. Mrs Wilkinson, the Burne-Jones's cleaning woman, waged a continual battle with Ned, trying to introduce brooms and soap into his studio. His household included a butler, assorted parlourmaids, a studio-boy and the dwarf Pendry, who ran errands and was a great favourite with children.[56]

Although the status of women changed as dramatically as that of the artists themselves during the Victorian era, we may surmise that they were less successful than men both socially and materially. To practise the fine arts professionally demanded unwomanly attributes of ambition and strength of purpose. In defining the position of Victorian women artists, Deborah Cherry describes purpose-built studio-houses as 'key components in the display of masculine identity', and it is true that women rarely aspired to an architect-designed studio.[57] Alice Meynell was one of the few critics to discuss the situation of women artists. Her 1883 *Art Journal* article on Laura Alma-Tadema actually mentions that Laura has her own studio. A journalist and literary critic from financial necessity, Alice's sister was the famous military artist Elizabeth, Lady Butler, author of the panoramic *Roll Call* of 1874, bought by Queen Victoria.

The first 'female' government school of design was established in 1843; the Society of Female Artists was founded in 1856. Despite these gestures towards professional standing, women were less well paid for their efforts, and many a promising start foundered on the logistics of combining art with marriage.[58] Edward Burne-Jones remarked: 'A painter ought not to be married, children and pictures are too important to be produced by one man.'[59] Georgiana Burne-Jones studied at the National Art Training School in South Kensington, and was encouraged by no less a supporter than John Ruskin; but on her marriage in 1860 she said, 'I stopped, as so many women do, well on this side of tolerable skill, daunted by the path which has to be followed absolutely alone if the end is to be reached'.[60] A poignant memory of her exclusion after the birth of her first child stayed with her for the rest of her life:

*The difference in our life made by the presence of a child was very great, for
I had been used to be much with Edward – reading aloud to him while he worked,
and in many ways sharing the life of the studio – and I remember the feeling of
exile with which I now heard through its closed door the well-known voices of friends
together with Edward's familiar laugh, while I sat with my little son on my knee
and dropped selfish tears upon him as 'the separator of companions and the
terminator of delights'.*[61]

66. E. BURNE-JONES, *Love*, design
for an embroidery panel, about 1880, for
the panel worked by Frances, Lady Horner
now at Mells Church in Somerset
(V&A: E.838–1937)

The women bore the burden of a label that has resonances even today, that of the 'Angel in the House'. Coventry Patmore's 1854 poem of that title belongs with the art and literature of the Pre-Raphaelite Movement. As a vision of the model wife it fettered women in domestic thrall and unselfishness and produced a direct conflict with the pursuit of creative fulfilment. Laura Alma-Tadema, Kate Perugini, Fanny Fildes, Louise Jopling and Helen Allingham managed to combine marriage and a career, while struggling for acceptance at exhibitions. The Grosvenor Gallery was markedly biased towards women artists, as was the Fine Art Society, also in Bond Street and founded in 1876, the year before the Grosvenor. Many of the women who persisted did so largely out of financial necessity. Beautiful women are a vivid presence in the Pre-Raphaelite circle, their beauty and femininity dominating the paintings, but their contribution at a more practical level was crucial. The often employed romantic medievalizing subject of the woman at her embroidery frame had its counterpart in reality, and wonderful embroideries are the material legacy of this artistic device (pl.66). The idea that women could beautify their homes through their own artistic efforts was liberating, and much anecdotal evidence attests to the extent to which they did so. The feminine touch was commercialized by Morris, Marshall, Faulkner & Co., where the women of the family undertook the embroidery and female relatives of the partners did tile-painting and raised gesso decoration on furniture.

Dress was a key element in the Art Movement and in the *mise-en-scène* of the artistic milieu, but the recognizable style of 'artistic' or Aesthetic dress which emerged from the wider Pre-Raphaelite community was driven by practicality.[62] Fashion is intentionally class-conscious and the modes of the mid-nineteenth century were highly impractical, particularly for women who shouldered the complex and demanding role of artist's wife. Adopting tight lacing and voluminous skirts would have been an unimaginable handicap in the domestic life of the artist's household. Agnes Macdonald, Burne-Jones's sister-in-law, complained when on a visit to Morris's Red House that the doors were not wide enough for a crinoline. This would not have merited a moment's consideration to the inhabitants of the house, for whom fashion was an irrelevant luxury.

Rossetti provided detailed specifications for the softly flowing peacock-blue silk dress worn by Janey Morris, his muse and favourite model, for her portrait of 1868 (pl.68): 'About the blue silk dress', he wrote, 'it occurs to me to say that I think the sleeves should be as full at the top as is consistent with simplicity of outline, and perhaps would gain by being lined with some soft material, but of this you will be the best judge'. He wanted a panel of embroidery on the yoke of the dress, both back and front, but as far as it is possible to tell, this was not carried out. He ends the letter with a postscript: 'I hope you will wear the dress to take away the stiffness'.[63] Janey is seated at a table on which lies an open book. Flowers in a vase and scattered on the table convey a variety of coded messages: for the carnations, 'passionate declarations' – or more specifically, 'refusal' in the case of striped carnations; 'injustice' for the hop garland. The roses have a variety of meanings: 'love' or 'beauty', with more precise messages of 'secrecy' when a full-blown rose is placed over two buds, and 'silence' for a white rose. The inscription on the painting reads: 'Jane Morris AD 1868 D. G. Rossetti, pinxit. Conjuge clara poetâ et praeclarissima vultu, Denique picturâ clara sit illa meâ' ('Famous for her poet husband, famous for her face, may my picture add to her fame'). The painting may have been planned as early as 1866. It belonged to Mrs Morris and then to May Morris, and passed via her will to the University of Oxford; it then reverted to the Society of Antiquaries with the Kelmscott estate.[64]

Timeless, anti-fashionable, Rossetti's presentation of Janey in a long series of literary and mythical images as a suffering, imprisoned wife-victim did little to allay suspicions about the intimacy of their relationship. Her taste in dress inclined naturally to this loose, flowing style designed by Rossetti, as is apparent from photographs actually posed by him (pl.67). Rossetti's presence caused the

67. Jane Morris in the garden at Tudor House, posed by Rossetti for a photograph by J.R. Parsons, 1865 (V&A: 1751–1939)

photographer, a professional named John Pearson, to transcend his normal banal approach to portraiture: he never took anything else as intense and interesting as his images of Mrs Morris. The date is 1865, when fashionable dresses were immensely bulky and lavishly trimmed, although the crinoline had just begun to shrink from its widest circumference. Henry James was betrayed into near caricature when struggling to express his exact impression of Janey's appearance:

> *Oh, ma chère, such a wife! Je n'en reviens pas – she haunts me still. A figure cut out of a missal – out of one of Rossetti's or Hunt's pictures – to say this gives but a faint idea of her, because when such an image puts on flesh and blood, it is an apparition of fearful and wonderful intensity. It's hard to say whether she's a grand synthesis of all the Pre-Raphaelite pictures ever made – or they a 'keen analysis' of her – whether she's an original or a copy. In either case she is a wonder. Imagine a tall lean woman in a long dress of some dead purple stuff, guiltless of hoops (or of anything else, I should say), with a mass of crisp black hair heaped into great wavy projections on each side of her temples, a thin pale face, a pair of strange, sad, deep, dark Swinburnian eyes, with great thick black oblique brows, joined in the middle and tucking themselves away under her hair, a mouth like 'Oriana' in our illustrated Tennyson, a long neck without any collar, and in lieu thereof some dozen strings of outlandish beads – in fine complete. On the wall was a large nearly full-length portrait of her by Rossetti, so strange and unreal that if you hadn't seen her you'd pronounce it a distempered vision, but in fact an extremely good likeness.*[65]

68. D.G. Rossetti, *Jane Morris*
(The Blue Silk Dress), oil painting, 1868
(Society of Antiquaries, Kelmscott Manor)

69. W.P. FRITH, *The Private View
at the Royal Academy,* oil painting, 1881
(Private Collection)

This is Frith's satirical view of the
artistic set, seen at the Private View of
the Royal Academy Summer Exhibition.
Eye-witness and press reports suggest
that many of the costumes are no
exaggeration. The inclusion of Lillie
Langtry, acknowledged mistress of the
Prince of Wales, and Oscar Wilde, already
the butt of cartoons in *Punch*, shows that
Frith is also commenting on the new
social order.

James was no admirer of this fashion, seeing its wearers as 'the worldly semi-smart ones, and the sickly frumpy lot who wear dirty drapery'. Their privileged position allowed artists considerable latitude with conventional social usage, but they often attracted unkind comments from more conforming members of society. However much the artistic set might revel in unconventional tastes, opinion remained on the whole hostile. A possibly exact but unkind impression of Laura Alma-Tadema's appearance at a Royal Academy reception in 1873 was expressed by the American Mrs Henry Adams:

> *Mrs Alma-Tadema … looked like a lymphatic tigress draped in Japanese
> embroidered silk, bracelets at the top of her arms, hair the colour of tiger lilies and
> that fiery flower hanging in bunches from it. She waved up and down the room like
> a serpent and we trotted round after her.*[66]

Oscar Wilde, just making his mark on London society, was afforded a prominent position in W.P. Frith's satirical *Private View at the Royal Academy*, 1881 (pl.69). Frith represented his group portrait as a satire on artistic pretensions, claiming that it showed 'some of the eminent men and women of our time who might have been present'. The scene includes easily recognizable portraits of Millais, Leighton, Ellen Terry and Lillie Langtry. Du Maurier is standing, a constant observer, to the left of Wilde's group. Frith explained:

> *Beyond the desire of recording for posterity the aesthetic craze as regards dress,*
> *I wished to hit the folly of listening to self-elected critics in matters of taste whether*
> *in dress or art. I therefore planned a group, consisting of a well-known apostle of*
> *the beautiful, with a herd of eager worshippers surrounding him. He is supposed to*
> *be explaining his theories to willing ears, taking some picture on the Academy*
> *walls for his text.*

The description continues: 'A group of well-known artists are watching the scene'; Frith also draws attention to 'a family of pure aesthetes absorbed in affected study of pictures'.[67]

For the increasing numbers of women who were practising artists, either amateur or professional, the situation was straightforward. They preferred to design something practical and original, and there are many sightings of the more striking artistic fashions in Victorian memoirs. The pioneer photographer Julia Margaret Cameron confronted enormous difficulties in her pursuit of success, but she reached a measure of professional acceptance in the end. Her eccentricity in all areas of life was marked, no less so than in her dress. She was an apparition in 'silken folds and glittering decoration', and she 'confronted the common world of convention and habit, not only unrestrained by its normal boundaries, but unconscious of their very existence'.[68] In the moodiness and unspecific ambience of her photographs Mrs Cameron was far ahead of her time, and she was disappointed to find that 'detail of table cover chair and crinoline skirt were essentials to judges of that Art which was then in its infancy' (*Annals of my Glass House*, 1874). She also employed Indian shawls, floating draperies and exotic jewellery to suggest imaginary time and place (pl.70). Anne Thackeray Ritchie described her as 'a woman of noble plainness carrying herself with dignity and expression, and well able to set off the laces and Indian shawls she wore so carelessly'.[69] From 1863 Mrs Cameron's appearance was marred by staining on her hands and clothes from the photographic chemicals she used to pursue a new hobby. She managed by a great struggle to turn herself from an amateur into a professional, but she never made much money.

70. J.M. Cameron, *Marie Spartali as Hypatia*, photograph, 1867 (V&A: 1141–1963)

There were plenty of women prepared to imitate the subtle shade and simple lines of dresses worn in Burne-Jones's portraits, chosen by the artist himself. 'Grosvenor Gallery dresses' had a recognizable currency in reporting events, largely in a spirit of mockery. Coutts Lindsay's wife Blanche had her own way of dressing, probably inspired by Rossetti's paintings. Her aunt, Charlotte de Rothschild, much given to sharp observations, said of her: 'She wears neither cuffs, nor collars, nor crinoline, but mediaeval Italian sweeping skirts and innumerable chains, lockets, rings, bracelets, embroidered girdles and all the paraphernalia of Pre-Raphaelite pictures'. The taste for Aesthetic or 'Pre-Raphaelite' dress was mainly concentrated into the period from the late 1850s until about 1880; the danger was always that it would become as banal as contemporary fashion. As early as 1878, *Cassell's Family Magazine* suggested: 'Copy almost any old costume of the three last centuries and you will scarcely go wrong'. When it became mixed up with the Rational Dress Movement and early feminism, the picturesque qualities of 'Grosvenor Gallery dress' were sublimated into concerns for health, hygiene and freedom from corsets and tight-lacing, and its romantic associations with artists and the cult of the studio were lost.

At a domestic level, wild flowers and modest native plants also became a distinguishing feature of the artistic home and garden. Cissie Frith, daughter of W.P. Frith and later an author of books on household decoration under her married name of Mrs Panton, remembered her mother getting round the problem of what might otherwise have been a very expensive element in their entertaining:

> *She made her house and her entertainments brilliant and unique, and having a perfect genius for organization, left nothing to other people. Long before flowers were indispensable in a room – in the days when one had to go to Covent Garden or to Soloman's in Piccadilly for anything one required in the way of plants and blossoms – we were never without them, and I well recall the disgust expressed by my grandmother at a charming arrangement of ox-eye daisies and grass which my mother had gathered during a day in the country – I fancy Kew or Hampton Court – which would nowadays be admired for its appropriate lightness of touch.*[70]

A self-conscious modesty was one of the aspects of artistic life imitated by the cultivated upper classes.

THE ARTISTIC SUBURB

In 1877 E.W. Godwin, architect of Whistler's White House, was retained as the first architect to the artistic garden suburb being created by the cloth merchant and property speculator Jonathan Carr in London's Bedford Park.[71] He designed the modest prototypes but he was shortly replaced by Norman Shaw. Moncure Conway lived at Bedford Park: in *Travels in South Kensington* (1882) he asks:

> *Am I dreaming? Right before me is the apparition of a little red town made up of quaintest Queen Anne houses … I was almost afraid to rub my eyes, lest the antique townlet should vanish, and crept softly along, as one expecting to surprise fairies in their retreat.*[72]

Conway sees 'aesthetic houses', each one different, with children playing among flowers and fruit trees; the houses are gabled, with white-painted wood trim and fences and decorated with the ubiquitous sunflower, the front doors and window surrounds ornamented with tinted glass; medlars grow on the pavement. He decides that this is the place to make 'life worth living', adding: 'so far as the ladies are concerned it is true that many of the costumes, open-air as well as other, might some years ago have been regarded as fancy dress, and would still cause a sensation in some Philistine quarters'. The costumes to which he refers consisted of the simple, high-waisted flowered gowns illustrated by Walter Crane and Kate Greenaway (pls 71, 72). The style was appropriated by the inhabitants of Bedford

71, 72. K. Greenaway, 'The Tea Party' and 'Going to see Grandmamma', illustrations to *Marigold Garden*, 1885

Park, where the casual attitude to dress broke down social barriers and promoted a sense of community. Artistically decorated modern houses had hitherto been the preserve of rich collectors and artists, but, as Conway observed, people who 'most desired beautiful homes were those of the younger generation whom the new culture had educated above the mere pursuit of riches'.

Bedford Park was admired for solving artistic and economic considerations; it was the starting point for the affordable smaller, architect-designed house in suburban developments all over the country. The houses catered to the taste of the cultured middle class, academics and churchmen who, in the 1870s, filled their red-brick 'Queen Anne' houses with Morris wallpaper, a collection of blue china and some Japanese fans. In Bedford Park the owners of the new-built houses were allowed to select their wallpapers up to a certain sum. Conway commented:

> As a matter of fact, a majority of the residents have used the wall-papers and designs of Morris, the draught on whose decorative works has become so serious that a branch of the Bloomsbury establishment will probably become necessary in the vicinity of Bedford Park.[73]

From his Northern outpost, the Leeds painter John Atkinson Grimshaw sent bulletins on artistic furnishing and interior decorating in a series of paintings based on his two homes.[74] Of all the non-Metropolitan Aesthetes Grimshaw is the most impossible to ignore. Like Tissot, he made a speciality of artistic interiors and gardens occupied by pretty women in quasi-historical or supra-fashionable costume. In 1870 he took on the tenancy of Knostrop Old Hall, a seventeenth-century red-brick gabled manor house two miles outside Leeds. Here he was inspired by the success enjoyed by Alma-Tadema and Tissot to use the settings in the panelled rooms and the old garden for a series of interiors and garden scenes. They form the most important and complete record of a romantic artist's 'Aesthetic' milieu as

73. J. ATKINSON GRIMSHAW,
The Chorale, oil painting, 1878
(Private Collection)

74. J. ATKINSON GRIMSHAW,
The Cradle Song, oil painting, 1878
(Private Collection)

applied to domestic decoration and garden design of the later nineteenth century.

Of all Grimshaw's artistic interiors of the 1870s *Day Dreams* is the most chic and metropolitan (pl.77). The decor is more modern and exotic than the Leeds interiors. The picture hang on the dado directly references Whistler's advice and his own installations of his works at exhibition. Embroidery, lace, Japanese fans and porcelain and the sensuous fur covering of the chaise-longue closely echo Tissot's painted world. Like Tissot's very successful social pictures, these paintings celebrate the beauty of women and the aesthetic qualities of an eclectic range of *objets d'art*.

Grimshaw also had a house, Castle by the Sea, in Scarborough, in which two more of his paintings of this type are set, *The Chorale* (pl.73) and *The Cradle Song* (pl.74), both dating from 1878. Grimshaw shifted objects and furniture around, creating an idea rather than a record of an artistic house. Nonetheless, his interiors represent an Aesthetic ideal very clearly, using C.L. Eastlake's 'Solanum' wallpaper, a Japanese matting dado and a stained glass window (*The Chorale*), and wood panelling, antique furniture and latticed window panes (*The Cradle Song*) to convey a strong message about interior decorating in the artistic milieu. Like Tissot's very successful social pictures, Grimshaw's celebrate the beauty of women and the aesthetic qualities of an eclectic range of *objets d'art*. The intensity with which he approached Knostrop and Scarborough was certainly responsible for their powerful effect. A financial crisis forced him to give up the Scarborough house, but he retained Knostrop until his death.

AESTHETICISM IN THE GARDEN AND CONSERVATORY

Conservatories and winter-gardens were new, a valued amenity attached to the villas springing up in the developing areas of London in which many artists' houses were located. Tissot used his large attached conservatory to great effect, for his paintings of modern life (pl.80). In yet another echo of Tissot, Grimshaw set *Il Penseroso* (1875) in the Knostrop conservatory (pl.76). Here Grimshaw is painstakingly realistic: these are identifiable plants showcasing the new English gardening-style of growing new introductions and rarities. The image includes a fashionable collector's table and a mock seventeenth-century chair. Again, a woman is depicted, claiming the territory as feminine, perfumed, coloured and enclosed. Reluctant to abandon such a popular vein, Grimshaw painted *The Rector's Garden* (pl.78) as a perfect example of the 'Aesthetic' garden as it influenced the artistic ambitions of the cultivated professional middle-class.

Even in London, still-extensive gardens provided idyllic subject matter. Walker's garden at the family house at 3 St Petersburgh Place in Bayswater, where he lived from 1863 until his early death in 1875, was the setting for a number of his paintings, including *Autumn* (pl.75), painted in 1864. The back garden also accommodated Walker's studio, which was built around this time in 1865 – a great improvement on his previous arrangement, which was to paint in one of the rooms in the house. The garden was protected from the road by a typical Victorian shrubbery; in front there was a flower bed filled with colourful flowers in a semblance of bedding-out, but more free-growing and untidy than Victorian gardening conventions demanded. The window boxes and the bright display on the verandah at the back of the house were much noticed by visitors. The inhabitants were deeply attached to their London garden, which was lovingly tended by Walker's mother and sister. He writes with a passion of nostalgia about a posy sent from there when he was painting in the country:

> *As for the sweet little bouquet, it is Bayswater all over, and ten times more precious than any made of Maidenhead blossom. The mignonette was hanging its head, but the jasmine and the carnation all right, and to-day they are all fresh as when picked ...*[75]

75. F. WALKER, *Autumn*, watercolour, 1864 (V&A: P.3–1911)

The scene is set in the back garden of the Walker family house in Bayswater.

76. J. Atkinson Grimshaw, *Il Penseroso*,
oil painting, signed and dated 1875
(Collection Lord Lloyd Webber)

The scene is the conservatory at
Knostrop Hall, Leeds, filled with exotics,
orchids and begonia plants with distinctive
markings of the kind so much disliked
by William Morris.

77. J. Atkinson Grimshaw, *Day Dreams*,
oil painting, signed and dated 1877
(Private Collection)

The Hammersmith garden of the Arts and Crafts architect Charles Spooner and his artist wife Minnie Dibden Davison, a miniature painter, was illustrated in *The Gardens of England* (1908) by Beatrice Parsons and E.T. Cook. The book was aimed at the middle class and marks a break with formality, to a nostalgic rural look fostered by the immensely successful genre of garden watercolour by artists like Helen Allingham and Beatrice Parsons herself (pl.79). The house and its garden at Eyot Cottage, Chiswick Mall, formed part of an artistic enclave on the Thames that included William Morris's last London residence, the eighteenth-century Kelmscott House. This kind of garden is deliberately rural, designed to imitate nature's profusion, with 'old-fashioned flowers' – hollyhocks, gladioli, marigolds and the like. Minnie Spooner lived on a long time and left the house to a friend, thus ensuring the garden's survival into the 1980s, with its espaliered fruit trees and cottage flowers.

78. J. ATKINSON GRIMSHAW, *The Rector's Garden*, at Yew Court, Scalby, Nr Scarborough, oil painting, 1877 (Harris Museum and Art Gallery, Preston)

79. B. PARSONS, *A London Garden in August*, watercolour, about 1898–1900 (Geffrye Museum)

An illustration made for Beatrice Parsons and E.T. Cook, *The Gardens of England*, 1908.

80. J.J.J. TISSOT, *The Bunch of Lilacs*, oil painting, about 1875 (Private Collection)

RURAL IDYLL: ESCAPE TO THE COUNTRY

In London, Bedford Park was a practical compromise between the claims of town and country, always a dilemma for artists who needed rural scenes for their paintings but feared to lose their contacts and networks if they moved from the urban centre. The arrival of a rail network around London made it actually practicable for artists who specialized in rural genre subjects to live in the country. Orbital suburban development was still in the future, and it was possible to settle not too far from the nerve-centre of the art world, still firmly concentrated in the Capital. Eventually a number of artists' colonies formed in a ring around London, congregating in Surrey, Kent and Berkshire where quaint rustic communities still survived with their cottage architecture in picturesque decay. Not long after the arrival of the railway in 1859, the area of Surrey around Guildford and Godalming saw a great influx from the art world. Alfred Tennyson built a house at Aldworth; Henry Cole, Director of the South Kensington Museum, rented at Shere before building at Witley; George Eliot and her companion George Lewes lived there too. The watercolourist Myles Birket Foster discovered this part of Surrey while on holiday in 1862 and decided to settle there (see p.164). He was one of the most successful painters of his time, with dealers so anxious to acquire works by him that they would travel down to his rambling Surrey house, The Hill (pls 81, 82), and buy straight off his easel. The great popularity of these rural watercolours by Birket Foster and his numerous successors brought many urban businessmen to the country, and with them the very developments that would finally obliterate the country scenes that inspired the idyllist genre.

In 1881 Helen Allingham and her husband William (poet and intimate of the Pre-Raphaelite circle), herself one of the most successful of the rural idyllists, moved from Chelsea to a house in Witley named Sandhills. The house was an example of red-brick vernacular style, but not as consciously quaint as The Hill. It was too plain and modern to provide a subject for its owner's watercolours, but the interior was a useful background for domestic scenes (pl.83). It was furnished with a mixture of plain eighteenth-century pieces and Morris rush-seated chairs. The equipment in the house was old-fashioned and the Allinghams did nothing to change this; it remained without lighting, heating or bathroom, even long after they had departed. The dark hallway gradually filled with perambulators and other impedimenta, but it opened out into a sun-filled parlour overlooking the garden and a great wooded valley; the dining room and the nursery were picturesque settings for the paintings of family life that found favour with the artist's patrons. The clothes worn by the children, long-superseded traditional smocks and sunbonnets, can hardly be regarded as normal wear for the date.

The attraction of this part of Surrey was that even in the 1880s it remained

81, 82. C. KEENE, interiors at Myles Birket Foster's house, The Hill, Witley, etchings, 1860s (British Museum)

83. H. ALLINGHAM,
Pat-a-cake, watercolour, 1884
(Private Collection)

A mother is teaching her children the
nursery rhyme in the corner of a room
in the artist's house.

almost untouched by development; it might have been a hundred miles from
London. Change was not long in coming (in no small part prompted by the artistic
invasion), and the local views began to have the additional charm of nostalgia for
a vanishing world. Mrs Allingham was in fact an accomplished portraitist, but her
countryside cottage and garden pictures were so popular that she was forced by
financial necessity to concentrate almost exclusively on that one strand of subject
matter. She had ten exhibitions at the Fine Art Society in New Bond Street, starting
in 1886. Her rural scenes tapped into a new public consciousness of the fragility of
the country's heritage of ancient buildings. The first catalogue shows evidence of
missionary zeal, probably not unconnected with William Morris's campaigning on
behalf of the Society for the Protection of Ancient Buildings, founded in 1877. The
introduction to the catalogue was provided by William Allingham, who remarked:
'In the short time, to be counted in months, since these drawings were made, no
few of the Surrey cottages which they represent have been thoroughly "done up"
and some of them swept away'. The exhibitions of Mrs Allingham's work proved
successful, importantly for the artist since she had to support her family after
her husband's death in 1889. When the Allinghams returned to London shortly
before William's death, Sandhills was taken by the wealthy semi-amateur painter
and writer W. Graham Robertson, who also left it unchanged in all his 40 years'
residence.

Fred Walker had discovered the Upper Thames in the 1860s, and some of his most successful works were painted in the still unspoilt villages clustered along the river around there. When he died tragically early of consumption in 1875 he was buried at Cookham-on-Thames. George Dunlop Leslie, who was Walker's friend from their days as members of the St John's Wood Clique, acquired a house on the Thames at Wallingford in 1884. He had been exploring the river for years, and once established there he continued to people his sunlit rooms with innocently occupied women dressed in a form of Regency revival dress. In *Sun and Moonflowers* of 1889 (pl.84), the vista of trees suggests the wider horizons of the countryside around his Wallingford house.

84. G.D. LESLIE, *Sun and Moonflowers*, oil painting, shown at the Royal Academy, 1889 (Guildhall Art Gallery)

85. K. HAYLLAR, *Sunflowers and Hollyhocks*,
watercolour, signed and dated 1889
(Guildhall Art Gallery)

It seems unlikely to be mere chance that his near neighbours the Hayllar family
– James Hayllar and his four artist daughters – used the interiors of their rented
house, The Priory, at Wallingford, as a still life in a very similar way to Leslie.
Kate Hayllar's *Sunflowers and Hollyhocks* (pl.85) includes many of the ingredients
of a middle-class idea of artistic taste: the heavily carved furniture, 'old-fashioned'
flowers, sunflowers and hollyhocks, blue and gold Chinese vases, Japanese screen
and flowered brocade, pale yellow silk shawl and Oriental-pattern carpet.[76] These
interiors are less reflective of their rural situation than the idyllic subjects by
Walker and Helen Allingham.

FIN DE SIÈCLE

By the end of the nineteenth century the idea of artist's house as an individualistic
and modern architectural concept attracted patronage at the highest level,
notably from Queen Victoria's grandson Ernst Ludwig, Grand Duke of Hesse at
Darmsdadt. In 1897 he retained Charles Rennie Mackintosh and another British
modernist, M.H. Baillie Scott, to remodel rooms in his Grand Ducal palace.[77]

86. M.H. BAILLIE SCOTT,
competition design, double-height hallway
from the *Haus eines Kunstfreundes*, 1901

87. F.C. VARLEY, *The Studio at
74 Cheyne Walk*, watercolour, about 1900
(Private Collection)

88. F.C. VARLEY (attrib.), *The Dining Room at
the Magpie and Stump*, watercolour, about 1900
(V&A: E.1903–1990)

This commission was followed by the creation of an artists' colony in the park of Matildenhöhe, with each architect-designed house conceived, like Red House, as a work of art complete in itself, in which every detail from furniture and decoration to the most humble household articles followed a master plan. This architectural type effectively encoded an idea which had developed organically in the living arrangements of Victorian artists. With the packaging of the 'artist's house' for 'ideal' suburban development its position at the architectural cutting edge was at an end.

Mackintosh and Baillie Scott's ideas for the palace of the artist Duke were closely paralleled in their 1901 competition designs for a '*Haus eines Kunstfreundes*' (an art-lover's house), neatly reflecting the situation as it developed through the second half of the century, in which amateurs and patrons were emulating the ideas and fluid spaces of artists' houses in their own homes (pl.86). Baillie Scott was also interested in the design of 'artistic' gardens, another concept intimately connected with the overall concept of the artistic house.[78] As the Arts and Crafts Movement gained adherents the way studios looked underwent a considerable change. In 1891 Charles Francis Annesley Voysey intruded an attenuated urban roughcast studio house, self-consciously different from the established style of red-brick and white-painted wood, into South Parade at Bedford Park. Just a year later his low-built, gabled studio-house – more a cottage, also roughcast – for the decorative painter W.E.F. Britten was built in St Dunstan's Road, Hammersmith.

With arrival in 1893 of the cosmopolitan and cultivated *Studio* magazine – whose proprietor, Charles Holme (one-time partner of Christopher Dresser), now lived in Morris's Red House – the tone of reporting on artistic decoration changed:

> *It is given to few men to paint pictures or to walk in the paths of pure art; but the sphere of home decoration is open to all. The result of personal labour in this direction may be more interesting than valuable from an artistic standpoint; as, for example, in the case reported in the newspapers some weeks ago of a philatelist who covered the walls of a room with postage stamps. The money value of those stamps was no doubt considerable, but their artistic value, as a wall covering, must be nil; and it is to be regretted that any approving criticism of such an example of depraved taste should be diffused amongst an undiscerning public.*[79]

The perception of the artist's milieu changed to a fastidious simplicity. Watercolours made at the turn of the twentieth century provide a valuable record of rooms in the Magpie and Stump, the house at 37 Cheyne Walk built for his family by the architect and silversmith Charles Robert Ashbee (pls 87, 88) and in his married home at 74 Cheyne Walk. Ashbee himself spent a few years before his marriage in the house at number 37, an ambience redolent of his artistic aims and crafts experiments.[80] The dining room is remarkably austere, with a narrow X-frame trestle table made by Ashbee's Guild of Handicraft, and plain rush-seated ladder-back chairs. The frieze above the plain, light-coloured panelling was in collaboration with his sister Agnes. On the sideboard there is blue-and-white china – still a benchmark of artistic taste – and on the side table silver plate by Ashbee himself. The studio at 74 Cheyne Walk is hardly more comfortable. The circular light-fitting and furniture were designed by Ashbee and made by his Guild. Rumpled Oriental rugs strike a suitably casual note, as does the curtained opening leading to the double-height space beyond. If the method of recording them is somewhat old-fashioned, the rooms themselves are very modern in their unstructured and uncluttered approach to decoration. Ashbee's interior designs were given wide currency when they were described in *The Studio* in 1895; the watercolour of the dining room was reproduced in the Viennese periodical *Kunst und Kunsthandwerk* and the studio at 74 Cheyne Walk in the Stuttgart publication *Moderne Bauformen* in 1903.[81] Scandalously, the family house at number 37 was demolished in 1968 (see p.219).

THE MARCHIONESS OF GRANBY
By H. S. Mendelssohn.

CHAPTER THREE

Amateurs and Aesthetes

Queen Victoria was brought up with all the polite accomplishments, including watercolour painting, but her attachment to art and its practice was far beyond mere dabbling. By her own account she tried to do a little drawing or painting every day. Despite this empathy and real appreciation, she was anxious to discourage her artistically talented daughter Princess Louise from an artistic career. She was not keen to see her children frequenting artistic social circles: 'Beware of artists [*Künstler*]', she told her daughters, 'they mix with all classes of society and are therefore most dangerous'.[1] The Queen, ingenuous as ever, had hardly set an example in this respect; she and Prince Albert – himself a talented artist – were avid studio visitors. Certain of their favourite artists were even admitted to something approaching friendship. This spirited exchange, it is said, took place at Landseer's studio in St John's Wood Road; Her Majesty enquired:

'How much do you pay for a tube of ultramarine?'
'Fivepence' replied Landseer.
'Oh!' exclaimed the Queen, 'Albert and I only give fourpence.' [2]

Victoria and Albert visited Landseer on two occasions, in 1849 and 1851. This possibly apocryphal story does indicate that, as a favourite of the royal couple and drawing teacher of Victoria and her daughters, Landseer could dispense with the formalities of address. He was on terms of easy familiarity with the aristocracy, having conducted a liaison with the Duchess of Bedford for many years.[3] His friend W.P. Frith, however, believed this to be a disadvantage to him:

Edwin's genius elevated him into the society of what is commonly called 'the great'
to a degree equalled only, perhaps, by Sir Joshua Reynolds. I venture to think that the
advantage of the connection was entirely on the side of 'the great,' whose scrapbooks
and albums were enriched by gratuitous sketches, and whose pockets were often
replenished by the profits obtained on the sale of pictures for which absurdly small
prices had been paid.[4]

There was, of course, still considerable confusion over the position of artists who were born gentlemen, since they were regarded as having lowered their social status.[5] Less exalted origins could be an advantage in making an artistic career. The lure of social acceptance was matched by a genuine need for financial reward and security.

Among the Victorian royal children, many of them accomplished and well-taught, Princess Helena (Princess Christian of Schleswig-Holstein) was one of the founders of the School of Art Needlework, which gave a valuable royal imprimatur to the embroidery revival – a very important element in Aesthetic home decoration – pioneered by William Morris and his wife, and sister-in-law Bessie Burden. Her sister, Louise, who married the Marquess of Lorne, strove to be conspicuously professional in her approach. She painted, as they all did, but also practised as a sculptor, a much more serious proposition for the amateur, studying with the Queen's 'sculptor-in-ordinary', Sir Joseph Edgar Boehm (baronet and owner of a handsome red-brick house in Wetherby Place, with a modelled terracotta porch by himself). One of Princess Louise's best-known works is the seated full-length of her mother in front of Kensington Palace. She was made an honorary member of the Old Watercolour Society and exhibited at the socially acceptable Grosvenor Gallery,

89–92. Portrait photographs
(clockwise from top left):
89, Princess Louise Caroline Alberta, Duchess of Argyll, by W.D. Downey, albumen print, 1868
90, (Marion Margaret) Violet Manners (née Lindsay), Duchess of Rutland, by H.S. Mendelssohn, 1892
91, Caroline Blanche Elizabeth, Lady Lindsay, and Sir Coutts Lindsay, 2nd Bt, by Thomas Buist, albumen carte-de-visite, September 1864
92, John Roddam Spencer Stanhope by Lewis Carroll (C.L. Dodgson), 1857
(National Portrait Gallery)

among other places.[6] Her story was repeated in many aristocratic and professional families. Others who occupied this uneasy territory include her husband's sculptor uncle (and, as was common with large Victorian families, near contemporary), Lord Ronald Sutherland Gower, also condemned by birth to amateur status in spite of his considerable achievements in public sculptural commissions. Aristocratic artists who enjoyed a measure of professional respect include George Howard, 9th Earl of Carlisle; Violet, Duchess of Rutland; Sir Coutts Lindsay and his wife, Blanche (née Fitzroy).

Although Victoria and Albert were truly dedicated to their various artistic activities, the idea of claiming professional status was completely unthinkable for Princess Louise. However, it was the Princess who enticed her siblings, notably the Prince and Princess of Wales and the sensitive Prince Leopold, into the world of exhibitions and studio visiting. She built her studio with the help of Godwin, friend of Whistler and Oscar Wilde and a leading Aesthetic Movement architect and decorator. For the interior decoration of Kensington Palace she turned to Leighton's architect, George Aitchison. She may have seen Aitchison's decorations for Ernst Benzon at 10 Kensington Palace Gardens, just opposite the palace, completed three years earlier (pl.93).

It is possible that the equivocal professional status of Sir Coutts and Lady Lindsay made them sympathetic to the quasi-amateur exhibitor when they opened the Grosvenor Gallery in 1877. For whatever reason, it became the venue for public exhibition for many of these aristocratic Aesthetes, like George Howard, a pupil of Alphonse Legros. He took his artistic career as seriously as his responsibilities as a landed aristocrat permitted. Coutts Lindsay's cousin, Violet Lindsay, who married the future Duke of Rutland, made a career out of her talent for delicate pencil portraits, and had to endure a reputation for eccentricity as a result. Much

93. G. AITCHISON, design for the decoration of the drawing room at 10 Kensington Palace Gardens for the banker Ernst Benzon: ceiling, parquet floor and wall, watercolour, 1871
(Royal Institute of British Architects)

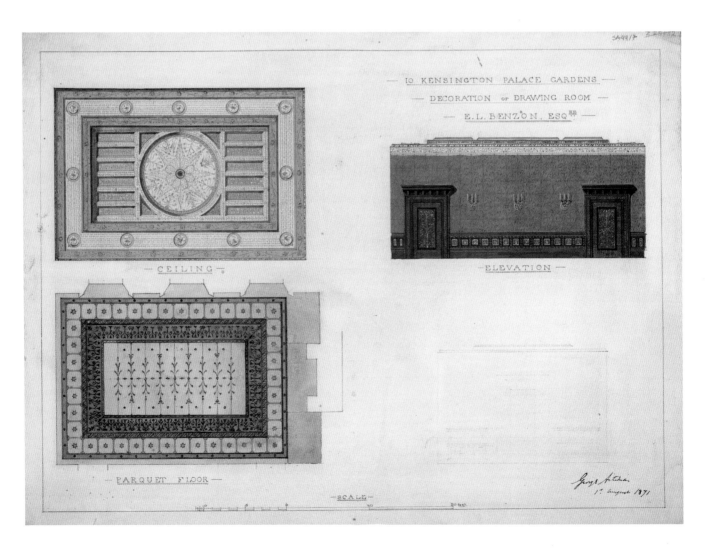

potential artistic achievement was frittered away in domestic decoration and ladylike pastimes of watercolouring and embroidery.[7] It is sometimes difficult to discover whether aristocratic amateurs were ever paid for their work, even when it was commissioned.

In fact at the Grosvenor Gallery the amateurs are, almost without exception, members of the self-elected Aesthetic elite, a fact easily explained by the close family ties of many of the protagonists. Another common thread is the Watts–Prinsep coterie at Little Holland House, a number of whom escaped from the brink of amateurism by sheer determination to overcome family prejudice and social pressure. One obvious example is John Roddam Spencer Stanhope, patron of Philip Webb, and Watts's protégé who assisted with the decorations of Holland House; his mother, Lady Elizabeth, was violently opposed to his choice of career.

Val Prinsep, another Webb patron and Watts protégé, slipped back into a comfortable well-off existence, with no need to earn his living, when he married the daughter of the shipping magnate F.R. Leyland, Whistler's patron and owner of the notorious 'Peacock Room' in his Aesthetic showcase in Palace Gate. Prinsep was over 40 when he married; it seems that he had previously had a long affair with Kate Collins, artist daughter of Charles Dickens and wife of the Pre-Raphaelite painter Charles Collins, who married Carlo Perugini, one of Leighton's protégés, as her second husband.[8] In fact the Little Holland House set and the Holland Park artists' community acted very much as a crossover social milieu, neatly summed up by Mrs Stirling: 'Roddam, an apostate from the traditions of his class, with the elasticity of an adaptable temperament, was equally at home in Bohemia or fashionable society.'[9]

Webb, Norman Shaw, Godwin and Aitchison are prominent among the architects patronized by this group; the common thread uniting the taste of wealthy and aristocratic patrons with that of the less moneyed artistic community lies in this choice of architect and style. William Morris was their decorator, sometimes a strongly visible presence, sometimes a figure in the background like any true professional. Leyland added a relatively unknown Aesthetic architect-designer, Thomas Jeckyll, to devise a setting for his collection of blue-and-white porcelain. Under Whistler's ruthless sway, this would be transformed into the 'Peacock Room' and imperil Jeckyll's sanity (pl.94). Leyland's drawing room acted as a shrine for some of Rossetti's most lush late works on the subject of female beauty, termed by F.H. Myers 'the sacred pictures of a new religion'.[10] Other spaces were dedicated to Burne-Jones and Albert Moore. This is not the place to re-tell the story of the notorious 'Peacock Room', but it must rank among the most ambitious decorative undertakings of the Aesthetic Movement.[11] Jeckyll also worked on a sophisticated Aesthetic dwelling at 1 Holland Park for Alexander Constantine Ionides, a leading member of the artistic Anglo-Greek community (pl.95).

Rosalind Stanley, wife of George Howard, was introduced to G.F. Watts and the Little Holland House circle by her sister Blanche. Blanche Ogilvy, Lady Airlie, enticed artists and men of letters into her social circle as a distraction from the gambling and hard drinking cronies favoured by her husband, the Earl of Airlie. Their London house, Airlie Lodge, was not far from the Prinseps' and it became one of the centres of artistic social life in Kensington. Rosalind's familiarity with the world of art was one of her attractions for the young George Howard, whose only interests since early youth had been painting and drawing. The Burne-Jones's became their intimate friends. The Howards decided to build their studio-house in 1867, and, almost certainly as a result of visiting Val Prinsep in Holland Park Road, chose Philip Webb as their architect.[12] The house was built on the west side of Palace Green, a still-rural wooded lane behind Kensington Palace. The design for the tall red-brick house was a contrast to the predominantly Italianate style of the grand houses lining Palace Green. Inevitably it fell foul of the Commissioners of Woods and Forests, who solicited opinions from other architects and made reports deeply offensive to Webb. In fact the external details in stone and moulded

94. J. MᶜNEILL WHISTLER and
T. JECKYLL, the 'Peacock Room',
completed 1877, at 49 Prince's Gate,
photograph by Bedford Lemere, 1892
(V&A: 240–1926)

At the end of the room over the fireplace
hangs Whistler's *Princesse du Pays de
Porcelaine* (Christine Spartali).

95. T. JECKYLL, perspective design for the
billiard room at 1 Holland Park, watercolour,
about 1870 (V&A: E.1797–1979)

The room as executed was much more
overtly Japanesque, designed to conform
to the generally Anglo-Japanese character
of the house.

96. Dining room in the Howards' house at Palace Green, *The Studio*, October 1898

brick have an elegance and refinement that more conventional 'Queen Anne' quite misses. Finally, some kind of compromise was hammered out, and the work began in June 1868. The house was at last ready for occupation in February 1870.

The Howards' Palace Green house was decorated and furnished by Morris and Burne-Jones with minute care. Many of the rooms had Morris wallpapers, 'Daisy' in the day-nursery, 'Pomegranate' in blue for the library and in green for George's dressing-room. The drawing room on the first floor had a yellow and white ceiling, Morris patterns on the walls and Persian rugs on white matting covering the floor. The furniture was picked up around town, with the help of the ubiquitous Charles Augustus Howell, a fixer who had insinuated himself into the innermost artistic circles via a friendship with Rossetti. On the first-floor half-landing there was an organ decorated by Burne-Jones. The conservatory had flower-boxes made of Dutch tiles. Unusual arrangements of pampas and dried grasses replaced conventional bouquets of hot-house and garden flowers.

The showpiece was the dining room, said to glow 'like a page of an illuminated missal': doors and walls were panelled in blue-green painted and gilded wood, the frieze was decorated with a leaf and flower pattern in raised gesso (pl.96). Above the frieze ran a series of panels painted by Burne-Jones with the story of Cupid and Psyche, adapted from designs he had made in 1866–7 for Morris's *Earthly Paradise*, a collection of twenty-four tales intended for publication as a large folio but never realized during his lifetime. When Burne-Jones dallied, the panels were finished by Walter Crane. The coffered ceiling was also decorated with flowers and foliage. In 1898 *The Studio* devoted an article to the house:

It would be a rash statement to affirm of the decoration of any single apartment, that it was absolutely the best example of the style it obeyed. Yet if ever it was safe to speak thus unreservedly, it might be concerning the beautiful dining-room at the Earl of Carlisle's House, Palace Green, representing as it does the united efforts of Burne-Jones, William Morris, and Philip Webb.[13]

While Palace Green was in the making the Green Dining Room opened in the South Kensington Museum. The work of Webb, Jones and Morris, it confirmed Rosalind Howard in the rightness of her choice.

The guiding principle in planning a Palace of Art was that of a harmonious whole, including fitting costume for the inhabitants. One of the most conspicuous borrowings by the upper-class intelligentsia from the art world was a distinctive way of dressing. In 1865 the diarist Lady Frederick Cavendish wrote of Rosalind: 'she dresses madly in odd-coloured gowns with long trains, which cling around her *unbecrinolined*'.[14] Wilfred Scawen Blunt in his diary for 1872 was more precise:

I found her ... dressed as I remember well in a way then absolutely new to me, and contrary to all the fashions of the day ... a green stuff gown, with tight sleeves slashed at the shoulders, and skirt looped up, while at one side a satchel hung from her girdle by a chain attached to her waist.

The chained 'satchel' hanging from a girdle raises the subject – beyond the scope of this account – of the taste for quaint accessories and artistic jewellery, and paved the way for the success in this area of the Arts and Crafts Movement.

Arthur Lewis, moving spirit behind the Arts Club in Hanover Square, established his own brand of mixed society from 1862 at nearby Moray Lodge on Campden Hill. Here the Prince of Wales was welcomed among artists and collectors, writers and musicians, and a smattering of business associates of the host. Watts was one of his guests, with Leighton, Val Prinsep and Millais. Lewis had artistic ambitions himself, and although his business responsibilities prevented him from taking up art professionally, it was as something more than an amateur he exhibited his work at the Royal Academy. For his Saturday evening parties he had elegant invitation cards designed by Fred Walker, offering 'Music' and 'Oysters'. Walker was a member of the St John's Wood Clique, and they too accepted Lewis's invitations.

Lewis's guests provided the music by singing and playing instruments with true amateur fervour: the gatherings of the 'Moray Minstrels' were immortalized by Du Maurier in *Trilby* (published in 1894). One of the popular social amenities of Moray Lodge was its tennis court. Until Lewis married in 1867 the 'merry clan' seems to have been entirely male, but after the actress Kate Terry (elder sister of Ellen) became his wife a more conventional regime was put in place. Kate was 23 years old, beautiful and charming. She had agreed to retire from the stage in order to mollify Lewis's formidable mother, and she set about entertaining artists, actors, patrons, dealers and musicians at Moray Lodge, which became, according to one historian of the Victorian social scene, 'a central gathering point where widely distinct circles meet on common ground'.[15]

Aitchison and Leighton continued their artistic partnership in the houses of the amateurs and aesthetes who congregated in the close-knit circles comprising the cultural elite of London. Together they worked on decorations in houses for the Hon. Percy Wyndham at 44 Belgrave Square in 1870 (pl.97), and Stewart Hodgson in Mayfair in 1881; both were important patrons of the artist. The Wyndham family

97. G. AITCHISON, design for the interior decoration of the staircase well of Percy Wyndham's house, 44 Belgrave Square, 1869 (Royal Institute of British Architects)

Aitchison designed the frieze of birds for the upper landing. The three dancing figures, painted by Leighton, survive as separate panels.

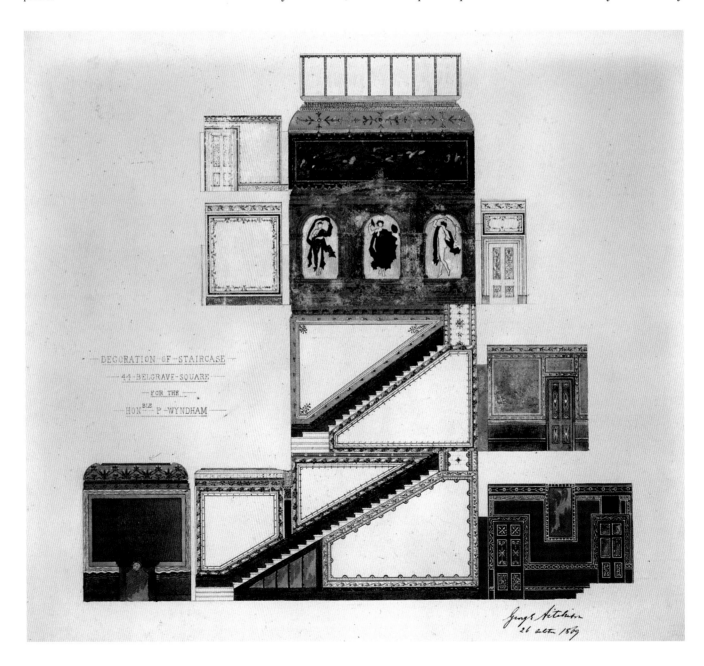

DECORATION OF STAIRCASE
44 BELGRAVE SQUARE
FOR THE
HON^BLE P WYNDHAM

probably best exemplified the crossover between the aristocracy, politics and the art world.[16] The Hon. Percy and Mrs Wyndham were noted patrons of contemporary art; Percy Wyndham was one of the earliest purchasers of Whistler's 'Nocturnes', buying one shown at the first Grosvenor Gallery exhibition. Leighton painted decorations for the hall and stairway of their Belgravia townhouse. Webb was the architect and Morris the decorator of their Wiltshire mansion, Clouds. Madeline Wyndham was, with Princess Christian, among the founders of the School of Art Needlework. In Burne-Jones's studio the Wyndhams' daughter, Mary (shortly to become the wife of Lord Elcho, heir to the Earl of Wemyss), met Arthur Balfour, future Prime Minister and the man she wished she had married, with whom she was to conduct a lifelong intimate friendship.

The Wyndhams were pioneers of antique collecting as a way of furnishing; they claimed that the contents of Clouds had been collected over the course of 25 years. They loved old Oriental rugs and antique textiles. Madeline Wyndham, who was a more than competent amateur artist, possessed true flair, and she was adept at the art of contriving original decorative results from old and unusual fragments. Her advice was often very practical and down-to-earth, and she bombarded her daughters with lengthy instructions on the use of remnants and silk turned wrong side out to produce a particular effect.

Aesthetic partnerships in the Leighton-Aitchison circle made an outstanding contribution to artistic interior decoration. Looking at the client/artist relationship, a picture of friendships across a particular area of artistic culture begins to emerge. Aitchison's patrons were, like the Wyndhams, significant collectors of High Victorian art; many were themselves talented amateurs. The similarity of their artistic voyage of discovery is striking, with the figures of Ruskin, Morris and the Pre-Raphaelites looming large in the genesis of many programmes of beautification for the 'Palace of Art'. The mural schemes for members of the cultivated upper class mirror the decorative schemes carried out for the more modest homes of artists, and were certainly inspired by them. The network of cross-fertilization between the artist-protagonists of this study and their patron-friends is nowhere more clearly exemplified than in this explosion of interest in domestic mural decoration for the 'Aesthetic' house.

One of Aitchison's finest achievements, the decoration of Frederick Lehmann's early eighteenth-century house in Berkeley Square, dating from 1873–5, did not involve Leighton; in this instance his collaborator was Albert Moore (pl.98). As well as the schemes with their beautiful friezes, Aitchison designed all the furniture. There was no wallpaper in the house, all the pattern being executed by hand. The Lehmanns, who were also patrons of Leighton and of Millais, crossed the boundaries of artist and amateur. Frederick, a businessman from Hamburg, was a Member of Parliament and connoisseur of music who married the pianist Nina Chambers. His father and two of his brothers, Henri and Rudolf, were artists; the brothers made successful careers for themselves and Rudolf married Nina's sister Amelia. Nina and Amelia were childhood friends of the Dickens family and had moved in artistic and literary circles all their lives.

Rudolf Lehmann had known Leighton since they were both in Rome in the mid-1850s; in 1866 he settled on Campden Hill where he pursued a career as a portrait painter. However, when the Frederick Lehmanns wanted portraits of their daughter (also Nina), they turned to Leighton and Millais. For Millais Nina is dressed in white, a deliberate echo of – or even challenge to – Whistler's *White Girl* (1862; National Gallery of Art, Washington, DC), and one of his most Aesthetic portraits. The Lehmanns were very much part of the musical culture of the Kensington artists' colony. Frederick's sister Eliza was married to the steel magnate Ernst Benzon, yet another of Aitchison's patrons (for the decoration of the drawing room at 10 Kensington Palace Gardens, 1871, see pl.93) and owner of Leighton's *Golden Hours* (1864; Private Collection). The wealthy Benzons were a useful source of patronage and great hosts of lavish musical entertainments.[17]

98. G. AITCHISON, design for the decoration of the front drawing room at 15 Berkeley Square, 1873 (Royal Institute of British Architects)

The frieze of a continuous band of peacocks on a gold ground was painted by Albert Moore.

For the Eustace Smiths' Princes Gate house Aitchison collaborated with two other Aesthetic artists, Thomas Armstrong and Walter Crane.[18] Eustace Smith was heir to a ship-building fortune; his wife, Martha Mary Dalrymple, a connection by marriage of the Prinsep clan, was an heiress in her own right. She changed her name to Eustacia and embarked enthusiastically on the artistic life, buying works by Watts, including *Choosing* (see pl.121), his portrait of his wife, Ellen Terry. The Smiths had been introduced to the Aesthetic ideal through visits to the Prinseps at Little Holland House and to Leighton. Leighton's devoted admirers, they owned the nude *Venus Disrobing* (1866–7; Private Collection), for which it was rumoured 'Eustacia' herself had sat. This was not very likely, since the painting had belonged to Frederick Leyland, who sold it in 1872. As Moncure Conway remarked,

> It is, indeed, a very significant thing that such men as Albert Moore … should have been found ready to undertake work of this description; for though it is a return to such work as Giotto and Michael Angelo were glad to do, we have heard of late years occasional sneers at 'mere decoration'.[19]

The boudoir was decorated with a frieze by Crane of white cockatoos on a gold ground (pl.99).

The hallway in the Wyndham's Belgrave Square house had set up a model for decorative figures embodying music and dance which was to be developed by Leighton in other, more ambitious programmes of decoration. James Stewart Hodgson, a wealthy patron of the arts and banker – a partner in Baring Brothers – had been a valued friend of Leighton's since the late 1850s, owning several of his

99. G. AITCHISON, design for
the boudoir for Mrs Eustace Smith,
52 Princes Gate, 1877
(Royal Institute of British Architects)

The frieze with cockatoos was designed
by Walter Crane. The ebony door-frames
and wainscoting inlaid with ivory and
mother-of-pearl survive in the house.
With its lavish use of precious inlay, this
scheme showed off Aitchison's debt to Owen
Jones, particularly to Alfred Morrison's
townhouse at 16 Carlton House Terrace.

important works. The decoration of his London house at 1 South Audley Street
was undertaken by Aitchison in 1881, and included friezes of *Music* and *The Dance*
(pls 101, 102) by Leighton, as well as mosaic panels illustrating *The Elements* by
Crane (pl.103).

Stewart Hodgson also owned several important works by Leighton, including
Lieder Ohne Worte (1861; Tate Britain), as well as the huge *Daphnephoria* (1874–
6; Lady Lever Art Gallery, Liverpool), which hung in his country house, Lythe
Hill at Haslemere in Surrey; *Sisters* (c.1862; Private Collection), of two girls in
ivory satin dresses; and a portrait of his two daughters (1888; Private Collection,
Australia), also wearing dresses of ivory satin. He had a number of oil-sketches
relating to other important works. Letters from the artist to Hodgson excuse the
slow progress of the two friezes, which Leighton blamed on their size, each, as
he pointed out, being as long as the *Daphnephoria*.[20] The figures in *The Dance* and
Music are static and simply modelled, in a style reminiscent of Greek vase painting.
In spite of further delays caused partly by work on the much larger and more
complicated South Kensington Museum frescoes, *The Dance* was completed in time
to be exhibited at the Royal Academy in 1883 (no.158); *Music* was completed by
1885 (RA, no.344). Stewart Hodgson owned a colour sketch for *Music*, which was
shown in the Royal Academy Winter Exhibition in 1897. The scheme was initially
undertaken by F.P. Cockerell and taken over by Aitchison after Cockerell's death in
1878, along with Watts's studio at 6 Melbury Road.

Princess Louise's uncle-in-law, Lord Ronald Sutherland Gower, artist, writer,
collector and dilettante, promoted the social rise of the young Oscar Wilde when

100. G. AITCHISON, design for
Stewart Hodgson's drawing room,
1 South Audley Street, 1881
(Royal Institute of British Architects)

Aitchison's interior designs are among the
most exquisite and colourful among an array
of talents in Victorian decorative art.

101–2. F. LEIGHTON, decorative friezes:
101, *Music* (above) and
102, *The Dance* (below),
painted for Stewart Hodgson's
London house at 1 South Audley Street,
oil painting, 1881–3
(Leighton House Museum)

The friezes were removed from South
Audley Street to Leighton House Museum
in 1975 and replaced with copies.
The surviving decoration in the house
has been restored.

103. Sitting room in Gower Lodge, home of Lord Ronald Sutherland Gower, illustration from *Bric-a-Brac*, Lord Ronald's description of his house and its contents, published in 1888, p.19

he first emerged from Oxford as a prize-winning poet. Wilde's friendship with Lord Ronald has a special interest as providing the model – in part, at least – for the decadent and cynical aristocrat Lord Henry Wotton in Wilde's scandalous novel *The Picture of Dorian Gray*, published in 1891. Lord Ronald was the fourth and youngest son of George Granville, 2nd Duke of Sutherland, and Harriet, Duchess of Sutherland, Mistress of the Robes to Queen Victoria. It was an awe-inspiring milieu and not one in which the idea of a profession as artist would flourish. Lord Ronald, with dogged determination, followed the career of sculptor, one of the hardest for the amateur. His relationship with the professional art world was often difficult as he was apt to adopt a condescending tone with other artists. He gradually gained recognition for his work, the best-known example being the large-scale Shakespeare monument at Stratford-on-Avon.

Lord Ronald met Wilde through the portraitist Frank Miles, with whom Wilde was to share the Chelsea studio-house designed and built by E.W. Godwin. Lord Ronald had encountered Miles in 1876 at a party given by Millais, and Miles carried him off to meet Wilde soon after. Visits quickly followed to Lord Ronald's newly acquired house at Windsor. Lord Ronald had transformed the half-timbered gabled cottage, which he named Gower Lodge, into a perfect setting for his books, pictures and antique bibelots, many of them associated with Marie-Antoinette (pl.103). Wilde, introduced, probably for the first time, to the aristocratic artistic ambience, was entranced, declaring it 'one of the most beautiful houses' he had ever seen. When he was composing *The Picture of Dorian Gray* this house provided the perfect ingredients for Lord Henry Wotton's Mayfair house. Dorian Gray, left alone in the library, examines its contents; it is packed with precisely the precious trifles that appealed to Lord Ronald. The ticking of the 'Louis Quatorze' clock irritates Dorian, and when Lord Henry arrives belatedly his excuse is that he has been in Wardour Street, bargaining for a piece of old brocade. The whole atmosphere conjures up Lord Ronald and Gower Lodge perfectly. Gower Lodge was, in fact, inspired in turn by the house of the stained-glass artist Charles Eamer Kempe, a much-admired example of the artistic Olde English style.

It is hard to apprehend fully the achievements of those Victorian artists who undertook public and domestic decorative schemes, since so many of them

104. E. BURNE-JONES, *The Garden of the Hesperides*, decorative panel in coloured and gilded gesso, 1880–1 (V&A: Circ.525–1953)

are invisible or even destroyed. Burne-Jones's lovely gesso and gilded panel, for example, is all that remains of a scheme for his devoted friends and patrons Mr and Mrs George Lewis (pl.104). It was made to go over the fireplace in their country retreat, Ashley Cottage at Walton-on-Thames, the Dower House of Ashley Park, in a room lined with blue linen which, it was said, William Morris had dyed with his own hands. George Lewis, eminent Victorian solicitor, disentangled the affairs of the highest in Society from the Prince of Wales downwards.[21] He was involved with nearly every *cause célèbre* of his time. His highly cultivated and artistic second wife, Elizabeth (née Eberstadt), was a noted hostess who was passionate about all the arts; they were 'breath of life' to her. The Lewises' Portland Street house was the centre of an artistic and musical circle which included nearly all the main players in this book: Whistler, Du Maurier, Alma-Tadema, Henry James and all their musician friends, as well as the Lewises' most intimate friend, Burne-Jones. Elizabeth also took up the young Oscar Wilde when he first arrived in London. The Burne-Jones panel was presented to the Victoria and Albert Museum by Miss Katherine Lewis, their youngest daughter, who as a child had been the recipient of a series of charming letters from Burne-Jones.[22]

A rambling Tudor mansion once inhabited by Cardinal Wolsey, Ashley Park belonged to the widow of Sassoon David Sassoon, senior member of the fabulously wealthy Sassoon dynasty, who had arrived in England from Persia in 1858. It was a rather eccentric selection by Mrs Haweis for inclusion in *Beautiful Houses* (1882). By the date of her publication, S.D. Sassoon had been dead since 1867, having succumbed at the age of 35 to a heart attack, and his widow lived at Ashley Park in some financial straits, having run through the considerable fortune left to her by her husband. In spite of the creeping dereliction, however, the house was a dream of Aesthetic perfection, being full of original Queen Anne features but furnished with modern artistic pieces and ornamented with collections of porcelain and Japanese works of art. It was the centre of an artistic circle that had many features in common with the Anglo-Greek coterie which formed around the Ionides family. Additionally, the Sassoon sons were members of the Prince of Wales's Marlborough House set, who relied on Lewis to protect them from scandalous publicity about their gambling and extra-marital affairs.

Next door to George Howard's London house, 2 Palace Green was built by W.M. Thackeray in 1860, widely identified as a pioneer in the red-brick 'Queen Anne' revival.[23] Next to Thackeray's new mansion, inspired by Christopher Wren's Marlborough House shortly to house the newly married Prince and Princess of

Wales, there remained a genuine remnant of the Queen Anne period: 3 Palace Green, an increasingly rare type like a cottage in London, had once been the laundry to Kensington Palace. From 1886 it belonged to Francesco Enrico Canziani, a senior member of the now largely forgotten Italian colony, who lived there with his artist wife Louisa Starr Canziani and their daughter Estella, also an artist. The house became a meeting place for Italian artists in London and the Anglo-Italians such as Walter Crane, Henry Woods and Luke Fildes, who had great success with their Italian – mainly Venetian – subject matter. Crane persuaded Louisa into the campaign for dress reform, and she herself was a great proponent of artistic dress.

As a small child, Estella Canziani visited the Kensington studios with her parents.[24] On one Show Sunday they managed to see 20. She remembered the Prinseps' 'magnificent' house, with its entrance hall of gold panelling and rooms filled with *'objets d'art*, furniture, tapestry, and pictures'.[25] Her mother had been much less impressed by W.P. Frith's studio when she visited in in 1867: after waiting in

one of the most elegant drawing-rooms I have seen, we were conducted into one of the shabbiest studios I have seen, considering that it is the studio of an R.A., and one who must be one of the richest R.A.'s. There was not a thing of beauty in the place, a room not large, very lofty, with papered walls, nothing on them, only over the fireplace an engraving or two ...[26]

Artists of Frith's era were slow to buy into the 'show studio' ethos, but the up-and-coming generation already expected something better in the 1860s.

105. G.F. WATTS, *Alexander Constantine Ionides and his wife Euterpe, with their children Constantine Alexander, Aglaia, Luke and Alecco*, oil painting, about 1841
(V&A: Ionides Bequest CAI.1147)

This is a small version of Watts's Ionides family portrait now at the Watts Gallery, Compton, Surrey.

106. The Antiquities Room at
1 Holland Park, London, photograph by
Bedford Lemere, about 1898
(V&A: E.1:13–1995)

107. The Morning Room at
1 Holland Park, photograph by
Bedford Lemere, about 1898
(V&A: E.1:17–1995)

The head of the Anglo-Greek community, Alexander Constantine Ionides, who was born in 1810, was one of the earliest and most important patrons of G.F. Watts. It is probably no coincidence that the Anglo-Greek circle bears a distinct resemblance to the Holland Park circle. A member of the second generation of an Anglo-Greek textile trading family, Alexander Ionides was by the early 1840s well on the way to the great family fortune which enabled himself and his successors to become collectors and builders on a noble scale. He was recently established in a beautiful and expensively equipped and decorated house at Tulse Hill, near Dulwich. Watts was a wonderful mentor and generous in bringing his fellow artists to the notice of his patron. It was through Watts that Ionides came into contact with Whistler. From Tulse Hill Alexander Constantine moved in 1864 to a newly built house at 1 Holland Park, close to Watts at Little Holland House. This was the very year in which Leighton and Val Prinsep built their studio-houses in nearby Holland Park Road.

The three Ionides boys in Watts's portrait (pl.105) all collected art, the eldest, Constantine Alexander on the grandest scale – contemporary French paintings and sculpture as well as works by Rossetti and Burne-Jones. It is his collection which is now in the Victoria and Albert Museum. Alecco and Luke both studied art in Paris with the 'Paris Gang', Poynter, Thomas Armstrong and George du Maurier among them; Alecco features as 'the Greek' in Du Maurier's art world novel, *Trilby*. It was Alecco who introduced his Paris friends into the Ionides circle. He succeeded to the house in Holland Park when his parents retired to Hastings in 1875; he made extensive alterations, creating a notable 'Aesthetic' ensemble (pls 106, 107). From 1881 Morris was decorating there: the wallpaper used for the Antiquities Room was 'Chrysanthemum' (1877) and a more informal sitting room was papered with 'Garden Tulip' of 1885. The 'Forest' tapestry, designed by Philip Webb with Henry Dearle, was in the study (pl.108). It was one of the most splendid schemes to be undertaken by Morris & Co., with gilded gesso panels by Walter Crane in the dining room.

108. MORRIS & CO., *Forest*,
woven wool tapestry designed by
Philip Webb and Henry Dearle for
the Study at 1 Holland Park, 1887
(V&A: T111–1926)

Constantine, Alecco and their youngest sister Chariclea, who married the
musician and conductor Edward Dannreuther, all employed Philip Webb and
William Morris. The whole Ionides–Coronio–Spartali clan, which headed the
Anglo-Greek community – their attachment to their cultural origins is indicated
by the fact that the two older boys in the family portrait by Watts are wearing their
national dress – were to prove generous in their patronage, and their exquisitely
decorated houses were looked upon as inspiring examples of artistic taste. The
group in the portrait offers an early glimpse of some of the key members of the
Greek artistic coterie, Aglaia in particular developing close friendships with Morris
and Burne-Jones. She grew up to be a great beauty, much in demand as a model,
and took a practical interest in Morris's textile ventures. She married Theodore
Coronio, another member of the Anglo-Greek business community.

The young women were noticeably free in their manners. Du Maurier
observed:

109. Illustration of the sofa in
the portrait of Mrs Luke Ionides from
Mrs Haweis, *The Art of Decoration*, 1884

110. W. BLAKE RICHMOND,
Mrs Luke Ionides,
oil painting, 1879
(V&A: E.1062–2003)

111. E. BURNE-JONES, *The Mill*,
oil painting, 1870–2
(V&A: CAI 8)

Owned by Constantine Alexander Ionides,
this painting was traditionally said by
the family to include portraits of the
'Three Graces', Marie Spartali, Marie
Zambaco and Aglaia Coronio.

*The women will sometimes take one's hand in talking to one, or put their arm round
the back of one's chair at dinner, and with all the ease and tutoiement, or perhaps
on account of it, they are I do believe the most thoroughly well bred and perfect
gentlefolks in all England.*[27]

This sort of intimacy was quite unheard of in polite Victorian middle-class
society. In the 1860s the delicate fabric of this social circle was riven by the
scandalous love affair between Burne-Jones and a ravishingly beautiful Ionides
cousin, Marie Zambaco (née Cassavetti). The convolutions within the artistic
community were considerable, but on the surface everything remained the same.
Family tradition suggests that the dancing women in Burne-Jones's painting, *The
Mill* (pl.111) are Marie Spartali, Marie Zambaco and Aglaia Coronio.

A quintessentially Aesthetic portrait of Mrs Luke Ionides, carefully calculated
down to the last detail of setting and costume, by the High Victorian classicist W.B.
Richmond, son of George Richmond RA, was exhibited at the Grosvenor Gallery
in 1882 (no.186; pl.110). Mrs Ionides was born Elfrida Elizabeth Bird in 1848, and
married Luke Ionides in 1869. Both Constantine and Luke lived in Holland Villas
Road, not far from Holland Park. Luke's volume of *Memories* is a valuable record
of the family milieu and the art world of his time: Whistler and Burne-Jones were
among his particular friends. Like Burne-Jones, Luke also fell in love with Marie
Zambaco, his cousin; the strain of this eventually ended his marriage to Elfrida.
The background of Blake Richmond's highly ambitious painting is filled with a
bold piece of Japanese embroidery, a Kimono silk. Elfida's dress is in the fashionable
'artistic' style, soft silk, real lace, smocking detail on the sleeves and jewellery in
the form of a Renaissance Revival silver-gilt belt buckle and long Indian bead
necklace. The sofa, featured by Mrs Haweis in *The Art of Decoration* (pl.109), is the
kind of overblown neoclassical design admired by Whistler; the occasional table is
of an inlaid Moorish type much favoured in artistic circles.

One of the highly detailed, miniaturist watercolour interiors painted by
Alma-Tadema's artistically gifted daughter, Anna, shows the drawing room at 1a
Holland Park (pl.112). She was influenced in technique and subject matter by her
father and his second wife Laura, her stepmother, but her interior views are her
most individualistic works. This example was painted in April 1887 at the house
owned by the Coronio family, adjoining Alecco Ionides' much admired Morris-
decorated 'Aesthetic' dwelling. Rossetti's red and black chalk study of *Marianna*,

112. A. ALMA-TADEMA,
Drawing Room at 1a Holland Park,
watercolour, 1887
(Russell-Cotes Art Gallery and Museum,
Bournemouth)

The painting was exhibited at the
Grosvenor Gallery in 1887.

113. S. BOTTICELLI, *Smeralda Brandini*,
tempera on panel, 1470
(V&A: CAI.100)

One of the Old Masters from the Ionides
collection, formerly owned by Rossetti.

visible on the left of the painting, was owned by Aglaia Coronio; it is now in the Metropolitan Museum, New York. The drawing room painting was shown at the Grosvenor Gallery in 1887, along with Laura Alma-Tadema's *Always Welcome* (1887; Russell-Cotes Art Gallery and Museum, Bournemouth), in the style of a Dutch seventeenth-century interior.

The head of the Spartali clan was Michael Spartali, a wealthy merchant who was Greek Consul-General in London 1866–82. His daughter Marie, born in 1844, who lived first in Hornsey and then at The Shrubbery, a large Georgian house on Clapham Common, spanned the two worlds of patron and artist. A painter herself, she was favourite model-muse of Rossetti, Burne-Jones and Ford Madox Brown. Along with the Ionides and Cassavetti girls, the striking good looks of Marie and her sister Christine – model for Whistler's *Princesse du Pays de la Porcelaine*, centrepiece of the Peacock Room (1863–4; Freer Gallery, Washington, DC; see pl.194) – made an enormous impression on the artistic community. They were among the legendary 'stunners' of the Pre-Raphaelite circle, the women who were responsible for a major shift in the perception of feminine beauty. After a garden party at the Ionides house in Tulse Hill, Thomas Armstrong recalled: 'We were all *à genoux* before them and of course every one of us burned with a desire to paint them'. Marie made a name for herself as a follower of Rossetti, exhibiting from 1867 at the Dudley Gallery, the Royal Academy and elsewhere. In 1871 Marie married a friend of Rossetti's, the American journalist William Stillman, a widower with three young children; the following year their daughter Euphrosyne, or Effie, was born. The marriage was not easy, but Marie was able to continue painting and was still in demand as a model.

The Constantine Alexander Ionides Collection was a strikingly generous benefaction to the nation in 1900. It was bequeathed to the South Kensington Museum, and when in 1904 it was exhibited at the Victoria and Albert Museum (as it had become), it was said by Tiburce Beaugeard, reporter for *The Lady's Realm*, that there had been 'no artistic inheritance so rich, so varied and so comprehensive' since the Wallace Collection in 1898.[28] The paintings, ranging from Botticelli (a portrait of Smeralda Brandini once owned by Rossetti; pl.113) and Rembrandt to Whistler and Degas, were to put the V&A collections on a totally new footing. The coverage of the modern Aesthetic Movement was breathtaking, with masterpieces by Rossetti himself, Burne-Jones and G.F. Watts. Also part of the bequest was the magnificent Broadwood grand piano commissioned by Alexander Ionides and designed by Burne-Jones (pl.114).

The Misses Marshall, daughters of the distinguished surgeon and anatomist John Marshall FRS, doctor to a number of artists including Ford Madox Brown and Rossetti, were inspired to create an artistic milieu through their contact with the Ionides clan. They are particularly interesting since they saw this world from the viewpoint of outsiders looking in. They aspired to an artistic 'salon'. Jeanette Marshall, the eldest, left 22 volumes of diaries, an eye-witness account of London's new social order.[29] Although their conversion to the 'artistic' style was initially reluctant, the girls were prepared to go to considerable lengths to create the right setting for artistic soirées, and even a ball, shopping assiduously (all recorded in the diaries), dressmaking, doing certain decorating and furbishing tasks themselves, and hiring plants from a nurseryman. For all their origins in practicality – and cheapness – so-called 'Pre-Raphaelite' fashions did, in fact, achieve a respectable following outside bohemian circles; Jeanette Marshall remarked in her diary, 'as we cannot do the ultra-fashionable, we'll be artistic at any rate'.[30] Her minutely detailed commentary on the artists and their homes is a revelation of the tastes and decorating practices of the artistic coterie.

The upper-class aesthetes who were patrons of artists such as Rossetti and Whistler, both of whom had very strong views on interior decoration, took the artistic style of decoration into the realms of ancestral homes and grand London houses. Where the Wyndhams had led, their children and friends followed. In the

1880s and 1890s visitors to 'Studio Sundays' in Kensington included a select coterie known as the 'Souls', a group of friends combining wit and intellect who, like the Bloomsbury Group in a later generation, were given their nickname by an outsider. In her *Life* of Lord Leighton, Mrs Russell Barrington mused on the composition of the late Victorian art world:

> *Imbued with a rare, peculiar refinement all its own, a kind of aesthetic creed sprang up in the later days of the nineteenth century apart from the arid soil of commonplace respectability and tasteless materialism. Burne-Jones painted it, Kate Vaughan danced it, Maeterlinck wrote it, the 'Souls' (rather unsuccessfully) attempted to live it, the humourists caricatured it, the Philistines denounced it as morbid and unwholesome. Leighton was tolerant and amused, but could not be solemn about it. And, assuredly, already this creed has been whisked away into the past by fashions diametrically opposed to it in character.* [31]

In part the value of the Souls' participation in the Aesthetic Movement is that they provide a well-recorded microcosm of its diversity and plurality of influences. They were a mixture of old families and new money, country squires and successful businessmen. Politicians like future Prime Minister Arthur Balfour ('King' Arthur), George Curzon and George Wyndham were prominent Souls. The women provided artistic talent, among them Madeline Wyndham, subject of one of Watts's most magnificent portraits; Violet Granby, future Duchess of Rutland, herself an artist and a conspicuous eccentric in the social circles which she was obliged by her position to frequent; and Lady Plymouth, who inspired from Burne-Jones the quintessential Aesthetic portrait, of whom it was said that her costume was much imitated in artistic circles. Frances Horner, Burne-Jones's intimate friend and confidante, was the daughter of William Graham, a Scottish merchant and Pre-Raphaelite patron and collector of Old Masters. Their houses were a mixture of Renaissance-style aestheticism (Hewell Grange at Reddich, the Plymouth mansion based on the Gonzaga Palace in Mantua) and innovative architectural patronage (Clouds, the Wyndham house in Wiltshire, was a fine Webb-Morris collaboration).

114. Grand piano, made for
Alexander Ionides by John Broadwood,
designed by Morris & Co. and decorated
by Kate Faulkner for the Second Drawing
Room at 1 Holland Park, 1884–5
(V&A: W.23–1927)

H. Jamyn Brooks

115. H. JAMYN BROOKS, Violet Granby
(née Manners, later Duchess of Rutland)
at the Royal Academy in 1888
(detail from pl.26)

Violet Granby, holding the hand of her
daughter Marjorie, is at the centre of a
group including Millais at the left, with
Philip Burne-Jones behind him; Sir John
Pender, pioneer of submarine telegraphy
and important collector and patron; Baron
Ferdinand de Rothschild, collector and
owner of Waddesdon Manor; Humphry
Ward, husband of the celebrated author
and himself an influential art critic; and
the artist George Richmond. Violet had
a reputation as an eccentric 'artistic'
dresser, but her personal style brought an
indefinable chic to her chosen costume.
She showed her work at the inaugural
Grosvenor Gallery exhibition in 1877.

When Mary Wyndham married Hugo Charteris (Lord Elcho, heir to the 10th Earl
of Wemyss) in 1883, she became the chatelaine of Stanway, a lovely Tudor house
in Gloucestershire. There she entertained artists and writers, among them her
close friends Burne-Jones and Morris, as well as Wilde, who had earlier been a
guest at Clouds. She was an intimate friend of Morris and she actually persuaded
him to design special wallpaper for Stanway, which he hung with his own hands.
Burne-Jones designed an Aesthetic monument to Laura Lyttelton (née Tennant),
who died tragically in childbirth (pl.116). Lady Warwick estimated the Souls
highly: 'They were decidedly ambitious, clever, and well-read, and exercised great
influence on London Society for five or six years'.[32] This kind of endorsement made
artistic taste acceptable, and the distinctions that had previously existed between
the houses of Aesthetes and other members of the well-to-do upper middle class
largely disappeared.

116. E. BURNE-JONES, memorial to
Laura Lyttelton (née Tennant), wife of
the Hon. Alfred Lyttelton, MP, who died
in childbirth. The 'peacock' gesso relief
is a symbol of the Resurrection. 1886
(V&A: P.85–1938)

HOLLAND HOUSE, SOUTH SIDE.

CHAPTER FOUR

The Houses and their Owners

GEORGE FREDERIC WATTS, FREDERIC LEIGHTON AND THE HOLLAND PARK COLONY IN KENSINGTON

For 25 years from 1850 to 1874 Little Holland House, home of the Prinsep family, was the epicentre of the artists' colony that developed in the environs of Holland House in Kensington (pl.117).[1] Little Holland House was also, throughout the whole of that time, home to George Frederic Watts (pl.118): Mrs Prinsep was to say of him, 'I invited him for three days and he stayed for 30 years' – only a slight exaggeration. By 1850 the heyday of the old mansion was over. Lord and Lady Holland, important early patrons of the artist, had once kept open house for political and literary London, but it was now rather run down and Watts had little difficulty in persuading them to grant a lease on one of the estate buildings, the Dower House known as Little Holland House, to his new friends, Mr and Mrs Thoby Prinsep. The Holland House estate was still beyond the turnpike on the road leading out of London, and the parkland surroundings made it a haven of peace and cleanliness. It was ideally suited to Watts, who was considered to be in delicate health.

Watts was born in Marylebone, above his father's piano-manufacturing workshop, in 1817.[2] His general education ceased at a very early age when he was apprenticed at the age of ten to the sculptor William Behnes. He studied briefly at the Royal Academy Schools, but his natural talent and the attention he paid to the art of the past formed his real artistic education. From very early on Watts managed to find people who would nurture him and deal with the practicalities of life. First Lord and Lady Holland housed him in Italy and encouraged his work, and then Mrs Prinsep looked after him for nearly thirty years. In 1886 he married Mary Fraser Tytler, his devoted helpmeet. This was his second marriage: his first brief union to Ellen Terry in 1864 was effectively at an end after barely a year. Watts had ambitions for art but not for fame or money; money for its own sake was of no interest to him and he was saved from the consequences of this indifference by his devoted friends. He did not have his own purpose-built house and studio until after the demolition of Little Holland House in 1875.

At one time used as a farm, the gabled roof and rambling interior of Little Holland House fitted with its still semi-rural surroundings. It provided a suitably romantic setting for the artistic visitors who congregated there in droves. This finely tuned Aesthetic milieu was presided over by Sara Prinsep, pioneer of the new social order, welcoming artists, writers, actors and musicians to her Sunday afternoon salon at a time when their foothold in society was still precarious. Sara was one of the seven Pattle sisters; among them was the pioneer photographer Julia Margaret Cameron and the beauty Virginia, Lady Somers. Anny Thackeray Ritchie recalled the sweeping robes and trailing Indian shawls worn by the sisters. Of Mrs Cameron she said, 'I remember a strange apparition in a flowing red velvet dress, although it was summer time'. Later she summed them up, '[The Pattle sisters] were unconscious artists with unconventional rules for life which excellently suited themselves'.[3]

Their unconventional way of life did not impede the Pattle sisters' marital prospects. Mrs Cameron and Mrs Prinsep enjoyed money and standing from the distinguished positions held by their husbands in India. 'Pattledom' (W.M. Thackeray's genial coinage) became a social network to be reckoned with:

117. Holland House, south side, Princess Marie Liechtenstein, *Holland House*, 1875, plate opposite p.6.

118. Little Holland House, Nightingale Lane (demolished 1875) watercolour, signed 'E. Hutton', before 1875 (Royal Borough of Kensington and Chelsea)

119. J.J.J. TISSOT, *The Letter,*
oil painting, 1876–8
(National Gallery of Canada, Ottawa)

The subject is set in the Dutch Garden
at Holland House. The figure is wearing
the kind of fashionable costume disdained
by the residents and habituées of Little
Holland House.

Virginia, the acknowledged beauty among them, married Lord Eastnor, heir to the Earldom of Somers; their daughters Isabella and Adeline both married into ducal families. Eastnor was a rich young amateur artist and photographer, and friend of John Ruskin. His mother discouraged him from pursuing his art: 'it was not considered the thing for a gentleman to draw too well like an artist; a gentleman might do many things pretty well but nothing too well'.[4] Julia Margaret's husband Charles Cameron said of him, 'He is an accomplished man, however, in matters of taste and paints like a professional artist'.[5] The youngest Pattle sister, Sophia, was another beauty and a friend of Burne-Jones. She married into the ancient Scottish Dalrymple family, but this did not deter her daughter Virginia from pursuing her independence from the tyranny of fashion. In Watts's portrait (pl.120) Virginia's green velvet dress in the Venetian Renaissance style is worn with coral jewellery often used to denote 'Italian' in Victorian painting. The dress survives in the collection of the Watts Gallery at Compton in Surrey.[6]

Isabella (Lady Henry Somerset) recalled that the Pattle sisters had 'a love of beauty in colour and form they all seem to have expressed in a passion for dress. They scorned Fashion, wore neither crinoline nor stays, and in long flowing garments designed and made by themselves, they walked serenely like goddesses through the London streets.' They added to their exotic reputation by speaking Hundustani among themselves and were reputed to sit up all night 'pulling their robes to bits and sewing them up in a new way ...'.[7] Mrs Cameron made friendships among the Little Holland House habitués who later served her well in her photographic career.

Mrs Thackeray Ritchie had known Little Holland House since girlhood; its inhabitants and atmospheric surroundings, heavily laden with nostalgia, feature in her novel *Old Kensington*, issued in monthly parts in the *Cornhill Magazine* (1872–3). Holland House itself was the epitome of an admired architectural style, and it served as the model for the 'Elizabethan' Fine Art Court at the Crystal Palace in Sydenham. It defined an important aspect of artistic house design of the period. The grounds were extensive, the old-fashioned garden of Holland House being a favourite with artists for romantic paintings in the historical, anecdotal vein: Tissot's painting *The Letter* (pl.119) is set in the Dutch Garden. Even towards the end of her life Lady Holland kept up the tradition of the annual garden party,

120. G.F. WATTS, *Miss Virginia Dalrymple*, oil painting, 1872
(Watts Gallery, Compton, Surrey)

The artistic green velvet Renaissance-style dress, with its bows imitating the 'aglets' found on Tudor costume, contrasts with the fashionable figure in Tissot's painting of the Holland House Dutch Garden.

and many people were familiar with the Italianate terrace ornamented with great urns full of flowers. The Prinseps and their guests could wander in the park as well as enjoying the beautiful garden of Little Holland House itself. A former owner, Lady Caroline Fox, sister of the 3rd Lord Holland called it 'Paradisino'. The resemblance between the Prinsep milieu and that of Watts's other early patrons, the Ionides family (see p.126), is hardly likely to be coincidental.

There was the added interest of Watts's private life; it was there that he met and married Ellen Terry. His intimate portrait of Ellen with loose, flowing golden hair was painted at Little Holland House: he called it *Choosing*, and it is the quintessential Pre-Raphaelite fashion statement (pl.121). The date is 1864; Ellen, dressed for her marriage to the 47-year old Watts, is still not 17 years old (her birthday was a week away). Her Renaissance-style wedding dress was designed by William Holman Hunt, and it is an early example of artistic taste in dress, even down to the string of amber beads, the only acceptable ornament for a certain type of fastidious aesthete. The full sleeves of the silk dress have the distinctive criss-cross ribbon detail, taken from Renaissance portraiture, which was much imitated in artistic circles. The picture is also a morality tale. Ellen is seduced by the beauty of the scentless camellia with its hollow promises (symbolizing the stage and her career as an actress, which she had agreed to abandon), while crushing humble scented violets to her heart with her left hand.

Ellen Terry's marriage to Watts was short-lived. She moved on to live with the aesthete-architect and designer E.W. Godwin, one of the most important figures in the Art Movement. Watts's pupil Roddam Spencer Stanhope believed that it was Sara Prinsep who wrecked the marriage: 'She never ceased to treat Ellen as a naughty child who must be scolded and made obedient, and a high-spirited, unconventional girl naturally resented this treatment, while Watts, absorbed in his art, was little aware of the mischief which was preparing.'[8]

Little Holland House had a large number of literary and artistic visitors, such as Rossetti – who introduced Burne-Jones into the circle – Holman Hunt, Du Maurier, Thackeray, Tennyson, Ruskin, Thomas Carlyle, as well as the musicians Joachim and Hallé. The house cast a potent spell over them, and there is something over-blown about reports of the social life. Significantly, Du Maurier wondered if the inhabitants were 'sincere'; William Morris regarded the fashionable life of the Prinseps with suspicion. One of Watts's friends, the collector Lady Charlotte Schreiber, said ruefully: 'I know there cannot be a worse place to go alone than Little Holland House, amidst artists and musicians, and all the flattery and nonsense which is rife in that otherwise agreeable society'. However, the entire household revolved round Watts. The amenities of Little Holland House, and indeed, Holland House itself, were greatly enhanced for the cultivated throng who made the trip to what was then a fairly distant suburb, by his presence and by the decorations Watts had painted, with the help of Spencer Stanhope, in many of the rooms in the great house. With typical generosity Sara Prinsep swept Burne-Jones into her care when he was ill, and he remained at Little Holland House for a few months while he convalesced.[9] Georgiana Burne-Jones understood what such an ambience meant to her husband:

> *There for the first time, he found himself surrounded without any effort of his own by beauty in ordinary life, and no day passed without awakening some admiration or enthusiasm ... The lovely garden that surrounded the house was an enchanted circle separating it from other places: there in summertime, and especially on Sundays, came most people of note that made up the 'world' of England – old and young, rich and poor, each welcome for some reason recognized by the hostess. Part of the lawn was given up to croquet – the chief outdoor game of the time – and another to bowls, whilst elsewhere encampments could be seen of those who did not play; and all seemed happy. The very strawberries that stood in little crimson hills upon the tables were larger and riper than others.*[10]

121. G.F. WATTS, *Choosing,*
portrait of Ellen Terry aged 16 in her
wedding dress, oil painting, 1864
(National Portrait Gallery)

Watts attempted to destroy his portraits
of Ellen after the collapse of the marriage.
This one escaped and later belonged to
Mrs Eustace Smith.

In his 1868 landscape *The Cedar Tree* (pl.122) Watts focused on the seclusion of the extensive Holland Estate, which at this date still extended to 80 acres. The painting shows May Prinsep walking in the north part of the Holland House garden with her dog in an almost other-worldly atmosphere of peace and contemplation, although in reality there was a teeming social round. The image is romantic, moody, an 'aesthetic' and poetic idea of the garden with its famously beautiful ancient trees. Here the urban middle classes are annexing part of a wider vista, in this case an upper-class country garden, in order to maintain a rural dream.

As the costume historian James Laver observed, the 1860s version of bohemian wear for men 'was a polite modification of the French artist costume of 1830'.[11] Leighton, for example, was usually portrayed in a version of bohemian costume, with an unstructured velvet jacket and a loose, flowing silk tie; he had abundant hair which he wore long. Watts devised a costume with wide-brimmed hat and loose-fitting velvet jacket. He figured latterly as an elderly sage in skullcap and long robes. The official version of Watts, dedicated, venerable and spiritual, promoted by admiring biographers (one of them his widow), leaves one unprepared for

the young man who loved women – his passionate admiration often translated into paintings of great beauty and sensibility – and hunting (he was an intrepid rider up to an advanced age), and his welcoming sociability to his many friends and patrons. Watts aired his own views in an article for the *Nineteenth Century*, 'On Taste in Dress', in 1883, a diatribe mainly concerned with the distortions suffered through tight lacing. He also evinced distaste for flying, untidy hair and for the self-consciously medieval in modern dress: 'Medieval costumes were often grotesque enough, but they were seldom without some strange sort of dignity; for the so to speak solemnity of the materials resented frivolity of cut.' The shared preoccupations with dress by artists and aesthetes relate to the Dress Reform Movement, another important strand in upper-class intellectual attitudes. In a wider context, which embraced such concerns as anti-vivisection, vegetarianism and some of the wilder reaches of spiritualism and psychic experiences, corsets and their damaging effects play an incongruous but significant role.

The whole fabric of this seductive social milieu was more fragile than it appeared. For all its rural location, the Holland Park area resembled nothing so much as a building site throughout the middle years of the nineteenth century. Roads were driven ruthlessly through the parkland surrounding Holland House. Little Holland House was in a tumbledown condition; it was held on a lease which had run out, and the Holland Estate was in need of funds. Development became inevitable even though Lady Holland, agent of the transformation, was horrified when houses started to impinge on her once rural surroundings. The magical place vanished to the developer, and Melbury Road became a prosperous artists' colony drawing a once-distant suburb into the urban sprawl.

When the lease of Little Holland House ran out in 1871, the Prinseps found there was no appeal against their eviction. Their much-loved household was sacrificed to the inexorable development of Kensington. Watts was now able to return the hospitality which he had enjoyed for so long. He bought a piece of land at Freshwater on the Isle of Wight, adjoining the Tennyson's property at Farringford. There he built a country retreat, designed by Philip Webb, large enough to accommodate them all. In a romantic landscape painting he emphasizes the rural seclusion and rustic surroundings of the house, although the Isle of Wight, too, was a nest of artists and poets and the social round hardly less frenetic than in London.

The problem of his London residence was solved for Watts by the Prinseps' son Val, who in 1864 had built a studio-house very close to his parents in Holland Park Road. The large garden, about an acre in extent, was more than he needed. He agreed to lease the part of it abutting the newly created Melbury Road to Watts, and there in 1875–6 Watts built his studio-house, also confusingly named Little Holland House, at number 6 (pl.123). The architect was Frederick Cockerell, chosen following the example of Watts's gentleman-amateur assistant Reginald Cholmondeley, who built his studio-house near Millais in Palace Gate. Conceived in the prevailing architectural taste of the immediate neighbourhood, New Little Holland House was red brick, with a red tiled roof and Tudor-style chimneys. It was described by Maurice B. Adams in the *Building News* as 'unpretending like its owner, and mostly devoted to work'.[12] When he came to enlarge it, Watts turned to George Aitchison, who built the picture gallery and added a terracotta porch. The picture gallery was open to the public on Sunday afternoons, but contained nothing for the merely curious beyond a display of enormous paintings. A few hints of the interior come from Chesterton's sale particulars when the house was on the market in 1919.[13] Still *in situ* were the tiled stove and fireplace with figure subjects by Burne-Jones in the dining room and drawing room; the drawing room fireplace had a repoussé copper mount and painted mantelpiece. A vine still flourished in the small conservatory running the length of the drawing room.

T.M. Rooke, long-time assistant to Burne-Jones, made a record of Watts's studio in Melbury Road with the impress of the artist's personality still unmistakably

122. G.F. WATTS, *The Cedar Tree*, oil painting, 1868–9
(Watts Gallery, Compton, Surrey)

The extensive grounds surrounding Holland House were available to the inhabitants of Little Holland House.

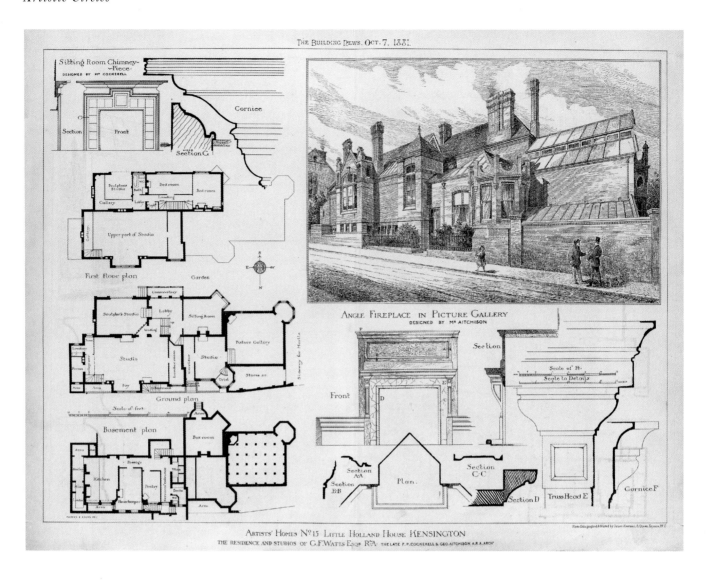

123. G.F. Watts's house, Little Holland
House, 6 Melbury Road, from *Building News*,
7 October 1881

124. T.M. ROOKE, *G.F. Watts's Studio,
Little Holland House, Melbury Road*,
watercolour, 1904
(Watts Gallery, Compton, Surrey)

upon it (pl.124). Watts seems to have risen only minutes before from the draped basket chaise-longue. Both windows are open and there is a vivid little bouquet of garden flowers on the table. In spite of the huge studio window and the high, narrow slit for getting vast canvases out, this is clearly a room for living and sociability: there were two fireplaces and a music gallery with a writing closet off it, and in the lobby was a fully equipped water-closet with hot and cold water for the models. On the easel at the back is a portrait of Mary Fraser-Tytler, Watts's second wife (and biographer). This watercolour was commissioned by Madeline, wife of the Hon. Percy Wyndham, as a memorial present for Mary, who was finally leaving the house (pl.125). It is a deeply poignant image, but it is a projection into the past because Watts lived out his last years in Surrey, visiting his London studio only rarely. The 'Queen Anne' house was scandalously demolished in 1964.

Val Prinsep's house was next door to Frederic Leighton's; they were built at exactly the same time, on plots of land leased from Lady Holland, and are recognized pioneers of the new genre of architecture. Prinsep, who had trained in Paris, stipulated a 'Parisian-style' studio taking up the first and second floors of the house. F.G. Stephens ventured one of his rare comments on the character of artists' houses about the Prinsep house, calling it 'sincere and picturesque'. The house was designed by Philip Webb and decorated in the new artistic style (pl.126), as described by Maurice B. Adams, its walls painted in Webb's signature 'Juniper green', with Morris papers and curtains and Japanese leather-paper panels for door panels and dados:

> *Mr Prinsep was one of the earliest to use this material, and obtained it specially from Japan … At the time Japanese leather-paper could only be had in small squares, and so its original quaintness for large surfaces is greatly increased by the varied character and colour which the many small squares insure – a variety which is almost entirely lost when continuous paper, such as that now imported from Japan, is used.*[14]

'Leather paper' was expensive but highly popular during the late nineteenth century. Like so much connected with artistic interior design, it was unveiled at the 1862 London Exhibition, and although not characteristic of Webb, it quickly entered the repertoire of architects and designers such as Burges, Godwin and Christopher Dresser. At the Vienna Exhibition of 1873 leather paper had a considerable success, and Japanese craftsmen were supplying retailers like Liberty's. Linley Sambourne used it in his house, making up for the expense by patching it carefully together and leaving bare spaces behind pictures. The British firm Rottmann, Strome & Co., whose founder, Alexander Rottmann, set up a factory near Yokohama in the 1880s, was one of the principal sources in the later period. In 1886 the wallpaper manufacturers Sanderson's set up a large department importing and selling Japanese leather papers. From modest beginnings in the artistic community, where it became almost a cliché of Aesthetic decor, Japanese leather paper migrated into the mainstream of fashionable decoration. Changes in fashion led to the decline of the industry and eventually the technique was lost. It has only recently been revived in Japan.

The houses built by Prinsep and Leighton present an interesting contrast in taste; the two men had known one another for several years, since the days when Leighton frequented Little Holland House. Webb had already demonstrated, in William Morris's Red House (1858–9) and Fairmile (1860) for Spencer Stanhope at Cobham in Surrey, that he was an admirer of English vernacular; Leighton's architect Aitchison was playing a different game, with a modernist Continental classicism. Godwin commented on the juxtaposition of the two styles, comparing Aitchison's 'barrenness of outline' with Webb's 'pleasing arrangement of gabled masses'.[15] However, it was Leighton's house that garnered the publicity, year in, year out. It is worth noting that these two early studio-house owners both received their early training on the Continent and would have been aware of the grand studio-houses being created by Parisian artists.

125. F. Hollyer, portrait of Mary Seton Watts (née Fraser Tytler), the artist's second wife, photograph, about 1890 (V&A: 7810–1938)

126. J.J.E. MAYALL, Val Prinsep in his studio, from F.G. Stephens, *Artists at Home*, 1884

Leighton was born in Scarborough, second child and only son of Dr Frederic Septimus Leighton. His mother's health was poor and the family travelled on the Continent in search of a suitable climate. Leighton's education was cosmopolitan and his art training accomplished largely in Frankfurt, Paris and Rome. He came to live in London more or less permanently in 1859, taking a house in Orme Square in Bayswater but nurturing dreams of a proper studio-house of his own: 'I wish I had a house', he wrote to his mother in 1862; by 1864 he was financially in a position to contemplate making his dreams a reality, and at that moment the ideal site became available in Holland Park Road. In spite of his growing professional success, Leighton still needed backing from his wealthy father, to whom he wrote in the summer of 1864:

> *I should not leave the place that I am in except to build; a mended house would be most unsatisfactory and temporary. I feel sure I shall get nowhere standing room for a house for less than £28 [per annum], still less room for a house and large garden. If I find the terms exactly as I suspect ... I shall, I think, close the bargain.*

Leighton first met his architect and lifelong friend George Aitchison, a man whose ideas were absolutely in sympathy with his own, in Rome in the 1850s.[16] It could be said that Leighton House was Aitchison's alpha and omega: it is the only house for which he was solely responsible, from first to last, and, as Leighton's bank records reveal, he and Leighton worked on it for more than thirty years, from 1864 until Leighton's death in 1896. The Arab Hall added in 1877–8 is a masterpiece of Victorian Orientalism. Leighton was an exacting client, immersing himself in every detail of the house and quick to pounce on any faulty work. This left Aitchison well prepared for the clientele that Leighton's patronage brought him, the wealthy connoisseurs and collectors – and sometimes amateur artists – who used his services as the most accomplished and refined interior designer of his time. The fullest – and most fulsome – description of Leighton's house comes in Mrs Haweis's *Beautiful Houses* (1882).

The house was designed as a 'Palace of Art' but in a rather different sense from Morris's Red House (p.158). As well as its function as a working studio, Leighton's house was deliberately designed around the needs of his collection. It seems that he was buying decorative furniture and objects while still at Orme Square.[17] Indeed, the creation of the Arab Hall was for the purpose of displaying his fine collection of Isnik tiles, some thousand or so, mainly from Damascus. The tiles were collected by Leighton's friend Sir Richard Burton and Caspar Purdon Clarke, who was also employed for the same purpose by the South Kensington Museum. Leighton directed Clarke to 'certain houses' in Damascus:

> *I had no difficulty in finding my market, for Leighton, with his customary precision, had accurately indicated every point about the dwellings concerned, and their treasures … Leighton made no difficulty about the price and insisted upon paying double what I had given. He never spoke of pricing things up cheap, and scouted the idea of 'bargains in Art Objects'* [18]

Mrs Haweis was at pains to enumerate the antique and exotic items throughout the house, including inlaid Italian chests and chairs and Persian rugs. The paintings in the drawing room included works by Constable, Delacroix, and Corot. Other works included a portrait of an old man by Tintoretto (now back in the house), an unfinished double portrait by Reynolds (Fitzwilliam Museum, Cambridge), a number of Old Master Drawings and a gilded Renaissance relief of the Madonna and Child in the manner of Rossellino (also now back in the house). She described the dining room as 'deep red'; recent paint analysis has revealed details she did not record, that both floorboards and ceiling ribs were painted red. The shelves of the dining-room sideboard were lined with blue-and-white 'Nankeen' (*sic*) and old English china. On the walls were great ceramic dishes or chargers of Iznik and Rhodian ware. A large Persian-style dish by the brilliant French ceramicist and Orientalist Joseph-Théodore Deck hung above Aitchison's sideboard in the dining-room (pl.127). It was bought at the sale after Leighton's death for the South Kensington Museum.

Collecting was a mark of educated taste, but that probably bore little weight with Leighton. He must have shopped on an epic scale. He was buying on his annual trips abroad and he had the help of friends like Burton and Purdon Clarke. Although he had quite a distinguished collection of Old Master and contemporary paintings and drawings, it was Oriental ceramics, rugs and exotic textiles that predominated. His entire collection was sold at Christie's in King Street shortly after his death.[19] The sale lasted for more than a week, 8–16 July 1896, and the catalogue, in its laconic way, gives a flavour of the massed objects in the house.[20] True to his personal taste for Middle-Eastern artefacts, the largest group of material comprises some 82 examples of 'Rhodian, Anatolian and Persian pottery'. There were Persian rugs, Japanese screens, no less than 55 chairs, and a large collection of textiles and costume. The furniture was more of a rag-bag: items no doubt considered to be from the Italian Renaissance are confections of old

127. Large dish or charger in the Iznik taste by J.-T. Deck, formerly belonging to Frederic Leighton (V&A: 226–1896)

128. Leighton's house, interior of the
studio, photograph by Bedford Lemere, 1895
(Leighton House Museum)

panelling and crude carving. Major pieces of furniture designed by Aitchison, including a massive dining-room sideboard-cabinet, have disappeared. The sale proceeds amounted to £31,549 9s 1d.

Aitchison was a highly accomplished interior designer, with a subtle sense of colour and texture. He could incorporate decorative motifs in a great variety of media seamlessly into his rooms. The colour scheme of the central block of the house was austere, glossy black relieved with gold, black-stained floorboards, black-and-white mosaic floors and pink-buff wall colourings stencilled with gold rosettes. Over the door leading into the dining room (pl.129) was inscribed the toast 'Prosit', which Mrs Haweis rendered in *Beautiful Houses* with an elongated 's', resulting in the word 'Profit', not at all appropriate to Leighton's carefully presented persona. The studio was also red, with a gilded semi-dome at one end and deep blue pillars and gallery.

In the studio Leighton's treasured cast of the Parthenon frieze (from the Elgin Marbles in the British Museum) was let into the upper part of the wall. A cast of Michelangelo's marble tondo of the Virgin and Child, owned by the Royal Academy, was there too (pl.128). Photographs taken during Leighton's lifetime show the array of paintings, ceramics and rugs in every room. The furniture was an eclectic mix, casually disposed about the rooms and the vast spaces of the studio. The more decorative pieces were used as props in his paintings. In the drawing room (pl.130) hung Camille Corot's romantic four paintings of the *Four Times of Day* (about 1858) which were sold, like everything else, after his death. A sketch by Delacroix was let into the ceiling of the window-bay. The walls were papered with a modern

129. Leighton's dining room,
engraved illustration from *Building News*,
1876

The large sideboard was designed by
Aitchison. The plates decorating the
room formed part of Leighton's extensive
collection of Middle Eastern and other
ceramics. The table-setting for a lone
diner is a poignant commentary on
Leighton's bachelor life.

130. Leighton's drawing room,
photograph by Bedford Lemere, 1895
(Leighton House Museum)

In this room, furnished with 17th-century
cabinets, can be seen three of Corot's panels
of the four times of day, *Morning, Noon,
Evening,* and *Night.*

131. The Arab Hall in Leighton House, photograph, about 1890 (Leighton House Museum)

The Arab Hall design was based on the entrance Hall of the 12th-century Moslem Palace of La Zisa at Palermo, which Aitchison had visited with William Burges in 1853–4, with the addition of other exotic elements from the Middle East.

design powdered with gold abstract motifs, probably influenced by the publications of the innovative designer Christopher Dresser,[21] who had a close connection with Purdon Clarke. Leighton employed Morris & Co., but there is little evidence of this other than the upholstery of the ottomans in the Arab Hall, which appear to have been covered with 'Willow' in silk (1876), the 'Tulip' curtains in the little sage-green Library off the entrance hall, and the cushions in the studio.

Enlargements in 1876–8 brought an exotic dimension to the house. Aitchison's Arab Hall (pl.131) made Leighton's house into one of the wonders of Victorian eclecticism. The architectural style is based, but not slavishly, on the Alhambraic Sicilio-Norman palace of La Zisa at Palermo, and incorporates elements taken from the Cairene houses that Leighton must have known from paintings by J.F. Lewis and Frank Dillon – he visited Cairo himself only briefly. The tiles, a mixture of valuable Middle-Eastern examples collected by Leighton, included a frieze with a quotation from the Koran and pictorial tiles mixed with filling tiles in peacock blue made by William De Morgan. These caused De Morgan endless trouble, with repeated unsuccessful firings, and – as his wife revealed – a substantial loss of £500, which he never disclosed to his patron.[22] Walter Crane provided the design for a mosaic frieze above the tiles; Joseph Edgar Boehm and Randolph Caldecott

132. G. AITCHISON, presentation drawing of the Silk Room, watercolour, April 1895 (Royal Institute of British Architects)

This was the last addition to Leighton's house and intended to house his art collection.

designed decorative capitals for the colonnettes in the Hall and the columns in the entrance. Externally the dome was fringed with a frieze of brick ziggurats derived from the stepped pyramids of ancient Mesopotamia. These were removed in 1959, but have recently been reinstated. In spite of this enlargement the house still had only one bedroom (other than the servants' rooms on the upper floor) and the domestic offices were consigned to the basement.

Leighton continuously embellished his house with carefully chosen pieces. Having admired embroidery exhibited by the young designer and craftswoman Gertrude Jekyll, he wondered if she would accept a commission. His delicate approach to this 'lady of independent means' is an indication of the difficulties still surrounding the status of the semi-amateur. Reassured, he settled on a tablecloth of 'some good design and rich tone' to be carried out in wool and silk on a serge base. The seat on the stairs, contrived from an antique inlaid wooden chest, was also eventually upholstered in Miss Jekyll's embroidery. His last addition to the house in 1894 was the 'Silk Room' (pl.132), designed to house his growing picture collection. The walls were hung with leaf-green silk and it was lit by a domed skylight. It may even have been incomplete at the time of Leighton's death; all trace of its original decoration was lost at the time of the Second World War, but much has been done to restore it and to recover some of the works of art that he owned.

133. F. DILLON, *A Room in the Harem*
of Sheikh Sâdât, watercolour and bodycolour,
about 1875
(Searight Collection, V&A: SD.332)

Leighton claimed that his house was built in 'a mews', and until quite some time after he arrived, the surroundings included a working farmyard. The fashionable portrait painter James Jebusa Shannon, a late arrival in the Kensington circle, bought the old square white farmhouse, with its farmyard and garden in order to build his new house, which became 10 Holland Park Road.[23]

Not far from Leighton's house, on the other side of Holland Park, Frank Dillon's London studio at 31 Upper Phillimore Gardens was also an exotic confection. It was fitted out with an Egyptian 'divan': Moncure Conway noted that 'Mr Dillon, an artist, has for some time had a studio in which every article came from Egypt'.[24] Like Leighton's Arab Hall, it had a frieze with a quotation from the Koran. The youngest son of a silk mercer, Dillon trained at the Royal Academy Schools. He was a widely travelled topographical painter: in 1861–2, when he was in Egypt for a second time, he shared a studio with George Price Boyce. While in Cairo Dillon made a number of finely detailed watercolours of rooms in the Harem of Sheikh Sâdât (pl.133): the seventeenth-century house was a fine example of a Mameluk residence, with elaborate *mushrabiyas*, carved wood 'stalactite' ceilings, Isnik tiles, coloured glass window lights, Oriental rugs, and rich silk-covered cushions. These studios promoted the taste for 'artistic' interiors fitted out with latticed screens, divans, rugs and tiles.

Dillon visited Japan in 1876 and remained there for more than a year. On his return in 1877 his Japanese subjects were exhibited at Agnew's in Bond Street. He was knowledgeable about Japanese painting and published his book *Drawings by Japanese Artists* in 1880. Boyce, who was a close friend of Rossetti, was himself a Japanese enthusiast and may have fired Dillon's imagination when they were travelling together earlier on. Dillon's painting *The Stray Shuttlecock* (pl.134) shows a number of objects – including the scrolls – that were actually in the artist's possession and were donated to the V&A at his death. It is possible that the whole of the interior was shipped to England and erected in his studio. Another view, in a private collection, shows the space from a different angle and with different decorative details. Orientalism and exotica had the longest legacy in the 'artistic' lifestyle, lingering well into the 1920s. These modes remained a defining characteristic of 'artistic' interior decorating long after the lavishly appointed 'show studio' had come to seem an irrelevance.

Another Kensington artist, Linley Sambourne, owned a handsome mid-Victorian town house in Stafford Terrace, close to Holland Park, as a result of his successful career as a Punch cartoonist. In 1874 he married Marion Herapath and with the help of her father bought 18 Stafford Terrace for £2,000. The house was, of course, a testament to the earning power of the successful illustrator, its fashionable 1870s decoration the epitome of well-to-do middle-class achievement. Marion Sambourne's diaries reveal the highly conventional – and strictly anti-bohemian – social life of the Kensington artistic community. Unlike the more raffish set around Whistler, the Sambournes' friends, among them the families of Luke Fildes and Marcus Stone, embraced Victorian conventions of entertaining on a grand scale and the endless, time-wasting round of calling and leaving cards on

134. F. DILLON, *The Stray Shuttlecock*, oil painting, about 1877
(V&A: P.6–1916)

135. The drawing room, Linley Sambourne's house at 18 Stafford Terrace, photograph, 1893 (Leighton House Museum)

friends and neighbours. Marion herself was fashionably dressed – more inclined towards Paris than 'artistic' styles – and she spent relatively large sums at her dressmaker's. Their daughter Maud made a good marriage to Leonard Messel, member of a wealthy banking family. In the words of Oscar Wilde: 'The Great superiority of France over England is that in France every bourgeois wants to be an artist, whereas in England every artist wants to be a bourgeois.'[25]

The Sambourne house is the antithesis of Leighton's sternly defined workplace. A tall, narrow, bow-windowed dwelling on the Phillimore Estate, it was not purpose-built but a conventional developer's speculation, designed to serve a genteel urban middle class. A family dwelling, it housed the artist, his wife and their two children, as well as being Sambourne's workplace. By a series of historical accidents (including its descent to the unmarried Roy Sambourne) it has been preserved virtually intact, with its decorative scheme of Morris wallpapers including 'Fruit' and 'Diaper' in different colourways, 'Reformed' furniture, stained-glass windows and copper and brass Benson lights (pl.135).[26] It offers an astonishingly detailed picture of a cultivated and artistically aware Victorian family: Marion Sambourne's diaries preserve details of shopping and decorating and entertaining. As a rare survival of unaltered mid-Victorian interiors, the house is inevitably perceived as archetypal, but it is a multi-faceted exercise in self-presentation, each of the living areas exhibiting different aspects of Sambourne's role as an artist and in society.

The dining room exemplifies 'Reformed' taste, showing some indications (not, incidentally, backed up by documentary evidence) of the influence of Charles Eastlake's seminal decorating manual *Hints on Household Taste* (1868). It seems safe to say that no-one moving in the artistic circles frequented by the Sambournes could have remained unaware of Eastlake's ideas. The dining table is a handsome architect-designed piece by A.W.N. Pugin's son, E.W. Pugin. The carved sideboard with its painted and gilded panels and inset tiles, most expensive of the Sambournes' furniture purchases, is by another prominent designer, Bruce Talbert, as are the dining chairs: they are examples of one of the most popular and widely available of Talbert's domestic designs. The reclining chair designed by Charles Bevan is another popular 'Reformed Gothic' Victorian domestic piece. The room was papered with two different Morris & Co. patterns, 'Pomegranate' and 'Diaper', with a bronzed relief-pattern ceiling paper. A plate-rail high on the wall displayed a fashionable array of blue-and-white china, Oriental ware and some Delftware.

A number of decorating instruction manuals appeared fast on the heels of Eastlake's *Hints*, many laying considerable emphasis on the decorating precepts followed at Stafford Terrace, most notably the judicious mixture of old and new. The morning room shows the sensitive antique collector at work; this was Marion's territory, conveniently near the backstairs leading to the servants' quarters. The double drawing room on the first floor displays ambitions towards the grandiose Second Empire style popular with the wealthy urban professionals who were colonizing Kensington in large numbers. By the mid-1870s this style was a little dated, having enjoyed the status of high fashion some ten years earlier. Intriguing evidence throughout the house suggests that Sambourne's tastes may have been formed at an early age, by the 1867 Paris Exposition Universelle, either having been a visitor himself or through the extensive reporting in the Press.[27] Several of his purchases – and they were his rather than hers – show awareness of the revived '*dix-huitième*', a popular theme at the exhibition. Edwards & Roberts, leading firm in the 'satinwood' revival and medal-winner at the exhibition, was one of the firms favoured by the Sambournes; there is a handsome inlaid desk in the Stafford Terrace dining room. The influence of Owen Jones's ivory-inlaid furniture for his millionaire patron Alfred Morrison, shown in Paris in 1867, is apparent in the Sambournes' choice of a painted and ebonized bedroom suite in the same style, from Maples.

The Sambournes were close friends of Luke and Fanny Fildes who lived in Melbury Road, within easy walking distance, and their decorating tastes are very similar – although Fildes's Italian bias is not reflected in Stafford Terrace. It is probably true to say that the Sambournes, like the Fildes, did not embrace Aestheticism as such, seeing their purchasing of antiques and art more in terms of refined 'good taste' pursued primarily as decor. A curious aspect of the work and life of the artist himself was secreted in boxes and only came to light quite recently: his hobby of photographing models for his illustration work extended into a gallery of nudes.

The American George Boughton commissioned West House at 118 Campden Hill Road in 1879 from Norman Shaw. The red-brick house was named after the American painter Benjamin West, because of Boughton's American roots. West House was distinguished by being included in *Beautiful Houses*, where it is described in detail. An Aesthetic showcase, it was exquisitely fitted out, according to Mrs Haweis with 'softness, refinement, harmony'.[28] The comfort of the house, unusual among artists' households, was ascribed by Mrs Haweis to Boughton's American upbringing. The colour scheme revolved round the typical Aesthetic palette of blues, greens and Indian red dado and woodwork below a pinky-red upper register. Every room was filled with Oriental china, Japanese embroideries, Spanish leather and tapestries in a characteristically 'artistic' medley. Walter Crane recalled the Boughtons' house-warming in 1878: 'There were a very large number of guests, and they included, I think, most of the artistic celebrities of London. The stream of many-coloured costumes on the picturesque staircase, where there was a tremendous crush, formed a curious sight.'[29]

Holman Hunt had been ensconced since 1857 nearby, at 1 Tor Villa, on Campden Hill, a house he shared with his sister and pupil Emily and two fellow artists, Robert Braithwaite Martineau and Michael Halliday, genre painters with distinct Pre-Raphaelite tendencies. He used the double reception room on the first floor as his studio. A portrait by the Scottish artist John Ballantyne (pl.136) shows Holman Hunt in Eastern dress, installed in the studio after his return from the Holy Land, hard at work on *The Finding of the Saviour in Temple* (City Art Gallery, Birmingham). This vast work occupied him for five long, weary years, being completed in 1860. The Holman Hunt portrait is one of a series of studies of artists in their studios painted by Ballantyne between 1862 and about 1867; during this time he painted more than twenty of them. He may have been inspired by Edward Matthew Ward, whose series of portraits of great writers in their studies (including Charles Dickens and Lord Macaulay) was carried out in the 1850s. Ballantyne's series is the ultimate expression of the Victorian fascination with the artist's studio.[30] However, his focus on the 'working' studio presents an interesting contrast with the 'lifestyle journalism' of F.G. Stephens and Maurice B. Adams that later developed round the artist at home.

The background of Holman Hunt's painting *The Festival of St Swithin* (pl.137) shows the view in the rain out of the window at Tor Villa. Before Airlie Gardens was built there was a long vista up the hill, with large skies and dense foliage from the many trees. Holman Hunt set up the dovecote especially for this subject, alluding to the superstition that if it rains on St Swithin's Eve it will continue to rain for forty days. When Holman Hunt left the house was taken by Alfred William Hunt, a landscape painter, although Holman Hunt continued to use the studio when his successor was away on sketching tours. Alfred Hunt's daughter Violet recorded revealing scenes from bohemian life in her memoirs, and an evocative description of the house which she used in two autobiographical novels entitled *Their Lives* (1916) and *Their Hearts* (1921), published many years later. The studio was left more or less as Holman Hunt had it, with a green enamel stove embossed with red fleurs-de-lis. The drawing room was papered with 'Daisy' wallpaper from Morris & Co., and the green woollen curtains bore gold scrolls. These things were expensive in comparison with the trade items of the time; it remained one of the foibles of artistic decorating to value the quality and taste of Morris & Co. over the dictates of economy.[31]

136. J. BALLANTYNE,
William Holman Hunt wearing
Eastern Dress in his Studio,
Tor Villa, Campden Hill,
oil painting, 1865
(National Portrait Gallery)

137. W. HOLMAN HUNT
and E. HUNT,
The Festival of St Swithin,
oil painting, 1865–6
(Ashmolean Museum, Oxford)

The view through the window
is from Tor Villa.

138. E. CANZIANI, *Mrs Holman Hunt's Drawing Room* (Melbury Road), watercolour and bodycolour on brown paper, 1925–8 (Birmingham Art Gallery and Museum)

Louisa Starr Canziani, Estella's mother was intimate with Leighton and the Little Holland House set.

In 1881 the Holman Hunts moved to Draycott Lodge, Fulham, a Regency villa with a large old walled garden and orchard, close to the houses of his friends Burne-Jones and William Morris. Alice Meynell described the house in some detail for the *Art Annual* of 1893, and included a contemporary photograph of the exterior. Adding to Mrs Meynell's unremarkable description, the historian of old Fulham C.J. Feret wrote that 'the chief rooms of Draycott Lodge are low and long. The drawing-room and the dining-room were turned by the great artist into veritable museums of Eastern art'.[32] Photographs of the interior show wallpapers and curtain fabric designed by Morris, Oriental rugs, a mix of furniture from different periods, including 'Egyptian' chairs designed by Hunt himself, and 'Sussex' chairs from Morris & Co. He also owned an impressive array of Eastern artefacts and Italian Old Masters, bought as an investment. In Florence with his first wife Fanny Waugh in 1856–7, for example, he acquired a *Virgin and Child with Saints* attributed to Bellini.[33] His granddaughter, Diana Holman-Hunt, recalled the profusion of objects in her grandfather's house, 'miniatures, jewellery, silver, rugs, embroidery, enamels, Persian and De Morgan tiles and Islamic metalwork'; and that was without considering the fine arts, furniture and ceramics.[34]

Hunt had to leave Draycott Lodge when it was compulsorily purchased in 1902. By that time both Morris and Burne-Jones were dead. From 1903 Holman Hunt lived at 18 Melbury Road, built about 1875 as a speculation in the prevailing red-brick Dutch manner.[35] Diana Holman-Hunt left an unforgettable description of the chests and cabinets in the Melbury Road house, crammed with things used in his paintings, which had been reverently preserved by her grandmother Edith (pl.138).[36] Her account is an evocation of the treasures hoarded by an artist, from costumes to a jumble of jewels.

In the early 1870s the Holland estate was broken up still further, and sold for building. This was when Melbury Road was created and, following the example of Leighton and Prinsep, a number of rising artists congregated in a series of distinguished studio-houses along the road. The Thornycroft dynasty of sculptors, Thomas, Sarah and their son Hamo, lived at number 2–4, built in 1876 by John Belcher. Watts's Little Holland House was at number 6. Marcus Stone lived at number 8, built in 1875–6 by Richard Norman Shaw; Colin Hunter was at number 18, built in 1876 by J.J. Stevenson; William Burges at number 9 (now 29) designed and built 1875–81. Luke Fildes followed quickly on Stone's heels, buying a plot at number 11 (now 31), on which he built a large red-brick house also by Norman Shaw, in 1876–7. The studios in Melbury Road were a considerable advance in Norman Shaw's career as an architect of artists' houses; before 1875 he had built just two in the country, Glen Andred for E.W. Cooke and Grim's Dyke for Frederick Goodall. These new commissions were seen as a crucial step for the artists themselves, and Shaw gained a reputation as the architect who put artists on the road to fame and prosperity. His suave essays for Marcus Stone and Luke Fildes, begun shortly after the house at the top end of Queen's Gate for the rich patron and collector (and amateur artist) J.P. Heseltine, slipped neatly into the prevailing character of the new colony.

The contrast between Burges and Norman Shaw as architects was strikingly illustrated in Melbury Road. Burges's eccentric early Gothic Tower House stands out among predominantly 'Queen Anne' studio-houses: he described himself as 'a thirteenth-century man'. Here Burges was able to indulge on his own account in the kind of fantasy that he was creating for his millionaire patron, the Marquess of Bute, at Cardiff Castle and Castell Koch in Wales. In scale, of course, Tower House bears no comparison with these magnificent follies, but it was far beyond the conventional expectations of the urban professional. The interior was decorated throughout with themed mural schemes designed by Burges and carried out by the team of skilled artists who had collaborated with him on other projects. Much struck by its brilliant and exotic effects, Mrs Haweis described the guest bedroom as 'made of fire and flowers … The windows glow with colours such as

139. William Burges's bedroom at Tower House, Melbury Road, photograph, 1884

140. M. STONE, *Aesthetic Interior*, probably in his Melbury Road house, watercolour, 1870s (British Museum)

the *Alhambra* has. Through *Moorish* trellis-work these colours shine … What is not pure gold is crystal … The whole room is like a shrine or reliquaire'.[37] Burges died just as his house was finished. Godwin, who much disliked Leighton's house, describing it in strong terms as 'altogether unsatisfactory', greatly admired Tower House (pl.139).[38] Architect of a number of artists' houses in Chelsea himself, he had a good deal to say on the subject in general.

The Kensington studio-houses had gardens, treasured amenities made possible by their semi-suburban location. These, too became showcases for the 'artistic touch', in addition to their usefulness as props. Stone used the nostalgic, old-fashioned garden of his Melbury Road studio-house in a number of his scenes of Regency romance and intrigue (pl.141). His house was brought near to the road frontage in order to keep as much garden as possible: three gates in the fence led to three entrances, one for guests and family, one for the artist's models and one for servants, neatly demarcating the social, professional and domestic activities within. The interior was pale, the off-white studio hung with tapestries. The furniture was antique, placed on large Oriental rugs (pl.140).

Describing Luke Fildes's house for the *Strand Magazine* in 1893, Harry How, wrote:

> *One house in Melbury Road cannot fail to cause both eyes to 'take it in'.*
> *You cannot mistake it. It stands next to a habitation of the Norman period.*
> *It is of red brick and its windows are brimming with scarlet geraniums and*
> *marguerites. It is of Queen Anne design and bears visible marks of the skill*
> *of Norman Shaw, who designed it some sixteen years ago.*

Fildes built somewhat in advance of his success. He was able to do this on the strength of a timely bequest from his grandmother which supplied most of the funds for his house. He insisted that the central feature of the house should be a broad 'triumphal' staircase leading up to his studio, in anticipation – well justified as it turned out – of the crowds that would visit. For his hugely successful painting *The Doctor* (1887; Tate) a poverty-stricken interior was installed in the large studio. The profits from the painting's exploitation in the print market went a good way to vindicating his extravagant studio-house.

Stone and Fildes indulged in fierce rivalry over their careers and through their houses, but their decorating tastes were broadly similar. According to his son, Fildes and his wife Fanny held 'Aestheticism' in dislike,[39] a defensive stance that may be explained by the fact that Aestheticism had joined the repertoire of *Punch's* comic butts barely a year before Fildes built his house. The Fildes bought a number of Italian Old Master paintings of somewhat dubious authenticity, and they had Morris & Co. wallpapers and chairs; otherwise the furniture was largely antique Chippendale and earlier Florentine and Venetian pieces. The decoration was more sumptuous than conventional 'artistic' taste, with a crimson and gold drawing room – the colour described as 'golden bronze' – and a Pompeian-red staircase hall hung with Flemish tapestries.

In 1892 Walford Graham Robertson, friend of Albert Moore and Burne-Jones and later of both Ellen Terry and the second Mrs Watts – a hazardous pairing that was negotiated with finesse – built himself a house in Melbury Road at number 13, facing the turning into Holland Park Road. A quirky exercise in nostalgic eclecticism by Robert Dudley Oliver, with a seventeenth-century front and Elizabethan rear elevation, it was soon overshadowed by the mansion built next door (15–17 Melbury Road) by Halsey Ricardo, William De Morgan's one-time partner, for the engineer Sir Alexander Meadows. Meadows was not, of course, an artist, but by virtue of his architect and the pioneering design, his house joined the parade of artistic houses in Melbury Road which remains, with its immediate environs, the most important showcase for the Victorian studio-house.

141. M. STONE, *Married for Love*, oil painting, 1882, set in the garden at Melbury Road (Guildhall Art Gallery)

WILLIAM MORRIS AND THE 'PALACE OF ART': RED HOUSE AND THE TWO KELMSCOTTS

In spite of the brevity of his residence there, no more indelible mark has been made on a house by its creator than that of William Morris on Red House, at Bexleyheath in south-east London. Designed by his great and lifelong friend Philip Webb, it was a groundbreaking artistic dwelling and the prototype artistic 'Palace of Art', the ideal which dominated Aesthetic architecture and interior decoration in the second half of the nineteenth century.[40] When he began the Red House project Morris was barely 25 years old and had just married Jane Burden (pls 143, 144); for the 28-year-old Webb, newly established in his own architectural practice, it was the first commission for a private house (pl.145). Morris and his wife moved into the house in the late summer of 1860.

Son of a wealthy stockbroker, William Morris was born in Walthamstow on the outskirts of London and educated at Marlborough College, the recently founded Victorian public school.[41] He went up to Exeter College, Oxford, intending to enter the Church, but his friendship with Burne-Jones and subsequent meeting with Rossetti deflected him first into architecture and then, via an unsuccessful foray into painting, to the design career which he followed for the rest of his life. Webb's collaboration with Morris is an important aspect of the Morris story – even the ways in which he diverged from Morris make their own contribution towards illuminating both men. His contribution to the Morris enterprise, the extent of which is often underrated even by himself, particularly his role in the founding of Morris, Marshall, Faulkner & Co., tied the fortunes of these two men together until the very end. With Burne-Jones they form an important trio in the history of artistic design.

Red House was designed to express a set of social, architectural and cultural values drawn from the past. Planned with its garden as a single entity, the site was an old orchard and many of the trees were retained, some of them growing so near to the house that apples would fall through open windows in the autumn. The house was constructed with the emphasis on natural materials, of warm red brick under a steep red-tiled roof. Like many artists' households, Red House was conceived as a communal project. Morris intended it to be shared with his dearest friend Burne-Jones and his family.[42] It was the breakdown of these plans that sowed the first seeds of doubt as to the practicality of his dreams for an idyllic rural existence, and forced Morris to abandon the house after only five years.

Inside Red House, by using a preponderantly white scheme of decoration, later owners have created a sense of space and light, giving the house a reputation as a radical departure from the dark, curtained and close-carpeted high Victorian style of the day. Morris, however, had plans for its decoration that verged on the sombre, with rich painted decoration covering every surface, embroidered hangings worked by Jane Morris and her sister, Bessie Burden, and stained-glass panels by Webb in the windows (pl.142). When it came to furnishing, to quote Morris's first biographer J.W. Mackail, 'not a chair or table, or a bed; not a cloth or paper-hanging for the walls; nor a curtain nor a candlestick; nor a jug to hold wine or a glass to drink out of, but had to be re-invented'. As Rossetti had remarked, Red House was 'the most noble work in every way, and more a poem than a house such as anything else could lead you to conceive, but an admirable place to live in too'.[43]

A taste for the solid and massive had already manifested itself in Morris's experiments with the furnishing of rooms, formerly occupied by Rossetti, that he shared with Burne-Jones in Red Lion Square in Bloomsbury. Rossetti reported,

Morris is rather doing the magnificent there, and is having some intensely mediaeval furniture made – tables and chairs like incubi and succubi. He and I have painted the back of a chair with figures and inscriptions in gules and vert and azure, and we are all three going to cover a cabinet with pictures.[44]

142. P. WEBB, panel of glass quarries, possibly from the nursery at Red House, 1859
(V&A: C.63–1979)

143. Photograph of William Morris aged 23 from J.W. Mackail's *Life of William Morris*, 1899

144. Photograph of Jane Burden at the time of her meeting with William Morris, 1858 (V&A: Ph.1735–1939)

145. P. WEBB, design for William Morris's Red House, 1859 (V&A: E.60–1916)

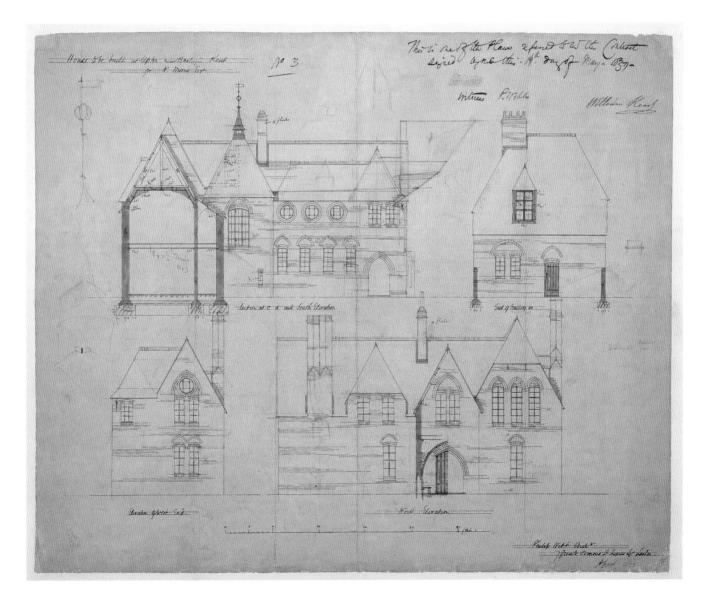

146. E. Burne-Jones, caricature
'self-portrait' of life at Red Lion Square,
Memorials, vol.i, 1904

The large round table and two great throne-like chairs painted by Rossetti with scenes from Morris's romantic poetry were transported to the country. The table and one of the chairs can be seen in a comic drawing by Burne-Jones of himself in the Red Lion Square room (pl.146). The 'cabinet' must be the large cupboard-cum-settle that could hardly be got into the house, and, when it was finally installed at Red House, took up the whole end wall of the drawing room, where it has remained. Webb topped it off with a minstrels' gallery. The other piece of painted furniture was a wardrobe, designed by Webb and painted by Burne-Jones with an episode from Chaucer's 'Prioress's Tale', a wedding present to Morris and Jane. The chairs remained at Red House after the departure of the Morris family, whereas the wardrobe stayed with them to become the centrepiece of their drawing room at Kelmscott House in Hammersmith (see pl.155).

The furniture at Red House was built to withstand Morris's violent personality, which sometimes resulted in savage attacks on tables and chairs; the massive oak dining table even had a band of metal round its edge.[45] The decoration was not to everyone's taste. William Bell Scott wrote after a visit that in the 'vast empty hall ... the adornment had a novel, not to say, startling character, but if one had been told it was the South Sea Island style of thing one could have believed such to be the case, so bizarre was the execution'. He came to the conclusion that 'genius always rushes to extremes at first'.[46] Whatever the shortcomings of the interior decoration, Morris's hospitality could not be faulted. In her 'Memorials' of her husband Lady Burne-Jones remembered: 'it was the most beautiful sight in the world to see Morris coming up from the cellar before dinner, beaming with joy, with his hands full of bottles of wine and others tucked under his arms.'[47]

Morris believed that the garden should 'clothe' the house, linking it with the countryside which then surrounded it (see pl.44): the climbing plants on the house were actually included in Webb's architectural plans. The garden was planted in a completely new style, with a profusion of old-fashioned native flowering plants: honeysuckle, briar roses, poppies and mallow, as well as blackberries and hawthorn and resplendent sunflowers in autumn. In addition to the orchard it had a productive kitchen garden. Morris was scornful of 'horticulture', which he equated with the Victorian passion for garish exotics: his idea was that a garden should be useful rather than ornamental. The courtyard garden was conceived as a medieval *hortus conclusus*, an enclosed plot with trellises and fruit trees and small, square, box-edged beds. Morris was proud of his gardening knowledge; as Mackail noted, 'Red House garden, with its long grass walks, its mid-summer lilies and autumn sunflowers, its wattled rose-trellis inclosing richly-flowered square garden plots, was then as unique as the house that surrounded it'.[48] The garden at Red House, when it was originally created in the 1860s, may have been more experimental than the house itself. The garden 'compartments' were made before this style became so significant in English garden design. Structurally, much survives, including some of the original fruit trees.

In 1883 Morris wrote an account of his earlier life in a letter to a socialist colleague:

> At this time the revival of Gothic architecture was making great progress in England and naturally touched the Pre-Raphaelite movement also; I threw myself into these movements with all my heart: got a friend to build me a house very mediaeval in spirit in which I lived for 5 years, and set myself to decorating it; we found, I and my friend the architect especially, that all the minor arts were in a state of complete degradation especially in England, and accordingly in 1861 with the conceited courage of a young man I set myself to reforming all that; and started a sort of firm for producing decorative articles.[49]

In fact, what makes the whole 'Red House' enterprise so important, including the massive furniture, was that it became the inspiration for the Morris decorating firm, which was to have such a profound influence on design and decoration in the

147. E. BURNE-JONES, *The Backgammon Players*, design for a painted panel for a cabinet inspired by the garden at Red House, pencil drawing, 1862
(Fitzwilliam Museum, Cambridge)

The cabinet is in the Metropolitan Museum of Art in New York.

148. W. MORRIS, 'Trellis' wallpaper, 1862
(V&A: E.452–1919)

later nineteenth century. *The mise-en-scène* itself provided ideas; the decoration of the medieval-style *Backgammon Players* cabinet (now in the Metropolitan Museum in New York; pl.147), for example, with its painted panels designed by Burne-Jones, is set in the Red House garden. Two of the four earliest wallpaper designs issued by Morris & Co. were inspired by Red House: an embroidered hanging was the origin of 'Daisy' (pl.149), and the Red House garden of 'Trellis' (pl.148). Overwhelmingly the most popular choice for artist – and 'artistic' – decorators were 'Pomegranate' or 'Fruit', and 'Daisy'. These early patterns lack the sophisticated, flowing quality of the later designs, but their crude naïveté may have appealed to the antiquarian tastes of this particular audience.

Morris, Marshall, Faulkner and Company, 'the Firm', as Morris liked to call it, was founded in 1861 and made its public debut at the 1862 International Exhibition in London. Morris had gathered some of the finest design talents from the wider Pre-Raphaelite circle, Webb, Rossetti, Ford Madox Brown and Burne-Jones. Given this round-up, the masthead is somewhat enigmatic; Peter Paul Marshall, an amateur painter, trained surveyor and sanitary engineer and Charles Faulkner, a mathematician, brought some organizational skills to the embryonic enterprise.[50] It was not a trouble-free start, one critic describing the furniture as

149. W. MORRIS, 'Daisy' wallpaper, 1862
(V&A: E.442–1919)

'Daisy' was a very successful design,
used in artistic households for decades.

'simply preposterous'. However, Morris understood that the way forward could not be through commissions for what he called 'state furniture', but must depend on a choice of articles for the decoration of the ordinary middle-class home. The prospectus offered a number of services: 'Mural Decoration, either in Pictures or in Pattern Work … Carving generally, as applied to Architecture … Stained Glass … Metal Work in all its branches … Furniture … Embroidery … besides every article for domestic use'.[51] The 'Sussex' chair of black-stained beech, costing about 7 shillings, remained in production until the 1940s. Mackail remarked that, 'of all specific minor improvements in common household objects due to Morris, the rush-bottomed Sussex chair perhaps takes first place. It was not his own invention, but was copied with trifling improvements from an old chair of village manufacture picked up in Sussex'.[52] The 'Sussex' chair became a symbol of the Morris look; combined with the 'Daisy' wallpaper it created an instantly recognizable statement of decorating principles of a very high-minded artistic character. Red House was indirectly responsible for creating an 'artistic' style, but it was 'work in progress' still when Morris had to leave and return to London in 1865, and no images survive of its decoration during the years of his residence.

Many of the exhibits from Morris's stand in the 'Mediaeval Court' at the

"The Hill," Witley, South Front.

150. M. BIRKET FOSTER, 'The Hill, Witley', *Art Annual*, 1890

1862 Exhibition found their way into The Hill at Witley in Surrey, the Firm's first domestic decorating commission, for the watercolourist Myles Birket Foster (pl.150). This commission presented Morris with opportunities to refine his notions of the 'Palace of Art'. Red House had provided endless ideas but had proved hard to finish; still embodying the handcrafted Palace of Art, The Hill was a more viable – even commercially sound – solution. As the earliest of the domestic decoration projects it was one of the most intense artistic experiences for the newly founded Morris, Marshall, Faulkner and Company. Architecturally, Birket Foster adopted the very look that he himself had made desirable through his idyllic rural subjects. It was a rambling house in the newly fashionable Olde English style, partly constructed from reclaimed materials from old buildings. Largely designed by its owner with the help of Decimus Burton, it was filled with works by Foster's artist friends.

The interior lived up to Morris's mission statement for his firm: to provide a complete interior decorating service, including murals and painted glass. He wished to create a glowing medieval painted interior, and every room was embellished with scenes from legend and fairy tale. In addition to the painted scenes tracing the *Legend of St George* by Burne-Jones were stained-glass panels with episodes from Chaucer's *Legend of Good Women*, also largely the work of Burne-Jones, separated by stained-glass quarries in the medieval style designed by Webb; tile panels and a painted screen were designed by Burne-Jones (pl.151). As Moncure Conway noted,

A very fine effect has been produced in the dining-room of Mr Birket Foster, at Witley, in Surrey, by inserting in the wall around the room a continuous painting by Burne Jones representing the legend of St. George and the Dragon. The stained glass which Morris & Co. have placed on the landing of the staircase, in the same beautiful residence, shows also that even a cottage-mansion of moderate size admits of a great deal more decorative color than is ordinarily supposed.[53]

His collection of ceramics, including much fashionable German stoneware, was disposed on elegant ebonized 'what-nots' designed for the Firm by Webb. A number of individual elements from The Hill project were duplicated for the South Kensington Museum, notably the stained-glass panels.

Morris went on to transform the way in which people of relatively modest means decorated their houses. In the 1870s, with furniture, metalwork, printed and woven textiles, wallpaper, tapestries, carpets, tiles and ceramics all in production, the 'Morrisian look' could be achieved in any artistic household. The easily recognizable wallpapers and 'Sussex' chairs announced Aesthetic allegiance. Walter Crane remarked that

> *The great advantage and charm of the Morrisian method is that it lends itself to either simplicity or splendour. You might be almost as plain as Thoreau, with a rush-bottomed chair, a piece of matting, an oaken trestle table; or you might have gold and lustre (the choice ware of William De Morgan) gleaming from the sideboard, and jewelled light in the windows, and the walls hung with arras tapestry.*[54]

This passage conjures up a picture of an artist's home, specifically a residence well known to Crane, that of Burne-Jones (see pl.178).

The Morris operation was held in awe even by confident Aesthetes. Louise, artistic and intellectual wife of Mandell Creighton, future Bishop of London, remembered her first home in Oxford:

> *With us both, yellow was a favourite colour; my best evening dress was yellow silk, and our drawing-room wallpaper was yellow … Our future house was quite new, so we did not go to the expense of Morris wallpapers on walls which might prove damp, but got our papers from Woollam & Co., who was reviving some of his old fashioned blocks, and we look forward to Morris papers in the future.*[55]

151. E. Burne-Jones, panel of tiles, 'The Sleeping Beauty' by Morris & Co., 1864 (V&A: Circ.520–1953)

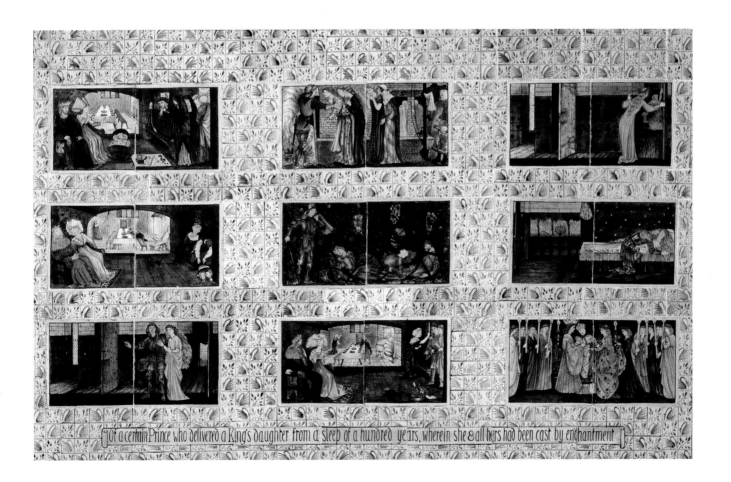

THE MANOR HOUSE, KELMSCOTT, FROM THE ORCHARD.

152. E.H. NEW, 'The Manor House, Kelmscott, from the Orchard', illustration to J.W. Mackail's biography of William Morris, 1899

This was a real piece of self-denial, since her husband was an ardent admirer of Morris; but what is so intriguing is why the by no means negligible firm of Woollams should be relegated to the status of stop-gap.

Plentiful evidence survives in letters and memoirs of the 'artistic' taste of churchmen and academics, but they were not the kind of people to be the subject of informal portraiture, so the visual evidence is hard to find. There was an aura of gravitas surrounding this style of decoration, with its emphasis on frugality and culture. The clergy had an intensive exposure to design reform, through the massive Victorian church-building programme and the efforts of the Ecclesiological Society. They were also the inhabitants of reformed Gothic vicarages, which have claims to rival Morris's Red House as the first modern middle-class homes. As Mackail pointed out, the early commissions for the Morris firm were for church decoration, 'and the movement was just beginning to spread from ecclesiastical into secular life, and become what was afterwards called Aestheticism'.[56]

153. C.M. GERE, 'Kelmscott Manor', wood-engraving, frontispiece to William Morris's romance of the future, *News From Nowhere*, Kelmscott Press, 24 March 1893

Red House was the first and only modern purpose-built house inhabited by Morris. It was an expense that he could not afford while the fortunes of the Firm were uncertain, and his later houses were rented. In the future his choices would be old dwellings, two eighteenth-century town houses and a Tudor Cotswold manor. The London house and workshop at 26 Queen Square, from which Morris conducted the business of the Firm and housed his family, was never close enough to his heart to be recorded. For his aesthetic sense to be engaged circumstances would have to await his acquisition of Kelmscott Manor in Oxfordshire (pl.152). He discovered the beautiful old Cotswold house in 1871, through an estate agent's catalogue. Ostensibly a country retreat for his wife and daughters, he took a joint tenancy with Rossetti and then, in an act of supreme unselfishness, departed for Iceland on 6 July 1871, leaving Rossetti and his wife to conduct their secret love affair in the seclusion of the country. It was one of those intensely mysterious Victorian relationships, with both parties in love but, as far as can been certainly ascertained, with no consummation. Opinions about this differ; the conclusions are, in the end, speculation. Nonetheless, it was deeply distressing to Morris and an enormous sacrifice to exile himself from the place that was to be his passion for the last 25 years of his life.

Rossetti was delighted with the house – even ecstatic – as his correspondence from this time reveals: he described the garden as 'a perfect paradise'. For his studio he commandeered the still intact Tapestry Room, a feature which had commended the house to Morris, the entire room being hung round with ancient, faded tapestries depicting the biblical story of Samson. Rossetti came to dislike the subject matter of the tapestry, particularly the episode where Samson's eyes are gouged out. Furniture surplus to the needs of the Morris family and from Rossetti's Chelsea house in Cheyne Walk was brought down and installed 'rather chaotically', and Rossetti took up shopping again, having rather abandoned his trawling of the London junk dealers when Tudor House was adequately equipped. The dealer Murray Marks, who had helped Rossetti to assemble his collection of blue-and-white porcelain, was roped in to find things that were needed, such as Pembroke tables. Application was made to Philip Webb for the components of paint colours for the rooms in green, grey and red. The green colour, Rossetti stipulated, should be 'a good tint of green ... I suppose something of the same sort as in that little dining-room of mine [in Chelsea]. How that was made I quite forget ...'.[57] During his next prolonged stay, in September 1872, he sent for 'an immense quantity of figured green Utrecht velvet rolled up somewhere at Chelsea' in order to make curtains. In the event it could not be found: Rossetti may have forgotten that much of it had already been used at Tudor House for curtains and upholstery.[58]

Morris made brief visits during these years; he finally took possession of his dream house in 1874, when Rossetti suffered a breakdown and was never able to return. Unlike Rossetti, Morris loved the Tapestry Room; it was one of his reasons for taking the house and it embodied an idea he first tried at Red House of covering the walls of a room with hangings. Through the Tapestry Room Morris had his bedroom, where embroidered hangings also took pride of place. The curtains and cover for the four-poster bed were designed and made by Morris's daughter May in 1891. The bedroom wallpaper was Morris's 'Lily' (1874).

At Kelmscott Manor Morris finally managed to recreate a domestic environment that reflected his ideals of art and rural loveliness in combination, as well as what was in effect a proto-Arts and Crafts garden. The frontispiece of Morris's romance *News from Nowhere*, drawn by Charles March Gere under the supervision of Morris himself, is an accurate representation of the Manor in its garden setting (pl.153). In spite of Morris's rather cautious reception of the trial drawings, one of them was followed faithfully for the final woodcut version. The much-reproduced image is only rarely credited to the artist, but late in life he was sought out by the writer Edmund Penning-Rowsell and interviewed about his relations with Morris. Gere stayed frequently with the Morris family, both in the country and at Kelmscott House in Hammersmith, while making drawings for the frontispiece and other illustrative projects connected with the Kelmscott Press. He remembered that both Morris and his wife had white hair, and that Mrs Morris was 'very reserved'. He got on well with her, however, and stayed with her after Morris's death to make delicate portraits of her on vellum.

Shortly after the interview he wrote down his memories of both Kelmscotts:

At Kelmscott Manor I slept in the little powder closet which opens from the Tapestry Room. Morris used to bring me in a can of hot water in the morning. He used to tumble out of bed, have his tub, slip into his blue shirt and blue suit, thrust a brush – or maybe only his hands – through his curly hair and beard – all the work of a few moments – and was ready for the day's adventure.

Morris liked everything solid and large; the wash basins and jugs were of massive proportions in earthenware; his tea cup and porridge bowl the same. He liked his bread in solid chunks; on one occasion I cut some bread at breakfast far too thin for his taste. A moment later he arrived and with a shout of disgust roared 'Who cut this bread?'… In London I slept in a little room approached by a step ladder from Morris's study. It was over a room in which the Fabian Socialists held their meetings, which often kept me awake until a late hour.

After supper Morris would generally play a game of draughts with his wife; if she beat him several times he would stop playing and sweep the draughtsmen from the board. After the game Morris went down to his study and I would go to bed hearing the squeak of his quill pen – he kept a dozen or so ready cut – as he drove it through a new poem late into the night. In the morning I saw the pages of his splendid script lying there on the table.

I believe that when Morris first set up house in London the servants mealed with the family, in accordance with socialist ideas: but this practice had come to an end when I stayed there.[59]

Drawings of rooms in the Cotswold Kelmscott and the London house by the river at Hammersmith were made from photographs by Gere's friend, the accomplished topographical artist Edmund H. New, for the official biography of Morris by Burne-Jones's son-in-law, J.W. Mackail (pl.154). This account of Morris's life was necessarily discreet about a number of private matters, but the picture of Morris himself is a faultless evocation of a remarkable personality.

Kelmscott Manor was connected by the shining thread of the Thames to Morris's town residence, the eighteenth-century Kelmscott House on Upper Mall at Hammersmith, home to Morris from 1879 until his death. Mackail described it without enthusiasm:

It is a larger Georgian house, of a type, ugly without being mean, familiar in the older London suburbs. … Behind the house a long rambling garden, in successive stages of lawn and orchard and kitchen-garden, still preserves some flavour of the country among the encroaching mass of building which is gradually swallowing up the scattered cottages, low and roofed with weathered tiles, that then lay between the river and the high road.[60]

Morris believed that he could make this new house beautiful without great expenditure (pl.155). He achieved the closest approximation to the lost Red House, with some furniture dating back to that time and hangings of his own wallpapers and woven double-wool textiles, 'Pimpernel' in the double-height dining room and 'Bird' in the drawing room (pl.157), designed 1876–8. The 'Peacock and Dragon' curtains from Hammersmith were transferred to the Tapestry Room at the Manor after his death (pl.156). His important collection of books and manuscripts formed the decoration of his study: for Morris this was embellishment enough; he never had many pictures, as can be seen in old photographs of the house. Souvenirs of Queen Square were a table by Philip Webb and the pillared grate used in many of his

WILLIAM MORRIS'S BEDROOM AT THE MANOR HOUSE, KELMSCOTT, FROM THE TAPESTRY ROOM.

154. E.H. New, 'William Morris's Bedroom at the Manor House, Kelmscott, from the Tapestry Room', illustration to Mackail's biography of William Morris, vol.ii, p.268

155. The drawing room at Kelmscott House, Hammersmith, photograph, 1896 (V&A: M.2–1973)

architectural commissions. After Kelmscott House was given up, the 'Bird' tapestry hangings found their way into another artist's house belonging to Morris's fellow printer and typographer Emery Walker, just a few hundred yards downstream at 7 Hammersmith Terrace.

In its relative austerity (compared to conventional taste of the time) and dedication to useful pursuits, Kelmscott House exemplified many of Morris's most cherished ideas on house decoration. In a lecture on 'The Beauty of Life', delivered in 1880, Morris spelled out his thoughts in detail:

Believe me if we want art to begin at home, as it must, we must clear our houses of troublesome superfluities that are for ever in our way: conventional comforts that are no real comforts and do but make work for servants and doctors: if you want a golden rule that will fit everybody, this is it: 'have nothing in your house that you do not know to be useful, or believe to be beautiful.' ...

Perhaps it will not try your patience too much if I lay before you my idea of the fittings necessary to the sitting-room of a healthy person: a room, I mean, which he would not have to cook in much, or sleep in generally, or in which he would not have to do any very litter-making manual work.

First a book-case with a great many books in it: next a table that will keep steady when you write or work at it: then several chairs that you can move, and a bench that you can sit or lie upon: next a cupboard with drawers: next, unless either the book-case or the cupboard be very beautiful with painting or carving, you will want pictures or engravings, such as you can afford, only not stopgaps, but real works of art on the wall; or else the wall itself must be ornamented with some beautiful and restful pattern: we shall also want a vase or two to put flowers in, which latter you must have sometimes, especially if you live in a town. Then there will be the fireplace of course, which in our climate is bound to be the chief object in the room.

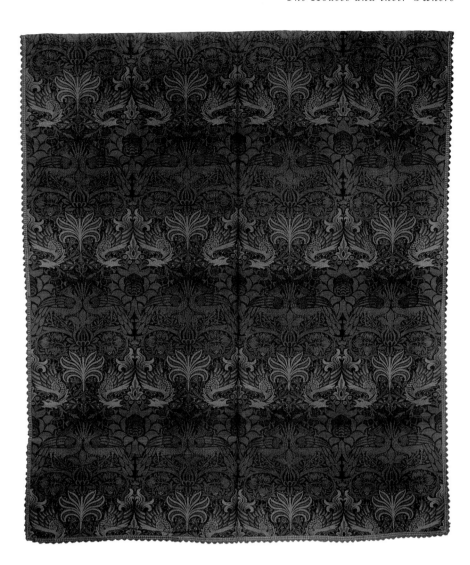

156. W. Morris, designed for
Morris & Co., 'Peacock and Dragon',
woven double-wool cloth, 1878
(V&A: T.64–1933)

157. W. Morris, designed for
Morris & Co., 'Bird', 1878,
woven double-wool cloth
(V&A: Circ.501A–1962)

That is all we shall want, especially if the floor be good; if it be not, as, by the way, in a modern house it is pretty certain not to be, I admit that a small carpet which can be bundled out of the room in two minutes will be useful, and we must take care that it is beautiful or it will annoy us terribly.

Now unless we are musical, and need a piano (in which case, as far as beauty is concerned, we are in a bad way), that is quite all we want ... [61]

True to his precepts, Morris had neither carpet nor curtains in his study. The other rooms were more luxurious; of the first-floor drawing room with its five windows overlooking the river, Mackail wrote that it was

quite unique in the quietness and beauty of its decoration. The painted settle and cabinet, which were its chief ornaments, belonged to the earliest days of Red House; the rest of the furniture and decoration was all in the same spirit, and had all the effect of making the room a mass of subdued yet glowing colour, into which the eye sank with a sort of active sense of rest. [62]

The products of the Morris Firm found their most sympathetic setting in the plain architecture and proportions of the house. Work on tapestry looms in the stables combined with spare elegance in the living quarters to satisfy Morris's artistic aims. However, he was disappointed with the way his utopian experiments developed, fearing that his products reached only the rich.

Furniture from all the houses found its way to the Cotswold Kelmscott after Morris's death. Mrs Morris managed to buy the manor house and estate in 1913 and it eventually became the property of her surviving daughter, May. The house and contents were bequeathed by May to the University of Oxford, and the contents, with their sources, were listed in her will. Red House is represented by a number of embroidered hangings, the painted jewel casket which had been a wedding present from Rossetti and Lizzie Siddal, and a half-tester bed; bedroom furniture in black painted wood designed by Webb; a 'very worn' Turkey carpet; a large round oak table (described as 'the first made'); a small round oak table ('Mrs Morris's work table at Red House') and a black Webb settle. Still surviving from Rossetti's tenancy of Kelmscott was a satinwood Sheraton table described as 'Dante Gabriel Rossetti's writing table'; also an oval mirror, a pair of 'Webb' candlesticks (presumably the copper candlesticks designed for the 1862 International Exhibition) and a number of his drawings of Mrs Morris and the girls. One or two items of useful furniture are listed as having been in Queen's Square. From the London Kelmscott came library furniture as well as an ivory and ebony cabinet from Morris's study and the 'Peacock' hangings from the dining room. Morris and Burne-Jones had lived all their lives with the products of the Morris firm, some from the earliest days; being completely outside fashion they never dated, and being sturdy and plain they never broke.

As time went by Oxford University found it could not make proper use of the house and in 1962 it devolved on the Society of Antiquaries who remain its custodians. It stands as a synthesis of Morris's tastes and beliefs about suitable domestic furnishing and decoration. He commented on his own 'conceited courage', but he achieved something remarkable when he harnessed the talents of artists like Rossetti and Burne-Jones to the service of interior decoration. He transformed the way in which people of modest means decorated their houses, by making art available not through an elaborate process of commissioning, but from a shop. Although the full-blown Morris & Co. treatment was not affordable by any but the very wealthy, Morris's influence was pervasive, particularly among cultivated professionals. The most popular of his wallpapers, 'Daisy', covered the walls of many of the little red-brick 'Queen Anne'-style houses that sprang up in garden suburbs on the fringes of London.

DANTE GABRIEL ROSSETTI, JAMES MCNEILL WHISTLER AND OTHERS IN CHELSEA

Old oak then became his [Rossetti's] passion, and in hunting it up he rummaged the broker's shops round London for miles, buying for trifles what would eventually (when the fashion he started grew to be more general) have fetched large sums. Cabinets of all conceivable superannuated designs – so old in material or pattern that no one else would look at them – were unearthed in obscure corners, bolstered up by a joiner, and consigned to their places in the new residence. Following old oak, Japanese furniture became Rossetti's quest, and following this came blue china ware (of which he had perhaps the first fine collection made), and then ecclesiastical and other brasses, incense-burners, sacramental cups, Indian spice boxes, mediaeval lamps, antique bronzes and the like. In a few years he had filled his house with so much curious and beautiful furniture that there grew up a widespread desire to imitate his methods; and very soon artists, authors, and men of fortune having no other occupation, were found rummaging as he had rummaged, for the neglected articles of centuries gone by.[63]

Artists as pioneers in a new style of collecting make up an important sub-plot in this narrative and in the wider context of art and the Victorian middle class. This is probably the area in which the closest crossover occurs between the tastes of the artists and their Aesthete patrons.[64] Leaving aside the systematic and intellectual collecting by, for example, Leighton, Victorian artists in general collected curiosities as props and these were absorbed into the production of paintings. Rossetti is a significant player in this arena in which artists seized opportunities that arose from their working environment, to assemble sometimes significant collections, notably of Oriental blue-and-white porcelain and Japanese art. The enthusiasm for Japanese art was fostered by the little confederacy of artists and collectors showing off their finds to one another, but it was also fuelled by the great variety of objects that quickly became available in London and Paris. Both Whistler and Rossetti were influential enthusiasts, whose possessions were part of their imagery, recurring from subject to subject, but also significant as collectors' pieces.[65] Some of Whistler's blue-and-white porcelain and his eighteenth-century

158. W.W. BURGESS, view of Rossetti's house, 16 Cheyne Walk, with Cecil Lawson's house adjoining, etching from a group of 110 published in 1894
(Royal Borough of Kensington and Chelsea)

159. Dante Gabriel Rossetti, portrait photograph, by C.L. Dodgson, October 1863 (V&A: 814–1928)

silver and plate are preserved with much archive material relating to his career in the Hunterian Museum in Glasgow.[66] Rossetti's most valuable possession was his Botticelli painting of Smeralda Brandini, once in the Pourtalés collection, which he bought for 20 guineas and sold to C.A. Ionides for 300 guineas; it is now in the V&A.[67] The painting was significant to Rossetti's art: it is the model for the series of female half-lengths that crown his later career; sometimes he employed the costume almost unaltered. The eminent Botticelli scholar Herbert Horne understood the importance of Rossetti's ownership of the painting: 'among the first to realise in some definite measure the peculiar character and charm of Botticelli's art were Dante Gabriel Rossetti and the Pre-Raphaelites'.[68] The painting has enjoyed a rather chequered reputation over the years, but is now firmly attributed to Botticelli.

Rossetti was born in Charlotte Street in Soho, son of an Italian professor and Dante scholar who was a political refugee. He found his artistic education at Sass's Drawing Academy and the Royal Academy Schools frustrating and in 1848 he became one of the founding members of the breakaway Pre-Raphaelite Brotherhood. By the time he arrived in Chelsea he had been briefly married to his beautiful model, Lizzie Siddal (herself an aspiring artist), and had joined with William Morris in the decorating firm of Morris, Marshall, Faulkner & Co., a collaboration that was to end in acrimony in 1876. In the autumn of 1862 Rossetti left Chatham Place, scene of his wife's tragic death, for Tudor House, a fine old building on Cheyne Walk on which he had set his sights for some time (pl.158). It was intended that the roomy house be shared with his brother William Michael Rossetti, his friend the poet Algernon Swinburne and the writer George Meredith; but the joint tenancy did not last or long, and essentially the house was Rossetti's alone from 1863 until his death in 1881.

Even after the embanking of the Thames in 1874 and the modernizing development of the riverside and Tite Street, Chelsea remained a more bohemian district than Kensington. It was seen as London's Latin Quarter, the nearest equivalent to the Parisian artistic neighbourhood in Montmartre. Of all the places where artists settled in London, Chelsea displayed the greatest contrasts between the old and the new, the respectable and the disreputable. It was still a largely undiscovered part of London, notwithstanding the fact that Thomas Carlyle had lived in a Queen Anne terraced house at 5 Great Cheyne Row (now 24 Cheyne Row) since 1834: fully conscious of the solid virtues of eighteenth-century building methods, Carlyle admired the house for the same features that would later attract artists to the 'Queen Anne' style, either genuine or re-created.

Chelsea's raffish character was partly due to the rough working life of the Thames waterfront and partly to Cremorne Pleasure Gardens, some hundred yards along Cheyne Walk from Whistler's first Chelsea house and rather further from Rossetti's. By the time of their arrival the Gardens were a notorious haunt of prostitutes and held a morbid fascination for both of them as they visited in search of models. One of the more ferocious animals in Rossetti's garden menagerie, a zebu, or Indian bull, came from a stall there.[69]

When Rossetti arrived in Chelsea he gathered around him a circle of artists and collectors of blue china, and created a cultured enclave in this still-remote location. His presence drew many of the intellectual elite to Chelsea, but it remained *terra incognita* to the fashionable set. Hall Caine believed its attraction for the artist lay in its fashionable neglect, remarking that 'Rossetti went so far afield, for at that period Chelsea was not the rallying ground of artists and men of letters'.[70]

Tudor House, which survives, is set back from the road behind railings broken by impressive gate piers and a fine pair of wrought iron gates. Rossetti annexed one of the reception rooms for his studio, reached via the white marble-tiled hall. The only concession to the studio's particular purpose was the enlargement up to the ceiling of the mullioned window. The full-width drawing room and Rossetti's bedroom were situated on the first floor, overlooking the river. The bedroom was exceedingly gloomy through the profusion of heavy drapery; the four-poster bed, sent by his mother when he moved into the house, was the one in which he had been born. For Rossetti a great attraction of Tudor House was its large old garden, shaded by ancient trees, originally part of Henry VIII's Chelsea palace. As his friend Hall Caine recalled, still in a state of shock after the death of his wife, Rossetti 'wished to live a life of retirement, and thought the possession of a garden in which he could take daily exercise would enable him to do so'.[71] The garden was deliberately unkempt, – 'a wilderness in most people's opinions' – but Rossetti preferred it that way.[72] It was populated by an extensive collection of noisy birds and beasts, a great annoyance to the neighbours; the peacock in particular was so loud that a clause was inserted into all future Cadogan Estate leases forbidding the keeping of peacocks.

It was to be expected that Rossetti would seize on the shopping and decorating opportunities afforded by the new place: his arrival at Tudor House had caused him to set off a flurry of shopping. The presence in Chelsea of numerous rag-and-bone merchants and cheap junk shops made it a perfect hunting ground for antiques and curiosities. Hall Caine noticed, 'His great grief notwithstanding, upon settling at Chelsea he began almost insensibly to interest himself in furnishing the house in a beautiful and novel style'.[73] He shopped all over the place, particularly for his beloved 'blue-and-white' – his friend George Price Boyce claimed that he even found furniture in a shop in Buckingham Street, near to his old lodgings – and he was a good customer of the London merchant Murray Marks. For him the chase was part of the process and the quarry an *objet trouvé* which he invested with his own perceptions of beauty and rarity: his belongings were enjoyed whether they were bric-à-brac or Renaissance portraits. His letters are full of contrivances, old curtains unpicked and put together again, embroideries mounted on new velvet backgrounds. Rugs were found in out-of-the-way places and the masses of blue-and-white pots proved irresistible, despite his chronic lack of cash. Rossetti was one of the first to collect Chinese furniture, having bought the huge carved wood and marble thrones owned by the famous 'Giant Chang' who was exhibited in London in 1865. Like many of his contemporaries (Leighton and Holman Hunt, for example), he collected, somewhat erratically, Old Master paintings, although the jewel of his collection, the Botticelli portrait of Smeralda Brandini (pl.113), was vastly superior to the other works he owned.

Ironically, this ad hoc, consciously anti-high-Victorian style was transported to the interiors of upper-class collectors and connoisseurs. Quite rapidly a consensus seems to have formed that Rossetti's house was the exemplar of a new and characteristically artistic way of decorating. Decorating advice from periodicals and popular instruction manuals of the time reflected many of the ideas embodied here, particularly the mixture of old and new. Echoing Hall Caine, H.C. Marillier, Rossetti's first biographer, saw the house and its contents as an important landmark:

> *Rossetti, in spite of his entire indifference to the outside public, had a wonderful way*
> *of infecting it with his own predilections and taste. He had borne a leading share*
> *in the Morris decorative movement; and now he was destined to pave the way for the*
> *modern craze for old oak furniture and blue china. Bric-à-brac was not of much*
> *account in England when Rossetti first began rummaging the dealers' shops ...*
> *it was a purely original idea in those days to buy up old furniture for use, and to*
> *enrich the walls of a house with panelled carvings and treasures from Japan.*
> *Those who follow the fashion to-day do it in many cases vulgarly and unintelligently,*
> *turning their houses into museums of costly and incongruous objects. So far as*
> *decoration went Rossetti knew to a hairbreadth what would harmonize and what*
> *would not, and however wide the range of his purchases might be he was never guilty*
> *of errors of taste. In such matters, it is generally conceded, his judgment*
> *was a touchstone.*[74]

Marillier had an interesting career, and as a commentator on taste he is certainly worth listening to. He fell in with Oscar Wilde while still a schoolboy, when he occupied rooms below Wilde's in a ramshackle house in Salisbury Street off The Strand. Wilde helped him with his Greek and he in turn brought up Wilde's coffee in the morning, while taking notice of the artistically decorated quarters. Wilde's long panelled room was painted white and the carefully assembled bibelots and souvenirs of travel – blue-and-white china, Tanagra figures, Greek rugs and hangings and Damascus tiles, drawings by Blake and Burne-Jones, and Edward Poynter's portrait of Lillie Langtry displayed on an easel at the end of the room – echo the Rossettian style. The top floor of the house was occupied by Wilde's Oxford friend the artist Frank Miles, who was later to commission a house from E.W. Godwin, in its own way quite the equal of Whistler's White House. Marillier joined Morris & Co. at a time when the firm's fortunes were in decline and it was he who set up the repair of old tapestries as a means of keeping the business solvent, becoming, as a result, a world-renowned expert on the subject. He made the first complete catalogue of Rossetti's work. He died in 1951.

First Edition

Dante G. Rossetti, deceased.)

16, CHEYNE WALK, CHELSEA.

CATALOGUE OF THE

HOUSEHOLD & DECORATIVE FURNITURE

OF THE ABOVE WELL-KNOWN ARTIST AND ~~LITTERATEUR~~, *Poet*

Comprising—In addition to the Furniture of the usual description, A LARGE AND RARE COLLECTION, among which will be found

A CARVED EBONY BEDSTEAD,

Reputed to have been **the Property of Queen Mary**;

A CARVED FOUR-POST BEDSTEAD,

Once the Property of the late Artist's Father, with Tapestry Hangings,

A LARGE VARIETY OF CABINETS IN CARVED OAK,

Also of the Painted Furniture Period and other styles;

COUCHES UPHOLSTERED IN GREEN STAMPED VELVET,

With Paintings in Panels by Dante G. Rossetti;

CHIPPENDALE CHAIRS & BOOKCASES,

A SMALL COLLECTION OF OIL PAINTINGS,

WATER-COLOR DRAWINGS & STUDIES OF CONSIDERABLE MERIT,

Old and Valuable Library of Books,

Many of particular interest to Artists, a portion being **Presentation Copies**;
Linen, China, Glass, Plated Goods, Ornamental Items, and Effects,

Which will be Sold by Auction, by Messrs.

T. G. WHARTON, MARTIN & CO.,

Upon the Premises,

16, CHEYNE WALK, CHELSEA,

On Wednesday, July 5th, 1882, and Two following Days,

At One o'clock punctually each day, (by direction of the Executor.)

There will be a Private View on the Saturday preceding the Sale, with admission by Orders only, (which may be had of the Auctioneers.) The Public View will be on the 3rd and 4th July, and Catalogues, price One Shilling each, may be obtained on the Premises, and of Messrs. T. G. WHARTON, MARTIN and Co., Auctioneers and Estate Agents,

1. BASINGHALL STREET, CITY, E.C.

Dandridge, Machine Printer, High Street, Deptford

160. Sale catalogue of the contents of Rossetti's house, T.G. Wharton, 5 July 1882, p.1

161. H. Treffry Dunn, *D.G. Rossetti and Theodore Watts-Dunton in the Sitting Room at Tudor House*, 16 Cheyne Walk, Chelsea, gouache, 1882
(National Portrait Gallery)

When the contents of Tudor House were dispersed at the sale following Rossetti's death, conducted by the auctioneers T.G. Wharton, Martin & Co. of Basinghall Street in July 1882, a number of these curiosities and pieces of antique furniture found their way into other artistic houses, notably the Cipriani-decorated sofa, which was bought by Wickham Flower, one of Rossetti's former patrons, for his handsome Norman Shaw house in Cheyne Walk. Millais bought the thrones of the 'Giant Chang'. Vernon Lushington, another former patron, bought a service of old 'Willow Pattern' china. The catalogue of the sale (pl.160) amounts to a virtual tour of the curiosities and knick-knacks that were crammed into every room in Tudor House. The pictures that remained after Rossetti's works had been removed were the usual mixed bag, the Old Masters mingled with works by friends of the artist, prints and photographs. Drawers and cupboards were full, with exotic jewellery and shawls, ornamental china, bronzes, tea-trays, statuary, candelabra and fragments of armour. Most of the rooms had a number of Turkey or Persian rugs.

Joe Comyns Carr, a director of the avant-garde Grosvenor Gallery, remembered that Rossetti's 'careless disposition of … simple furniture, though it bore some tokens of the newer fashion introduced by William Morris and by Rossetti himself, made no very serious appeal on the scope of deliberate decoration'.[75] The one item actually from the Morris decorating firm in Rossetti's green-painted ground-floor sitting room was the 'Rossetti' rush-seated chair; upstairs in the drawing room the five floor-to-ceiling windows were curtained in a Morris printed fabric. Henry Treffry Dunn's posthumous picture of the artist with his writer friend Theodore Watts-Dunton, painted from memory, is almost an inventory of artistic taste (pl.161; the 'Rossetti' chair is in the right-hand corner).[76] Significantly, Dunn assimilated the room at leisure before meeting its owner; he had already made

" Yet Nature is made better by no mean,
But Nature makes that mean; so o'er that art
Which, you say, adds to Nature, is an art
That Nature makes."—— SHAKESPEARE.

162. Frontispiece to *The Art of Decoration*
by Mrs Haweis, 1881

Mrs Haweis was aware of the place played
by appropriate dress in the Aesthetic house.

deductions about Rossetti's personality from his accumulation of curiosities. For Dunn, Rossetti was defined by his surroundings and his possessions. He first visited the house in 1863:

> I was ushered into one of the prettiest and most curiously furnished old fashioned parlours that I have ever seen. Mirrors of all shapes, sizes and designs, lined the walls, so that whichever way I gazed I saw myself looking at myself. What space remained was occupied by pictures, chiefly old, and all of a most interesting character. The mantelpiece was a most original compound of Chinese black-lacquered panels, bearing designs of birds, animals, flowers and fruit in gold relief, which had a very good effect, and on either side of the grate a series of old Dutch tiles, mostly displaying Biblical subjects treated in a serio-comic fashion that existed at the period, were inlaid. The firegrate was a beautifully wrought specimen of 18th-Century design and workmanship of brass with fireirons and fender to match. In one corner of the room stood an old English china cupboard; inside was displayed a quantity of Spode ware. I sat myself down on a cosy little sofa, with landscapes and figures of the Cipriani period painted on the panels; whilst admiring this curious collection of things the door opened behind me, and turning around I found myself face to face with Dante Gabriel Rossetti.[77]

Eighteenth-century portraits of collectors and connoisseurs represent objects to outline an intellectual journey. Dunn's portrait represents Rossetti as a creative artist through the medium of his personal and idiosyncratic setting. Theodore Watts-Dunton, his writer friend who lived for a while in the house, was to immortalize Rossetti as the 'Aesthetic' artist D'Arcy in his novel *Aylwin*, published in 1898. With hindsight we can see Dunn's as both a real room and a fictional 'artistic' setting; certainly there are many parallels with D'Arcy's rooms.

After Rossetti's death, the by-now celebrated Tudor House was taken by Mary Eliza Haweis, the writer and expert on modern aesthetic decoration. As the wife of a fashionable (and as it transpired, philandering) clergyman and daughter of Thomas Joy, painter friend and assistant to William Powell Frith, she frequented artistic circles. Although the house had been very much neglected by Rossetti at the end of his life and had been empty for a year, she determined to leave much of it untouched. The blue-tiled fireplaces and the subtle, time-worn colours in the panelled rooms were suitably artistic, and the long drawing room on the first floor remained the pale yellow that Rossetti had chosen. A Hispano-Spanish bureau at which Mrs Haweis did all her writing was installed there, and on this she placed a casket that Rossetti had depicted as 'Pandora's Box' in his *Pandora* of 1869.[78] She was enterprising enough to make a virtue out of this kind of artistic piety. The mystery of the Haweis' ever-diminishing finances (due to her husband's extra-marital escapades) had not yet been solved, and retaining the interior of Tudor House largely intact may have been dictated by penury. It was said that Catherine of Aragon had lived in the house and on this basis Mrs Haweis renamed it 'Queen's House'.

As the chatelaine of Queen's House Mrs Haweis expected to make her mark with her entertainments, including her own versions of artistic costume. She was a prominent figure in the promotion of 'artistic' dress. As well as writing on *The Art of Decoration* (1881; pl.162) and *Beautiful Houses* (1882) she had already published in quick succession *The Art of Beauty* (1878) and *The Art of Dress* (1879). In *The Art of Decoration* she muses on the subject of appropriate dress for historic decorating styles, citing particular paintings that might serve as useful models. In an article for *The Queen* in 1878 (the origin of what was to become *The Art of Beauty*) she had stated that 'the primary rule in beautiful dress is that it shall not contradict the natural form of the human figure ... one of the most important features in a graceful figure is the waist'.

Chelsea retained some fine historic architecture elsewhere, albeit much of it very run down. The talented and very much underrated landscape painter Cecil

DRAWING-ROOM OF BELLEVUE HOUSE.

163. W. Bell Scott's drawing room,
Bellevue House, Cheyne Walk, Chelsea,
from Moncure Conway's *Travels in
South Kensington*, 1882

164. William Bell Scott, John Ruskin and D.G. Rossetti,
photograph, about 1865
(V&A: 800–1928)

165. J. HEDDERLEY, *Cheyne Walk showing Belle Vue House* (detail), photograph, 1860s (Royal Borough of Kensington and Chelsea)

Gordon Lawson arrived to live next door to Tudor House in 1869; his house is shown in Walter Burgess's view of the Thames-side terrace (see pl.158). Further along Cheyne Walk, at number 4, Daniel Maclise lived in seclusion until his death in 1870; later George Eliot lived there, and died in the house in 1880. Herbert Horne, architect, poet, art-critic and collector lived at number 14 until departing for Florence, where he founded a museum.

Like Rossetti, William Bell Scott chose an old riverside house in Chelsea. The beautiful eighteenth-century Bellevue House at 92 Cheyne Walk (pls 163, 165) is described and illustrated by Moncure Conway in *Travels in South Kensington* (1882). Bell Scott's arrival had greatly added to the social amenities of the quarter as far as Rossetti was concerned, and he held numerous parties for chinamaniacs. Bell Scott respected the Adam-style architecture of Bellevue House, highlighting the drawing-room ceiling mouldings, in the form of fan-shaped ornaments and swags of foliage, in colours, mainly blue and white, producing an effect of Wedgwood ware. Fine 'Persian' rugs covered the floor. The scheme of the library, which was used as an evening sitting room, was consciously artistic, with Japanese-style friezes of birds and groups of blue-and-white china above the fireplaces. The dado, doors and other woodwork were all painted Indian red, and the wall above the dado covered with green-patterned paper.

Bell Scott maintained a curious *ménage à trois*, consisting of himself, his wife and his Scottish patron, Miss Alice Boyd of Penkill Castle in Ayrshire. Miss Boyd was a talented watercolourist and she painted a number of views from the house looking out over the river and the surrounding buildings, among them a view of Lindsey House at around the time when Whistler was living there (pl.166).

Rossetti shared his china collecting mania with many artist friends and cultivated patrons, but his principal rival was Whistler. The two men probably met through George Price Boyce, who eventually lived not far away at West House in Glebe Place, a studio-house built for him in 1869 by Philip Webb. It was Whistler, in fact, who introduced Rossetti to blue-china mania and the two maintained a sort of wary comradeship of shared interests and patrons. Like Tissot, Whistler, whose art also profoundly reflects his discovery of Japan, had started collecting in Paris, at La Porte Chinoise in the rue Vivienne and Mme Desoye's specialist shop in the rue de Rivoli. His friend and colleague Henri de Fantin-Latour said of Whistler's Parisian studio: 'We might be at Nagasaki, or in the Summer Palace'. Although many of the old blue-and-white wares collected by enthusiasts at the time were Chinese, chinamania was an aspect of the generalized Orientalism which included the Japanesque.

Boyce is hard to place in the artistic pecking-order. Painter and patron, he has much in common with the Aesthetic amateurs, including having a little money, which enabled him to collect works by his friends. He was a valued patron of Rossetti and Burne-Jones, and owner of Rossetti's *Bocca Baciata* (1859; Museum of Fine Arts, Boston), widely regarded as a groundbreaking image of early Aestheticism. Having trained as an architect, Boyce was a pioneer in Chelsea, purpose-building a new studio-house in preference to adapting an older house long before Whistler commissioned his modern White House from Godwin. As a young man Boyce lodged with William Burges in Buckingham Street; however, West House was probably inspired by Val Prinsep's house in Holland Park Road. The decoration was similar, with its Morris wallpapers, Webb's preferred 'Juniper green', and Delft tiles in the fireplaces. The sale of the house contents after Boyce's death gives an idea of the decoration:[79] the stairs were laid with blue Morris carpet, with Persian rugs on the landings; the studio floor was strewn with more Oriental rugs; at the windows were heavy tapestry curtains, and in place of doors there were tapestry portières. A large (7ft x 11ft) painted screen with Oriental figures and scenes had pride of place. Ceramics were dispersed throughout the house: large Japanese vases on stands and the ubiquitous 'Grès de Flandres' stoneware admired by so many of Boyce's fellow artists. In the drawing room, with its bordered Turkey carpet,

166. A. BOYD, *A View in Cheyne Walk,
Showing the Remains of Lindsey House
Riverside Stairs*, watercolour, 1874, from
Reginald Blunt (ed.) *The Crown & Anchor*,
1925, frontispiece

there hung a converted antique Dutch brass chandelier. So far so conventional, Boyce's taste was matched across the artistic spectrum. The interior of his house is little recorded, with just one photograph of the studio surviving in Webb's own collection.[80] Eventually the existing old houses in Glebe Place were demolished, to be replaced by red-brick studios lining the whole of one side of the road.

Whistler arrived in Chelsea around 1860, much the same time as Rossetti, chancing on part of another historic mansion, 7 Lindsey Row (96 Cheyne Walk), once the London house of the Earl of Lindsey, on the Chelsea riverfront. He had been brought up in St Petersburg where his American father was working as a railway engineer. When his father died the family returned to America. After an undistinguished period of three years at the Military Academy at West Point, Whistler departed for Paris and embarked on an artistic career. Expecting to make a better living in London, he lived in a number of addresses in Chelsea before building his studio-house in Tite Street, the revolutionary proto-modern White House designed by Godwin (pl.168).

167. Photograph of the White House, from the Pennells' edition of Whistler's journals, 1921

168. E.W. GODWIN, Whistler's White House in Chelsea, elevation, watercolour, 1877
(V&A: E.540–1963)

In 1863, while he was living at Lindsey Row, his mother arrived from America to live with him. She described the interior in a lengthy letter written soon after her arrival:

> *Are you an admirer of old China? This artistic abode of my son is ornamented by a very large collection of Japanese and Chinese. He considers the painting upon them the finest specimens of art and his companions who resort here for an evening relaxation occasionally get enthusiastic as they handle and examine the curious objects … some of the pieces more than two centuries old.*[81]

The grey tones of Whistler's studio, with accents of gold, opened up a vista of decorating style for Aesthetes. The effect can be seen in the backgrounds to his portraits of his mother (now in the Musée d'Orsay in Paris), of Thomas Carlyle (Glasgow Museums and Art Gallery) and of Cicely, the daughter of his patron, William Alexander. As she rested between sittings for her portrait, Whistler's early masterpiece *Harmony in Grey and Green* (pl.169), Cicely watched him putting a lemon tint above a gold dado on the walls of the hall and staircase at Lindsey Row: 'there were numberless little books of gold leaf lying about, and any that weren't exactly the old gold shade he wanted he gave to me'.

In his notes on 'Decorative Art and Architecture in England' (1882) Moncure Conway gives an evocative description of Whistler's rooms:

> *Mr Whistler dots the walls and even the ceiling of his rooms with the brilliant Japanese fans which now constitute so large an element in the decoration of many beautiful rooms; but in his drawing-room there were fifteen large panels made of Japanese pictures, each about five feet by two. These pictures represent flowers of every hue, and birds of many varieties and of the richest plumage. … There is also in the room an ancient Chinese cabinet with a small pagoda designed on the top, an old Japanese cabinet of quaint construction, and several screens from the same region, altogether making one of the most beautiful rooms imaginable.*[82]

169. J. McNeill Whistler,
Harmony in Grey and Green, portrait of
Cicely Alexander, oil painting, 1872–4
(Tate, London)

Whistler specified the exact fine white
muslin of the dress, putting forward
suggestions of shops where it might be
bought, and the accessories as well.

These panels are visible in a photograph of Whistler's drawing room at Lindsey Row illustrating an edition of his Journal edited by the Pennells. A photograph of the White House nearly contemporary with Whistler's occupancy shows its uncompromising exterior (pl.167).[83]

The architecturally avant-garde White House, designed for Whistler by E.W. Godwin in 1876 (pl.168), presents the greatest possible contrast with Rossetti's Tudor House. It was hardly lived in by its begetter and, unlike Tudor House and Leighton House, it no longer survives. It is a curious irony that William Morris's Red House and Whistler's White House, the most radical of the purpose-built artists' houses – and those with greatest influence on the architecture of the future – were so briefly occupied by the men who planned and built them. White House was a dwelling place and teaching studio. Godwin, its architect, was named by Max Beerbohm as 'the greatest aesthete of them all'. He and Whistler might have been made for each other: they were long-time friends and collaborators – indeed, they shared, successively, a wife, Beatrix Philip, who had been a student in Godwin's office. It was inevitable that Whistler's revolutionary new studio-house should be put into the hands of a man of such courageous ideas. With its top-floor studio running the whole length of the house, White House was starkly modern – too much so for the Metropolitan Board of Works, which rejected the initial design. The austere interior, decorated in the 'artistic' style, was described by dealer Walter Dowdeswell:

> *The house was a very strange one … The front door opened on to the pavement, and on entering one found oneself at once midway upon a flight of stairs – I was directed to descend, and found myself in a large terra cotta coloured room with white woodwork – very plainly furnished and very unusual. There were two long windows about 16 ft. high on one side of the room, looking upon a little bit of garden. They had small square panes of almost a foot square. The furniture consisted of a table and some large low chairs and a couch, covered to the ground in terra cotta serge.*[84]

In the articles on his London house for *The Architect* in 1876 Godwin remarked:

> *Personally I might go so far as to acknowledge that I like certain yellows of a tone akin to old satinwood; that light red or Venetian red brightened by white and pure, or nearly pure, white itself are favourites with me. Professionally, I have, of course, to assume a gloomier style.*[85]

In Whistler he had a client who shared his preferences. A collaboration between the two men, the 'primrose' room for furniture manufacturer William Watt's stand at the 1878 Paris Exhibition, gives a sense of Whistler's intentions for the White House interior. Godwin's design for the fireplace, inset with plain yellow Doulton tiles and polished brass grate surmounted by a pale mahogany overmantel for blue china ornaments, and flanked by dado and frieze, was decorated by Whistler with peacock and butterfly motifs.[86] Whistler's bankruptcy in 1879, brought about by the notorious libel case he fought against John Ruskin, forced him abroad and out of the house forever. A poster for the sale on the premises in May gives a hint of the contents: an ebonized and gilt drawing-room suite, Japanese cabinets and screen, Turkey and Persian carpets, a Japanese bath and a 'very valuable collection of Nankin & other China'.[87] It was a terrible fiasco; rolls of canvas were carried off for a few shillings and later yielded from their folds paintings by the artist. The pictures and china – and even the Japanese bath – were sold at Sotheby's in the following year, but the prices were still rock-bottom.

Little evidence remains of Whistler's much-valued decorating advice, apart from some colour-schemes dashed off for William Alexander, a discerning collector of Chinese porcelain, Japanese prints and lacquer, who lived at Aubrey House in Kensington. Whistler's own rooms often looked as if he had just moved into them. Louise Jopling recalled:

170. E. De Morgan, *Portrait of William De Morgan*, oil painting, 1909 (National Portrait Gallery)

We were shown into a nearly empty drawing-room, with only a large sofa, one or two occasional chairs, and a small Chippendale table. The floor was covered with fine, pale, straw-coloured matting. Some priceless blue china was distributed about the room, which had a wonderful air of refined simplicity.[88]

When Whistler returned to London he could not recover the White House from its new owner, but he moved into a block of studios, still in Tite Street. The interior was painted brilliant yellow, Wilde's 'colour of joyousness'. He later moved away from the river to The Vale, a little country-like enclave off the King's Road where the pioneer potter William De Morgan, friend and colleague of William Morris, lived with his wife at number 1. Theirs was a quaint, rambling house still at that date approached through a wooden gate down a mud path. Their garden retained part of an old mulberry grove, as well as an old fig tree and a vine (pl.171). Evelyn De Morgan's portrait of her husband (pl.170) was painted at The Vale in 1909: the covered vase he is holding was bequeathed by the artist to the V&A. The De Morgans' house was decorated with Morris wallpapers, lustreware by De Morgan himself (like the charger on the wall in the portrait) and Evelyn's richly romantic paintings.

The mantle of dandyism had fallen on the more flamboyant artists, most notably Whistler. He enhanced his already distinctive appearance with an eccentric personal style. Two and more generations after Beau Brummell and the creation of the Regency dandy, a much more sombre dress-code prevailed. Whistler, sophisticated and cosmopolitan and up in all the latest fashions, stood out because he exaggerated the cut and shape of his chosen costume, with his wide-brimmed hat, high-buttoned, close-fitting frock-coat, narrow trousers, patent-leather pumps – embellished on occasion with a bow of coloured ribbon – and his signature canary-yellow necktie. His dandified pose, with cane and monocle, and the exquisite fit of his jackets – over which he took infinite pains – marked him out in any gathering.

171. Photograph of William and Evelyn De Morgan in their Chelsea garden at The Vale, from Mrs Stirling's *William De Morgan and his Wife*, 1921

This was still an almost rural enclave of Chelsea, the house being reached down an overgrown dirt path.

De Morgan's study   Entrance to Drawing-room   Entrance to Studio, which is not shown in the photograph

THE VALE, CHELSEA

Where William De Morgan lived till 1910 when it was pulled down. It is the original of "The Retreat" in "The Old Man's Youth."

172. Oscar Wilde in the costume
he wore to lecture in America,
photograph by Sarony, 1882
(National Portrait Gallery)

In summer he wore trousers of white duck and a rakish straw hat. As much as
the velvets, flowing ties and soft silks of romantic artistic dress, Whistler's sharp
dandyism demonstrated his contempt for the sartorial shibboleths of fashionable
society.

Imitating Whistler, but with less finesse, Oscar Wilde made that kind of
dandyism grotesque, and he had the sense to abandon it quite quickly in favour of
a well-cut frock-coat of conventional shape, but not before his own romantic outfit
of velvet jacket, knee-breeches and silk stockings had earned him most welcome
notoriety (pl.172). His wife Constance, an aspiring writer, attractive, intelligent,
a good linguist and well-read, seemed prepared to comply with Wilde's fantastic
notions of dress – both for himself and for her. He designed her wedding dress,
'a delicate cowslip tint; the bodice finished with a high Medici collar', worn with a
saffron gauze veil and his gift, a silver belt. She bore the brunt of comments, often
derisory, about her clothes, which were regarded as too eccentric for the circles to
which the couple aspired.

In 1880 Frank Miles, Wilde's artist friend, arrived in Tite Street to live in a
striking modern studio-house commissioned in 1879 from Godwin (pl.173). He
and Wilde shared the house for a while, giving Wilde a model that he would later
try to replicate in his more modest terraced house. Tite Street had become the
site of the most extreme experiments in Aesthetic architecture. In a lecture to the
Architectural Association in March 1879 Godwin described the house for Miles:

173. E.W. Godwin, proposed design for
the front elevation of the house and studio
for Frank Miles (eventually rejected),
Tite Street, Chelsea, pen, ink pencil and
watercolour, about 1878
(V&A: E.556–1963)

It is for a bachelor, is unpretentious, containing about nine rooms besides a studio.
The latter is at the top of the house ... The whole house was designed with balconies
and other accessories to meet the taste of a lover of flowers ... I consider it the best
thing I ever did.

Godwin even specified the contents, down to the wineglasses from Powell &
Sons of Whitefriars. There are no surviving images of the interiors of Wilde's
later Tite Street house, but it was described often by visitors, enshrining Godwin's
ideas in an 'Aesthetic' model that was a considerable contrast to the picturesque
'Queen Anne' of so much studio architecture.

Whistler's White House and the house for Miles were pretty radical, even for
Godwin. The other studios he built in Tite Street were still highly original, but less
likely to fall foul of planning constraints. Many survive, making an artistic enclave
almost to rival the Holland Park area. Chelsea's artistic character was maintained
long after Kensington had settled into middle-class professional respectability.

EDWARD BURNE-JONES AT THE GRANGE IN FULHAM

Burne-Jones was born at Bennett's Hill in Birmingham, the son of a gilder
and frame-maker, who brought him up after the death of his wife within a
week of her son's birth. He was educated at King Edward's School, Birmingham,
and went up to Oxford, planning to enter the Church. Here he met Dante Gabriel
Rossetti in 1856, a momentous event which resulted in his leaving Oxford without
taking a degree. At Oxford he also met his lifelong friend William Morris, who was
also intended for the Church and together they started the voyage of discovery
that led them to the arts. Much of the house decoration undertaken by Burne-
Jones was on behalf of Morris, Marshall, Faulkner & Co., and his own houses
bear the unmistakable stamp of their joint ambitions for the beautification of the
domestic environment. Neither he nor Morris was much interested in comfort, as
their rooms demonstrate. After the plan to share Red House with Morris had fallen
through, Burne-Jones lived in old townhouses in London.

In 1860 he married Georgiana Macdonald, daughter of a Methodist minister
(pl.174). Ned Jones and Georgie Macdonald were very young and very hard-up
when they married: they had scraped together £55, and with this and the useful
wedding presents given by their friends and family, they set up house in Burne-
Jones's bachelor rooms in Russell Place. Their living quarters were austere but
the furniture was sturdy and survived in the succession of houses that followed.
It consisted of a solid oak dining table designed by Philip Webb and made at the
Industrial Home for Destitute Boys in Euston Road; chairs and a sofa, also of oak,
arrived from the same source soon after. The chairs were high-backed, with rush
seats; the sofa was of panelled wood painted black. Georgie recalled their history
when she came to record her husband's life:

The chairs have disappeared, for they were smaller articles, vigorously used and
much moved about but the table and sofa always shared the fortunes of their owners
and were never superseded: we ate our last meal together at that table and our
grandchildren laugh round it now.[89]

She continued her reminiscences of this first home in more detail – their later
living quarters were not given so much attention:

In the unsettled week before his marriage Edward had amused himself by painting
some figures upon a plain deal sideboard which he possessed, and this in its new
state was a delightful surprise to find. 'Ladies and animals' he called the subjects
illustrated, and there were seven pictures, three on the cupboard doors in front and two
at each end, which shewed them in various relations to each other ... Mrs Catherwood
[Burne-Jones's aunt] gave us a piano, made by Priestly of Berners Street: unpolished
walnut so that Edward could paint upon it.

Georgiana Macdonald aet.16
from a photograph.

174. Georgiana Macdonald, portrait
photograph aged 16, from *Memorials*,
her biography of her husband, 1904

187

175. E. Burne-Jones, detail of the decorated panel from an upright piano, 1860 (V&A: W.43–1926)

Not only did these treasured pieces survive throughout their owners' lives; some exist to this day (pls 175, 179).

Like Rossetti, Burne-Jones always chose to live in old houses. After the sad demise of the scheme for sharing Red House with Morris he rented briefly in Kensington Square and then, for 30 years from 1868, the Burne-Joneses lived in the eighteenth-century brick and stucco Grange (pl.176) on North End Road in Fulham, once occupied by the eighteenth-century novelist Samuel Richardson. The Grange was demolished as recently as 1957. Frances Horner (née Graham), daughter of the noted Pre-Raphaelite patron William Graham, remembered in her childhood she 'thought it rather dull when my father took to going to Burne-Jones's house at the Grange, North End Road, on Saturday afternoons, instead of to the mysterious romantic house in Cheyne Walk where Rossetti lived – unhappy solitary, but a king amongst men'.[90] She was not to find Burne-Jones dull for long. Their friendship developed into one of the long series of *amitiés amoureuses* pursued largely by correspondence throughout Burne-Jones's life. He was devastated when Frances married Sir John Horner and retired to lead the life of a country squire's wife at Mells Park in Wiltshire. Lady Horner made Mells a centre of artistic activity and one of the numerous country houses where artists (but rarely their wives) were entertained.

The garden at The Grange was large, containing magnificent old trees and a small orchard in which peaches, plums and apricots fruited in the shelter of a wall (pl.177). In the spring after their arrival Georgie was entranced to find a 20-ft border filled with lilies-of-the-valley; wild roses still grew in a turning off North End Road. Much of this rural character was swept away before the turn of the century.[91] G.D. Leslie went by invitation to visit the Burne-Jones household quite early on and, having noted that 'His wife looks like a girl of fourteen, pretty, and very unaffected', he described the house to George Augustus Storey, his neighbour in St John's Wood:

Burne-Jones' sitting-room is furnished entirely after his own taste – there is a jolly little oak piano, with paintings on the panels, on a gold ground, representing figures hunting and allegorical subjects. A stunning medieval sideboard, all beautifully painted, as fine as Chinese in colour. The curtains of delicate indigo blue, embroidered by hand by his wife.

There is a dark wainscot half-way up the wall, dull green paper, and lots of Chinese and Japanese ornaments; one a little looking-glass, with folding doors of blue silk.

His painting room has hardly any furniture in it at all, and was very untidy, I am happy to say, but then it led out of a stunning little sitting-room, which looked all the more cosy on account of it.[92]

The Grange.

176. The Grange, North End Lane, Fulham, photograph, from *Memorials*, 1904

177. F. HOLLYER, *The Morris and Burne-Jones Families in the Garden at The Grange*, photograph, 1874 (V&A: Ph.1813–1939)

178. T.M. ROOKE, *The Dining Room at The Grange*, watercolour, 1898 (Private Collection)

The 'dull green paper' was one of the popular Morris designs, the ubiquitous 'Fruit' or 'Pomegranate'. This was also used in the hallway, in a different colour. As well as the little painted piano there were two more of Webb's tables; the floor, like those in the rest of the house, was a patchwork of Oriental rugs. Only the stairs were carpeted, with a Morris pattern, but this was always hidden under a protective drugget.

The ground-floor drawing room, with its French windows leading out into the large garden, was recorded by Burne-Jones's long-time assistant and confidant, Thomas Matthews Rooke, in 1898. Rooke's painting shows an eclectic mix of artistic memorabilia: the Dürer engravings given to the artist by Ruskin in 1865 hang on the wall. There are casts of Theseus and Ilissus from the Parthenon pediments on the cupboard at the left. The green-stained bookcases were designed by the architect and metalworker W.A.S. Benson. Besides the many books and ceramic pieces (including a vase probably made by William De Morgan) there were touches of the exotic in a Moorish table inlaid with mother-of-pearl and a lamp of pierced metalwork. A cast of Michelangelo's reclining figure of *Dawn*, flanked by its companion, *Night*, stood on the mantelshelf, marking the impact of

179. E. BURNE-JONES,
the 'Ladies and Animals Sideboard', 1860,
from the dining room at The Grange
(V&A: W.10–1953)

180. W. MORRIS, 'Jasmine' wallpaper
designed for Morris & Co., about 1872
(V&A: E.770–1915)

Burne-Jones's first sight of his work on an epic trip to Italy in 1862. A portrait of Margaret Burne-Jones, his beloved daughter, by William Blake Richmond hung over the fireplace. The sitting room was papered with Morris 'Jasmine'(1872; pl.180), Georgie's own sitting room with 'Larkspur' (1874). Margaret's bedroom was papered with 'Lily', just like Morris's own bedroom at Kelmscott Manor.

Graham Robertson chose to describe the dining room when he first visited The Grange in about 1877:

> *The hall was dark and the little dining-room opening out of it even more shadowy with its deep-green leaf-patterned walls … At the end of the room stood a dark green cabinet with designs partly raised in gesso and enriched with gold and brilliant hues, wrought by Burne-Jones in the early days when he, with Morris and Rossetti, was devising wondrous furniture and house decoration.[93]*

The dining room was also recorded by T.M. Rooke in July 1898, just a month after Burne-Jones's death, but it had remained unchanged for decades (pl.178). The room is dominated by the trestle table given to the Burne-Joneses as a wedding present. The embroidered portière was a souvenir from Red House, one of the panels of Chaucer's 'Good Women' that were unfinished when the house was given up in 1865. The glass panels in the window were designed by Burne-Jones himself and made by the Morris firm. On the 'Ladies and Animals' sideboard (pl.179, now in the Victoria and Albert Museum) there is a small collection of earlier silver-plate, a taste Burne-Jones shared with Whistler. Above the sideboard at the right there hung a painting believed by Burne-Jones to be the work of Giorgione; it is now attributed to Palma Vecchio.[94] The rush-seated chairs are a variation on the 'Sussex' type, retailed by the Morris firm. The copper and brass chandelier by W.A.S. Benson is the only innovation in Rooke's painting: it was installed before 1887 (it is shown in the photograph by Frederick Hollyer, taking a similar view of the room, dating from that year). Walter Crane must have had this room in mind when he described the 'Morrisian method' of decorating (see p.165).

No-one was more qualified than Rooke to capture the essence of Burne-Jones's rooms. The two men first came into contact in 1869 when the young Rooke, who had trained as an artist at the South Kensington and Royal Academy Schools, applied to work for Morris & Co. This quickly led to his appointment as Burne-Jones's studio

181, 182. F. HOLLYER,
The Grange, Fulham, study
and first-floor sitting room,
photographs, 1887
(National Monuments Record)

assistant, a post he retained until Burne-Jones's death. In the 1890s Rooke started to keep notes of their conversations, some quoted in Lady Burne-Jones's *Life* of her husband, and selections published as a book by Mary Lago in 1981.

For all that they reveal, Hollyer's interiors cannot have been consciously stage-managed to imply the cultivated and subtle personalities of their inhabitants. The photographs are simply records; the rooms are intimate and lived-in (pls 181, 182). Burne-Jones himself had no liking for the show-studio and refused to join in; a casual form of open-house policy obtained at The Grange, largely for the benefit of close friends and family. The place fairly teemed with children: Rudyard Kipling had found it a haven of sanity when he was sent home from India to an unhappy time at a much-hated school. He hung the iron doorbell from The Grange on his own house in Rottingdean in the hope that children would continue to find it a symbol of happiness and refuge.

C.J. Feret, historian of Fulham, visited The Grange shortly after Burne-Jones's death:

> *Entering the house we find ourselves in a spacious vestibule, once a room. Facing us, a dining-room. Adjacent to this room is the kitchen. Beyond this, built upon what was once a portion of the garden, is an extensive addition to the house, made, probably, some sixty years ago. The bottom portion was, till recently, the great artist's drawing-room. Over it, on the first floor, is a large studio, originally a drawing-room.*
>
> *The grounds of the north part of The Grange are ... bounded by the old wall of Otto House. On the south side is the wall which divides the two gardens of The Grange. At the far end stands Sir E. Burne-Jones's garden studio. Facing the drawing-room is a pleasant lawn with here and there a notable tree. One is an old mulberry, which bears as good fruit as it did when North End was a rural hamlet. Another familiar friend in the part of the grounds of The Grange is a wonderful apple-tree, which, however, now year by year loses a limb. Nearer the house is fine old thorn, on which Samuel Richardson must have looked.*[95]

Until it was cut down in 1895, the neighbouring garden of the south half of the house harboured the 'lovely briar rose, which Sir E. Burne-Jones has immortalized in his picture of the "Sleeping Beauty"' (Buscott Park, Oxfordshire).

Philip Burne-Jones (who succeeded his father as the second Baronet in 1898) painted his father in his studio, as part of a series of writers and artists at work (pl.183), in the year of his death. Burne-Jones is here shown in a sympathetic and intimate portrait: he appears unaware of the scrutiny of the artist and no hint of posing as a famous personality has been allowed to compromise a truthful representation of the man immersed in his art. However, he is surrounded by works which do more than hint at his greatness. He is in the smaller of the two garden studios at The Grange, working on a cartoon for the series of Morris & Co. Arras tapestries woven at Merton Abbey. The tapestries, telling the story of the *Quest of the San Grael* from Sir Thomas Malory's *Morte d'Arthur*, were commissioned by the Australian mining-engineer William Knox D'Arcy in 1890 for the dining room of his house, Stanmore Hall in Middlesex. Burne-Jones is working here on 'The Achievement of the Holy Grail, Sir Galahad accompanied by Sir Bors and Sir Perceval'. The collaboration between Burne-Jones and William Morris on the great cycle of six huge tapestry panels marked the culmination of their obsessive exploration of the San Grael story which had started with their discovery Malory's works when they were up at Oxford in 1855. In the background is a version of *The Arming of Perseus*, another ambitious decorative project, commissioned by the politician and future Prime Minister Arthur Balfour for the dining room of his London house, which occupied Burne-Jones over a long period and was unfinished at his death.

His studios were entirely utilitarian, for working and not for show, with huge canvases stacked by the walls. He ridiculed the idea that the studio could feature as a mark of achievement: 'Is it fair for Carr [J. Comyns Carr] to publish interiors

183. P. BURNE-JONES, *Portrait of Sir Edward Burne-Jones, Bt,* oil painting, 1898 (National Portrait Gallery)

The first of a series of portraits of artists and writers at work, this was painted in the smaller studio at The Grange.

184. E. Burne-Jones, comic drawing of his studio, from *Memorials*, 1904

of all other studios except mine – Leighton's – Thorneycroft's [*sic*] – Marcus Stone's – all but mine? Do try and influence him – I should like my interior (of studio) published too – of course I should'.[96] This plaint is accompanied by a comic drawing of the said studio (pl.184). He had a terror of the mania displayed by his womenfolk for cleaning it.

At last, in 1890 Burne-Jones was photographed in his studio in the guise of an eminent public figure, turning to the viewer from a commanding position (pl.186). He is at work on his last, colossal watercolour, the *Star of Bethlehem* (Birmingham Museum and Art Gallery), in the garden studio of The Grange, Fulham. The *Star of Bethlehem* watercolour is a reworking of an earlier tapestry design, like the San Grael tapestries, which also dominated his last decade. His garden studio was built in 1882, positioned so as to mask the houses which had been built on what were once open fields at the back of the house. It was designed by Morris's associate W.A.S. Benson and was originally intended merely as a paintings store; however, the addition of a skylight made it into a usable workspace. Graham Robertson remembered the garden studio: 'It was a huge barrack of a place, like a schoolroom or a gymnasium, containing none of the usual properties and elegancies of the "show" studio.'[97] Ambrose Poynter, son of the painter, was brought in to make a record of the house studio, an intensely poignant memorial, the day after Burne-Jones died, aged 65, on 17 July 1898 (pl.185).

185. A. Poynter, *The House Studio*, 18 June 1898, painted the day after Burne-Jones's death, from *Memorials*, 1904

186. B. Leighton, *Edward Burne-Jones in his Garden Studio*, photograph, 1890 (V&A: PH.11–1939)

REGENT'S PARK AND ST JOHN'S WOOD:
LAWRENCE ALMA-TADEMA, JAMES TISSOT AND FRIENDS

Before Alma-Tadema and Tissot arrived there, artists' communities had been developing in Regent's Park and St John's Wood for a considerable time. Sir Edwin Landseer migrated to a farmhouse in St John's Wood Road, then a remote, undeveloped fringe of North London, in the 1820s. In 1844, when patronage by Queen Victoria consolidated his position, he commissioned a stately villa from the fashionable architects Cubitt & Co. He failed to oversee the plans and was rumoured to dislike the resulting pompous neoclassical building. The suave, witty and hard-working Ernest Gambart, leading dealer in contemporary painting and in some senses the creator of the Victorian art world, settled at 62 Avenue Road, Regent's Park, where he added a large room as picture gallery, ballroom and concert room. The house was subsequently owned by Mr Gillot of Birmingham, an enterprising collector-dealer, and then by Frederick Goodall, the successful Orientalist painter who installed an Oriental room. Gambart was the first to show French art on a regular basis in London, starting with an exhibition in Pall Mall in 1854. But his contribution to British art was to achieve unheard-of prices for the most popular painters; hardly a picture of any importance escaped him in his dealing years from 1853 to 1872.

Intimate groups of artists in the district who could visit one another frequently were almost club-like. One such group, which achieved the formality of a name and recognizable identity, was in St John's Wood: 'The St John's Wood Clique – what memories the name awakens! What sterling good fellows! What high hopes! What high spirits! What *camaraderie*! Shall we ever look upon the like of that Brotherhood again?'[98] A substantial part of the book on St John's Wood from which this quotation is taken concerns the artist inhabitants who followed Landseer. Many of the younger artists were members of the St John's Wood Clique, among them the pioneer photographer David Wilkie Wynfield, the bird painter Henry Stacy Marks, George Dunlop Leslie, Frederick Walker, George du Maurier and Valentine Prinsep. At some level all of them contributed to the special character of the Aesthetic Movement. They would run in and out of each others' houses, offering unsparing criticisms of work in progress. They were thought to be 'coming men', and embodied a kind of French sophistication. There were also sketching evenings: one of the members even made a drawing of a gathering at which they painted Shakespearean subjects on the walls of John Evan Hodgson's Hill Road studio. The Clique's preferred recreation was to walk to some not-too-distant hostelry, dine and drink, and return in the evening.

The area remained popular with artists and the Clique was succeeded in 1895 by the St John's Wood Art Club, bringing a new influx of young and hopeful painters and sculptors. When Alma-Tadema and James Tissot arrived in St John's Wood in the 1870s, they altered the balance towards full-blown Aestheticism. In its heyday the house at 17 Grove End Road, which Tadema took over from Tissot, was thought by some to be the most beautiful in London.[99]

The Dutch-born painter Lawrence Alma-Tadema settled in London in 1870; in 1873 he was naturalized as a British citizen. He owned two remarkable houses, among the most publicized and illustrated of Victorian artists' homes. Neither was purpose-built, although they were so extensively remodelled by the artist as to almost qualify as new-builds, and neither was particularly venerable: Townshend House in Regent's Park was part of a terrace (17 Titchfield Terrace at the North Gate) and 17 Grove End Road, to which he moved in 1885, was the St John's Wood villa dating from 1825 where James Tissot had lived with his mistress Kathleen Newton from 1876 until his return to Paris after her death in 1883.

Alma-Tadema wrote a much-understated description of the effect of light and colour on the succession of decorated studios he created in his houses:

I have always found that the light and colour in a studio had great influence upon me in my work. I first painted in a studio with panels of black decoration. Then in my studio in Brussels I was surrounded by bright red and in London – at Townshend House, Regent's Park – I worked under the influence of a light green tint. During the winter I spent in Rome in 1875–6 – when I was obliged to leave my London house by the destructive effect of the Regent's canal explosion – I tried the effect of a white studio. Now, as you see, the prevailing hue is silvery white, and that, I think, best agrees with my present temperament, artistically speaking.[100]

His studios were celebrated show-pieces. From 1871 he lived with his second wife, Laura, herself a talented artist, and his two daughters from his first marriage, in the artistic community growing up around Regent's Park and the newly developed St John's Wood. Noticeably eclectic in their use of materials, such as onyx, brass, ivory, ebony, Spanish leather, unvarnished gold-leaf and aluminium, the results transcended any rivals among the most exotic of Victorian studio-houses – even Leighton's house with its Arab Hall, or Carl Haag's Egyptian fantasy at Ida Villa, in Hampstead.

Alma-Tadema met Laura Epps, daughter of Dr George Napoleon Epps, a surgeon and practitioner of homeopathy, when she was only 17 years old. The occasion was a dance at Ford Madox Brown's on Boxing Day 1869, just seven months after the death of Alma-Tadema's first wife. He fell in love with Laura at first sight, and she became his pupil when he moved permanently to London in September 1870. A screen showing Laura's family remains unfinished, but its series of portraits records the artistic milieu of the Epps household with some accuracy (pl.188). The reverse of the screen is lined with Morris's 'Pomegranate' design, in keeping with its use in their first married home at Townshend House. They were married on 29 July 1871; Alma-Tadema started a portrait of Laura earlier that month, but it remained unfinished, possibly owing to preparations for the wedding.[101] The painting was given to Laura's sister Louisa (Mrs Roland Hill), and then returned to Anna Alma-Tadema, the artist's daughter, at Louisa's death in 1909.

The most complete account of Townshend House and the Grove End Road villa, the two houses decorated by Alma-Tadema, is by Julian Treuherz in the catalogue of the monographic exhibition held in Amsterdam and London in 1996–7.[102] Here he gives background and substance to the numerous accounts in contemporary periodicals: it is a measure of their importance in the context of Victorian taste that the houses were so extensively recorded. One frequently remarked aspect of Alma-Tadema's first house was the modest size of the studio. In fact the house was a warren of little rooms and spaces contrived from the standard London terraced-house layout. Moncure Conway illustrates a curtained opening between the dining and drawing rooms, draped with distinctive, possibly North African, woven textile in his *Travels in South Kensington*, captioning it 'Townsend [*sic*] House, residence of the distinguished artist Mr Alma Tadema' (pl.187). As Conway observed,

If a gentleman in London enters a house with the intention of decorating it in accordance with principles of art, his first work, probably, will be either to tear away doors that divide a drawing-room, and substitute a draping, or else frame it [the doorway] round with looped and corded drapery, which having in itself an artistic effect, shall change the barrier into beauty.[103]

A unique record survives of the Dutch Room (pl.189), one of the rooms severely damaged in the explosion on the canal in 1874, mentioned by Alma-Tadema in the passage quoted above, which almost destroyed Townshend House. The wallpaper is William Morris's 'Pomegranate', the dado is of Japanese tatami matting, and on the floor are Eastern flat-weave rugs over a geometric mosaic of tiles. The room had a papered ceiling and great oak cabinets, crowned with dishes and bowls of rare Oriental china (as on the left), containing linen. A piece of embroidery forms

187. D. Moncure Conway, curtained entrance to the 'Drawing-room in Townsend [*sic*] House', illustration from *Travels in South Kensington*, 1882

188. L. ALMA-TADEMA and L. EPPS,
Epps Family Screen, oil painting on a wood
frame backed with 'Pomegranate' wallpaper,
about 1870–1
(V&A: W.20:1–1981)

189. NELLIE (ELLEN) EPPS,
The 'Dutch Room' in Townshend House,
oil painting, signed, inscribed and
indistinctly dated, 'N.Epps/1873'
(Private Collection)

This room was partly recreated in the
Tadema's Grove End Road house as
Laura Alma-Tadema's studio.

190. A. ALMA-TADEMA, *The Drawing Room at Townshend House*, watercolour, 1885 (Royal Academy of Arts)

191. A. ALMA-TADEMA, *Interior of the Gold Room, Townshend House*, watercolour with scraping over graphite on paper, about 1883 (Nelson-Atkins Museum and Art Gallery, Kansas City, USA)

In the Gold Room is the gilded and gessoed Broadwood grand piano designed by George Fox for Alma-Tadema and shown at the Musical Exhibition at South Kensington in 1885.

the mantelshelf valance, a reminder of Alma-Tadema's extensive and valuable textile collection. Dutch seventeenth-century portraits and a drawing of Laura Alma-Tadema hang on the walls. The picture belonged to the Dutch collector H.W. Mesdag of The Hague, and remained in his family after the foundation of the Mesdag Museum, to which most of his collection was dedicated.

Alma-Tadema was still living at Townshend House when Mrs Haweis visited him to collect material for *Beautiful Houses*, so her particular magic was exercised on the less ambitious of his housing projects. As she noted, his tastes as a collector favoured seventeenth-century portraits, antique Oriental and Venetian textiles and Old Dutch inlaid cabinets. In the ante-room to the drawing room a row of seventeenth-century chairs was lined up against the wall. Old German glass and the inevitable blue-and-white pots filled little niches and corners in the labyrinthine plan, while the bulk of the textile collection was stored on shelves in Alma-Tadema's studio. Mrs Haweis remarked that the absence of doors between the rooms on the first floor gave the house 'an Oriental character wholly unusual'.[104] The description of his studio has it as dark-toned, 'decorated after the Pompeian taste', with panels of yellow and red, and the ceiling in 'deep Pompeian red, with many coloured arabesques, encloses panels and medallions of light blue … on which gods and goddesses disport – Apollo driving his chariot in the midst, amid the golden rays of the sun.'[105]

Views of the drawing room and ante-room at Townshend House were painted by the artist's daughter Anna, who was also his pupil, when she was only 17 (pl.190). The drawing room, with its striking black floor and Alhambra ceiling, was approached through an archway from the Gold Room (pl.191), which was entirely gilded and lit by a window with panes of thinnest Mexican onyx. The red velvet hangings of antique Persian appliqué behind the divan were once in a Venetian palace, part of the Alma-Tademas' large collection of antique and exotic textiles.[106] The Gold Room housed the Broadwood grand piano decorated by the artist and his wife. Mrs Haweis noted the niches filled with blue-and-white china above the entrance opening, the Chinese embroidered curtain and the parquetry floor in the Roman style. Beside the entrance, the Dutch cupboard from the dining room evidently survived the explosion. The wainscot (or dado) was decorated with a Byzantine design, and the walls above were covered with the gold leaf that gave its name to the room. The couple's entwined initials provided a decorative motif throughout, as elsewhere in the house.

The study (pl.192) was a practical space, with a sturdy table and cheap bentwood writing chair, but there were many artistic touches such as a chandelier designed by the artist and Japanese matting on the floor. The frequently remarked absence of doors in the house, removed by Tadema as a design feature, was particularly demonstrated here, where an outer wall was apparently pierced to reached the lobby or ante-room. In Anna's painting, what appears to be a Japanese embroidery can be glimpsed on the ceiling of the lobby to the left. William Michael Rossetti spotted Alma-Tadema as 'a devoted admirer of Japanese art – going, I think, as far as anyone I know'.[107] A portrait by her father shows Anna Alma-Tadema standing in the door of the study (pl.193). The portrait panels in the door, which had survived the damage caused by the explosion, can be clearly seen.

As children, Alma-Tadema's daughters wore variations on every kind of artistic fancy dress, from quaint, quasi-medieval to Kate Greenaway dresses, which must have made their friends mock. The date, 1885, of Anna's exquisite small paintings, is a clue to their purpose, as souvenirs. In that year the Alma-Tademas left the house on which they had lavished such loving attention – the house was fitted up, according to the *Art Journal*, 'to make it appear as much like a Roman villa as was consistent with the peculiarities of the English climate and the comforts of an English home' – to settle in a more imposing residence nearby, the detached villa at 17 Grove End Road recently vacated by Tissot.[108]

192. A. ALMA-TADEMA, *Sir Lawrence Alma-Tadema's Study at Townshend House*, watercolour, pen and ink, 1884 (Cooper-Hewitt National Design Museum, Smithsonian Institution, Eugene Victor Thaw Collection)

It was soon after he arrived in London in 1871 that Tissot lighted on 17 Grove End Road, one of the older houses in the neighbourhood, a late Regency detached villa built in 1825. It was a perfectly good house, not far from Townshend House, and it had a large, secluded garden. But before he set up in St John's Wood Tissot had lived in considerable splendour in central Paris, having made a large fortune from his art. He had an intensely personal vision, which he gradually refined into an immediately recognizable 'signature'. A number of his 'modern life' subjects from the 1860s are set in his fine house and studio in the avenue de l'Imperatrice near the fashionable Bois de Boulogne in Paris, a record of the splendour of the rooms with their Oriental rugs and Japanese art objects. His view of modern society is filtered through *japonisme*, the eighteenth-century revival and the influence of photography. His idea of fashion was idiosyncratic, but full of gaiety and not troubled by the distaste for modern dress expressed by Millais and Watts.

Tissot painted three Japanese subjects around 1869 in his *atelier japonais* in the Paris house (pl.194). The studio is filled with a collection of Japanese arts and crafts, some bought from Parisian dealers in Japanese objects, some probably acquired from the 1867 Paris Exposition Universelle, and others as gifts from his pupil the Shogunate Prince Akitake, whose portrait Tissot had painted in 1867. The carefully positioned objects include the large ship model which the women are examining intently, and a black and gold shrine, containing puppets rather than the expected idol. The ship model is sitting on a fine piece of patterned silk. When Rossetti visited a Japan dealer, the celebrated Mme Desoye in the rue de Rivoli in

193. L. Alma-Tadema, *Portrait of Anna Alma-Tadema entering the Study at Townshend House*, oil painting, 1883 (Royal Academy of Arts)

Paris in 1864, he was irritated to find that Tissot had got in before him and had snapped up all the costumes.[109] In a second picture in the series the two women have moved over to examine another shrine-like structure, again containing a puppet sitting on an elaborately carved table. Behind them is a Japanese screen. These paintings, coming at the beginning of the fascination with Japanese themes in art, enjoyed considerable success, but Tissot did not return to such overt use of Japanese influences, preferring the subtle employment of Japanese compositional devices and perspective.

Tissot came to London in the wake of the Paris Commune, in which he had played a role which made his departure prudent. He brought to English anecdotal realism a touch of French irony. He was inspired by Charles Baudelaire's key essay on *La peintre de la vie moderne*, calling on artists to seek beauty and serious themes in everyday life. He hoped that artists could be persuaded to treat modern life as thoughtfully as the historical, biblical and allegorical subjects, long regarded as the

194. J.J.J. Tissot, *Young Women looking at Japanese Articles*, oil painting, about 1869 (Cincinnati Art Museum, USA)

The setting is Tissot's Parisian studio.

195. J.J.J. TISSOT, *Reading the News*,
oil painting, about 1874
(Private Collection)

only proper material for 'high art'. Baudelaire's suggested themes form almost a blueprint for Tissot's paintings of fashionable middle-class life: *Manner and Modes, Beauty, Fashion and Happiness, Women: Honest Ones and Others.* To *Manners and Modes* Tissot added a highly topical gloss – the social unease of the newly wealthy middle class. The fashions he created were an instantly recognizable flurry of flounces, frills and furs with jaunty hats and muffs. One critic wrote of him: 'Mr Tissot points no moral; but his tales are certainly most skilfully adorned. He is no satirist. He takes Society as he finds it, and paints it in its habit as it lives; and Society, we conceive, ought to be very much obliged to so deft an expositor.'[110] Above all he charted the complexities of modern love, drawing endlessly on his own situation.

Tissot was an Anglophile from very early on (witness the use of the English James in his name) and he had colleagues in London. He thought that there might also be a ready market for his paintings, and he was right, as his friend Degas acknowledged: 'They tell me you are earning lots of money. Give me some ideas of how I might also get some advantage in England…' (letter of September 1871). The diarist Edmond de Goncourt heard that Tissot 'has a studio with a waiting room where, at all times, there is iced champagne, and … a garden where all day long one can see a footman shining the shrubbery leaves'. This impression was strengthened by some of his paintings, where servants were often present in both house and garden. But Tissot had to struggle for his success: the public were sometimes ambivalent about what was seen as his slightly racy French *chic*, and he had to endure some proselytizing on the part of the critics. The presence of his beautiful Irish mistress, the divorcée Kathleen Newton whom he met in 1876, hardly diminished speculation among members of the public.

In 1874, shortly after taking 17 Grove End Road, Tissot had a studio built under the direction of a talented young architect, J.M. Brydon. It was illustrated in the *Building News* in May, and described as follows:

As will be seen from the drawing, it is a large apartment, amply lighted, principally from the north and east. The whole of one side (the right in the view) is open to a large conservatory, from which it is separated by an arrangement of glass screens and Curtains. The floor is laid with oak parquet, and the walls are hung with a kind of tapestry cloth of greenish blue colour.[111]

One of the refinements that enabled Tissot to complete story-telling Thameside subjects in his studio was the installation of a bow window (on the left of the illustration in *Building News*) of eighteenth-century design, imitating one facing the river at Greenwich, which then featured in a succession of costume pieces with anecdotal titles and narrative genre scenes. It dominates the composition of *Reading the News* (pl.195), for example, and in *Lady at a Piano* (pl.196) it appears in a domestic context. Furthermore, backgrounds visible through the window could be varied to suit the narrative. The furniture and other decorative items from around Tissot's house feature over and over in these paintings: the mahogany drop-leaf table features frequently in his costume pieces, along with the Sussex-type chairs, reputedly designed by Rossetti, from Morris & Co. The elegant table is a much-used prop. Flowers dominate his paintings, evidence of lavish household expenditure of time and money.

Tissot loved to paint London parks and gardens (including Holland Park, see pl.119), but above all the Grove End Road garden and conservatory.[112] He was a pioneer in the use of a garden or conservatory setting to construct narrative fictions and suggest atmosphere. Although he did not employ the 'language of flowers' in the same way as the Pre-Raphaelites and the mid-Victorian narrative painters, there is nevertheless an emphasis on certain plants, not least the proliferating nasturtiums and geraniums and the dense panels of climbing ivy. The development of his personal gardening style was part of the appeal: his images show an intensively worked garden with well-established plants that are exotic, expensive, and require investment of skill, time, knowledge and money. The planting in the French taste, dense drifts of bright colours with pillars of trained geraniums and nasturtiums against a background of clipped ivy, was remarked on in notices of exhibitions featuring his work. Perhaps a subconscious recognition of the French style of his garden may have underpinned the frequently outraged tone of these comments: to the Victorians, 'French' could be used as a designation of nationality but also as a euphemism for things that were 'not done', unacceptable in a well-ordered and moral society. Although William Robinson had written on this topic, describing the use of ivy to clothe walls and pillars and the extensive decorative trelliswork, both features of the Grove End Road garden, Tissot had to contend with this attitude and at times seems to have encouraged it.

196. J.J.J. Tissot, *Lady at a Piano*, watercolour, about 1881 (Museum of Art, Rhode Island School of Design)

Through the window, Tissot has added details of shipping to suggest a port scene or one of the Wapping subjects for which he was becoming well known.

197. J.J.J. TISSOT, *L'Hamac*, etching, 1880
(V&A: E.851–1959)

Various different aspects of the garden appear in Tissot's *The Hammock* (1880; pl.197), *On the Grass* (1880; pl.198), *Rêverie* (1881; see pl.18) and *Le Banc de Jardin* (1883). Mrs Newton modelled for the figure reclining in a hammock in the many versions of this subject that he exhibited: no fewer than three were among Tissot's eight 'modern life' paintings included in the Grosvenor Gallery exhibition in 1879. As the *Spectator* remarked, 'these ladies in hammocks, showing a very unnecessary amount of petticoat and stocking, and remarkable for little save luxurious indolence, are hardly fit subjects for such an elaborate painting'.[113] The implication – perfectly correct, as it happened – is that this was a secluded retreat maintained by a man for his mistress. Tissot must have been laughing behind his hand at the critics. As a foreigner he was able to treat English class with amused detachment. Being French, his fashion sense was acute and he was evidently mindful of advice offered by Baudelaire to the 'Painter of Modern Life' to concentrate on the narrative of women, to observe her 'costume, gesture, bearing, gait, manners and morals'. Tissot's little paradise can be reconstructed in detail, using his paintings as a guide. The garden was fairly large and his paintings, with their many different viewpoints, make it look larger still. One of the most striking features of the garden can be seen in the background of his watercolour *Croquet* (pl.199): a marble colonnade copied from the one in the Parc Monceau in Paris.

The substantial conservatory which Tissot had added to the conventional stuccoed villa, leading off his studio, was used in his paintings on a number of occasions. This also had a loaded agenda, being associated in contemporary imagination with assignation and seduction. With *In the Conservatory* (1875–8;

198. J.J.J. Tissot, *On the Grass*,
etching, 1880
(V&A: E.1232–1936)

199. J.J.J. Tissot, *Croquet*,
watercolour, 1878
(Museum of Art, Rhode Island
School of Design)

The setting is Tissot's garden
at 17 Grove End Road, St John's
Wood. In the background, behind
the two girls on the grass, is the
colonnade, modelled on the one in
the Parc Monceau in Paris. The
larger oil painting of this subject,
exhibited at the Grosvenor Gallery
in 1878, is in the Hamilton Art
Gallery, Ontario.

pl.200), exhibition visitors found the ambiguous sexual messages to be exciting; in effect Tissot was staging his 'modern life' in the demi-monde. The conservatory merges inside and outside; with its exotics and rare flowering plants it is a show of wealth. Conservatories or 'winter gardens', being particularly suited to urban gardening, sprang up everywhere. Many newly built London villas had gardens large enough to accommodate a glasshouse, from which forced exotics could be brought in to decorate the house.

Tissot used the interior of his house as a background for his modern life paintings. *Hide and Seek*, of about 1880 (pl.201), depicting a woman and four little girls in the studio of his own St John's Wood house, shows a different social model: ordinary people in surroundings that are modern and eclectic but not pretentious. However, even with such an innocent subject as a children's game of hide-and-seek, every detail is capable of more ambiguous interpretation. This uxorious domesticity conceals an irregular ménage consisting of the artist, his beautiful mistress Kathleen Newton and her two children. Even though it is plainly a sunny day, they are all confined within a darkened room. Taken at face value, however, it is a faithful representation of a certain type of Aesthetic taste, which favoured Eastern carpets, fur rugs, Oriental porcelains, exotic – even menacing – tribal masks and embossed leather screens. The loving attention to the room and its contents provides a measure of how much Kathleen Newton's death and Tissot's subsequent flight to Paris would affect him, both at the time and long afterwards.

200. J.J.J. TISSOT, *In the Conservatory,* oil painting, 1875–8 (Private Collection)

Tissot used the large conservatory attached to his house for a number of his popular society pictures.

201. J.J.J. TISSOT, *Hide and Seek*,
oil painting, about 1880–82
(National Gallery of Art, Washington, DC)

The setting is the sumptuous studio in
Tissot's home with Kathleen Newton
reading while the children play.

The villa in which Tissot conducted his idyllic love affair all but disappeared in
a riot of alteration and aggrandizement in the hands of its new owner, Lawrence
Alma-Tadema.

When he moved to 17 Grove End Road in 1885 Alma-Tadema set out to create
something rather different from his maze of little rooms in Townshend House, less
cluttered and much more grandly conceived. Although he was altering an existing
house rather than building from scratch, the number of architects consulted and
the extent of the overhaul make this much like a purpose-built studio-house. The
original villa was completely encased and vastly enlarged to almost double its
original size. Very little remained from Tissot's occupation of the house other than
the garden colonnade, which survives even today. The materials cladding the house
were rich terracotta, Portland stone, marble, coloured tiling, some stucco rendering,
lead slate and bronze. A drawing from 1886 in the *Art Journal* by J. Elmsly Inglis,
one of the architects consulted by Alma-Tadema, gives a good impression of the
transformation (pl.202).[114] There were still examples of valuable textiles designed
into the decor, but the effect of endless little chambers leading from one to the

Principal Entrance : Studio Front.   From a Drawing by J. Elmsly Inglis.

202. J. ELMSLY INGLIS,
Alma-Tadema's house, principal entrance,
Art Journal Special Number, 1886

203. View from Alma-Tadema's studio
looking towards the Hall of Panels and the
atrium, *Art Journal*, Christmas 1910

other was lost; the result was undeniably impressive, but some of its former magic may have been lacking. The huge front door in its sculptural bronze frame led into an entrance hall with white panelled walls and a floor of Persian tiles. A brass staircase led to Tadema's triple-height studio which was silvered with aluminium leaf, the gallery lettered with the motto 'AS THE SUN COLOURS FLOWERS, SO ART COLOURS LIFE', one of the many such inscriptions throughout the house. An impluvium contained a marble sunken bath used by Alma-Tadema for his tableaux of naked women. The conservatory could be viewed from the studio gallery.

In the early 1880s Alma-Tadema had been engaged in one of his most lavish and important decorative projects, the music room in the Marquand Mansion in New York, home of the American millionaire Henry Gurdon Marquand.[115] The team involved with this remarkable project included Leighton and Poynter; the furniture was made in London by Johnstone, Norman & Co. and exhibited to the public in their premises in New Bond Street. This is the closest direct link between the artist-led British Aesthetic Movement and the 'Aesthetic' character of the great mansions created for American 'Gilded Age' collectors. Some of the flavour certainly worked its way into Grove End Road. Alma-Tadema installed a version of John La Farge's glass-mosaic design for the Marquand Mansion, of peonies blowing in the wind, in the dining room of his own house; it is now in the Museum of Fine Arts in Boston. Alma-Tadema's house was extensively publicized in art and architecture periodicals, confirming its reputation as the ultimate example of the artist's house.

His last studio was the epitome of artistic grandeur (pl.203). At a much more basic level quite divorced from considerations of interior decoration, the character

204. Panel showing Tadema's studio from the hallway at 17 Grove End Road, about 1883
(Fine Art Society)

This little panel of the studio at Townshend House was painted by Emily Williams and installed in the hallway at Grove End Road.

of the studio was crucial to the work which emerged from it. The silvery-white tone of Alma-Tadema's later work was the direct result of cladding the semidome in his studio with aluminium.

As at Townshend House, Laura Alma-Tadema had a suite of small rooms with her own Dutch-style studio; she used these as the setting for many of her genre scenes. Alice Meynell remarked of her work:

> *In details of domestic life, Dutch habits, Dutch furniture, and Dutch dress of the gentler and more courtly sort in the seventeenth century, Mrs Alma Tadema has found unconventional, honest and … homely grace … The artist has surrounded herself by relics and remains of the time and the country she loves … and thus her pictures seem to be produced within a genuine little Holland, in a genuine seventeenth century, without the blunders of ordinary historical research.*[116]

One of the most ambitious interiors in Alma-Tadema's Grove End Road house was the hallway. Inset into the wall were 45 panels, painted by the artists' friends to a uniform height and designed to reflect the style and subject matter of their creators (pl.204). Cosmo Monkhouse described them as the house's 'most remarkable feature';[117] the *Strand Magazine* devoted 15 pages to describing them in 1902.

Lady Monkswell describes in her diary a visit in 1893:

> *I took dear Lady Ripon to see Tadema's studio … Old Tadema was most attentive to us & showed her everything. I had seen before the studio with the apse lined with silver, & the upper gallery & the Pompeian Court where he writes his letters, & the recess looking into the greenhouse with the painted panels. But Tadema himself is as the hymn says 'new every morning'. I certainly had not seen the garden door; – the upper half is very thick inlaid glass in a sort of Japanese design with a broad border of what might well be uncut jewels. It faces the East, & Tadema said in his wonderful enthusiastic, eloquent & almost unintelligible manner (the manner of a genius) 'when the sun shines through it, it is like a hallelujah'.*[118]

The Grove End Road house was unquestionably superior to the terraced house by the Regent's Canal which Lady Monkswell had known well, but for all its grandeur it was not as lovingly portrayed as the quirky Townshend House. The flavour of this most remarkable of London's studio houses – and the enormous scale of Alma-Tadema's collecting activities – emerges in the catalogue of the sale of the Grove End Road contents after the artist's death in 1912.[119] The items speak of the interiors: the monogram 'LAT' decorating furniture and house alike, standing for both Lawrence and Laura, is a poignant reminder of this most successful marriage and artistic partnership.

Further down Grove End Road, at number 8, G.D. Leslie, like Tissot and Atkinson Grimshaw, made almost an industry out of his own Aesthetic 'Queen Anne'-style home, designed, in common with so many others, by Norman Shaw. It was furnished in an appropriate style, and its rooms provided settings of his hugely popular paintings in domestic genre. A subject called, appropriately, *Home Sweet Home* inspired the critic for the *Magazine of Art* to rather plaintive comment: 'Leslie chooses a purely feminine subject as usual. If this artist has ever painted a man, we do not remember it, but the pictures he paints find general favour in these elaborately idyllic days of ours.'[120] Here, in this clever phrase 'elaborately idyllic', we have another clue to the nature of the artist's domestic narrative: the widespread taste for episodes from the domestic life in some rather loosely defined 'olden time' finds an echo in the generally Olde English and 'Queen Anne' styles adopted for many artists' houses. Having found a supremely successful artistic domestic genre, Leslie stayed with it, painting his very similar *Sun and Moonflowers* (see pl.84) in 1889 when the first impact of the Aesthetic Movement was over and the style had long been annexed by commercial firms and decorators.

'SWEET HAMPSTEAD': NORTHERN RETREAT

Pockets of almost rural seclusion survived in unexpected places in London until well into the twentieth century. Mrs Caroline White published *Sweet Hampstead and its associations*, her nostalgic celebration of the rural character of the area, in 1901, but as the Preface makes clear it had preoccupied her for more than thirty years. She was tapping into the taste among cultivated and artistic people for immunity to urbanization that seemed to keep the modern world at bay. Although it had been the haunt of artists for generations, Hampstead also developed as a new-build artistic community in the wake of Kensington and Chelsea. Initially it was the old red-brick houses and the past artistic associations of the area that were congenial, and rent was cheap. Church Row, an elegant street of largely mid-eighteenth-century red-brick houses leading to the parish church of St John, became a favourite site. Haverstock Hill, too, was being rapidly colonized by artistic inhabitants. Many of the picturesque houses that cluster around the studio-houses survive, giving an idea of the romantic character of Victorian Hampstead. The 'Queen Anne' houses that were the choice of most of the Hampstead artists play an important role in its distinctive development. The area was developed by artists building studio-houses at much the same time as Bedford Park.

George du Maurier, chief chronicler of the eccentricities of the Aesthetic Movement, moved to Hampstead in 1869, attracted by the remaining wild, untamed quality in the landscape and the adjacent Heath. After moving from one rented Georgian house – staying in 27 Church Row for four years – to another, he settled for New Grove House, a renovated eighteenth-century house with a large, light studio.[121] Writing in *Harper's Magazine* in 1897, Henry James, who would walk all the way from De Vere Gardens in Kensington to dine with his friend, tells us 'that the Hampstead scenery made in *Punch* his mountains and valleys, his backgrounds and foregrounds'.[122] Du Maurier's house supplied the artefacts decorating the interiors in his cartoons and book illustrations and his family many of the *dramatis personae*. The rooms are decorated with the accoutrements of Aestheticism, Japanese fans and screens, blue and white pots, Regency convex mirrors, spindly chairs, rugs and watercolours or prints in wide white mounts.

Suburban pretensions were irresistible to *Punch*: Du Maurier invented the Jack Spratts in 1878, just as the first Bedford Park houses were completed. Du Maurier put them in 'an old suburb' in North London, presumably Hampstead, but the Spratts enjoyed typical pastimes described by Bedford Park residents: discussing art and painting pictures, playing newly fashionable games such as tennis and billiards, and putting on theatrical performances. The suburban development of Holloway in North London was less salubrious than Bedford Park, but the Grossmiths' Mr Pooter and his wife Carrie had their own aesthetic pretensions. In *The Diary of a Nobody*, which appeared in *Punch* from May 1888, the Pooters transform their drawing room for a party by hanging muslin curtains in place of the doors and adorning the corners of newly acquired tinted photographs with Liberty silk bows. Mr Pooter ridicules Carrie's attachment to fashionable smocking for her dresses, but actually supports her social ambitions. This is the ethos of the artist's house reduced to its lowest common denominator and an indication that the end of its architectural and social significance is in sight.

Hampstead was later to be the site of a 'garden suburb', but in the 1870s and 1880s the nearness of the Heath drew a number of watercolourists, among them the successful children's illustrator Kate Greenaway. Kate's father was a struggling wood-engraver who worked on the popular animal illustrations by Harrison Weir, among other things. He was a friend and colleague of Myles Birket Foster, and Kate was a frequent visitor to Birket Foster's house, The Hill, at Witley, where she painted rustic scenes alongside Helen Allingham. Kate, who had been Helen's friend from her art student days, attempted to alter her subject matter to country cottages, but their old and tumbledown character did not suit her essentially orderly

205. Helen Allingham in her studio,
Eldon Road, Hampstead, photograph, 1890s
(Burgh House Museum, Hampstead)

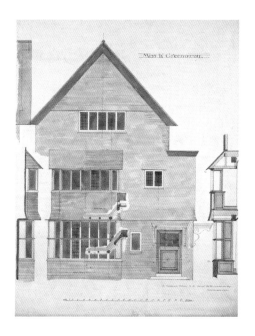

206. R. NORMAN SHAW, elevation,
39 Frognal, for Kate Greenaway,
watercolour, 1885
(Royal Academy of Arts)

207. W.E. NESFIELD and J. FORSYTH,
Anglo-Japanese screen, made as a
wedding present for Richard and Agnes
Norman Shaw, 1867
(V&A: W.37–1972)

artistic personality and so she returned to small children and flowers. Her four exhibitions at the Fine Art Society in New Bond Street relied almost entirely on the resale of illustrations for *Marigold Garden, The Language of Flowers, Children's Games* and *Little Ann*. The buyers were nothing to be ashamed of: two items went to the Art Gallery of New South Wales in Sydney, Leighton bought one and so did George Howard, Earl of Carlisle. She made £964 from her show in 1891, an excellent result as she acknowledged herself, since the illustrations had already been paid for once by her publisher, Edmund Evans. By 1881 she had made such a success of her career as an illustrator that she was able to pay £2,000 for plot at 39 Frognal, and to commission her studio-house from Norman Shaw (pl.206). The studio was designed to accommodate her parents and her brother, John, as well as her own working space.[123] The large slanting window on the side elevation proclaimed its function. The style of plain vernacular dwelling with decorative tile-hanging recalls the Surrey cottages around Witley. However, Kate felt compelled to apologize to Norman Shaw for the modesty of her commission in comparison to the splendour of his other artist-patrons. Kate had fallen under the spell of John Ruskin, and the elegant little tea-room leading from her studio was designed for entertaining him on his visits to London. Her one extravagance was a fireplace with tiles designed by Shaw. Helen Allingham herself settled in Hampstead, at Eldon Road, shortly before the death of her husband (pl.205). Her widowhood was made more bearable by the presence of artist friends. With Kate she made painting expeditions by railway to old Surrey haunts and to Kent.

The land in Old Frognal became available for building development in 1873 and the ambitious scale of the plans for streets of fine houses appealed to successful artists. The novelist Sir Max Pemberton, who lived at 56 Fitzjohn's Avenue, described the visitors on 'Show Sunday' as 'a source of inspiration ... to the makers of fashion plates': Webb and Shaw were both active in the area. Grander houses than Kate Greenaway's, designed by Shaw for heavyweight academicians Edwin Long (two) and Frank Holl arose in Fitzjohn's Avenue and Netherhall Gardens. These were more in keeping with the artistic development of Hampstead, though a cluster of eighteenth-century houses off the High Street and up by Hampstead pond were chosen by artists for their elegant settings. The artistic development of Hampstead benefited from being embedded in a historic urban setting. Shaw's own house in Ellerdale Road, the first of his Hampstead houses, was large but rather plain (but with certain 'signatures' in the jutting 'Ipswich oriels' that enliven the façade), treading a course between the modest Greenaway house and the extravagances of Holl's mansion. It was intended to be a family house: the plans were drawn up on the day in 1874 when his third and last child was born. The site was close to the elegancies of Church Row and had a view of the back of Hampstead Church. The interior was full of Aesthetic touches, in the William De Morgan fireplace tiles, the decorative raised plaster friezes and the scattered Persian rugs (pl.207).[124]

Hampstead artistic tastefulness was interrupted by Carl Haag, another Hampstead resident, with his fabulous Eastern fantasy in Ida Villa at 7 Lyndhurst Road (pl.208). Haag made a speciality of pictures of Oriental life. He was born in Bavaria and came to London in 1847 where he attracted the attention of Queen Victoria. In 1853 he was invited to paint at Balmoral. He travelled extensively in the late 1850s, in Egypt, Palestine and Syria. The Queen commissioned copies of a number of his Oriental views. In 1858–9 he spent the winter in Cairo with his friend Frederick Goodall, and there made a meticulous watercolour of the studio they shared. He inscribed it 'My painting room in Cairo', with the address, his name and the date, 1859; he was there again the following winter. In 1866 Haag married and set up house in Hampstead, where his rooftop studio was described as 'Cairo in London'.[125] It was a vast space, 40 x 30ft in extent with a 15-ft ceiling rising to 25ft at the central skylight. The studio was fitted up with furniture bought in Cairo, including the *mushrabiya* screens so beloved of artists, textiles,

208. Carl Haag's studio at
7 Lyndhurst Road, *Art Journal*, 1883

209. W. ORPEN, *The Mirror*,
oil painting, 1900
(Tate, London)

musical instruments, tiles and leatherwork. Haag's studio-style translated into a Turkish room he designed as a smoking room for the Prince of Wales at Marlborough House, London home of the Prince and Princess after their marriage in 1863.

The developer Richard Batterbury and his two sons were responsible for a number of Hampstead studio-houses, including the picturesque and relatively inexpensive Olde English grouping in Steele's Road, off Haverstock Hill. Hampstead's artistic character was particularly in evidence in the early twentieth century, but the scene had shifted back to the older houses. The completely open-ended eclecticism of the late Victorian artistic interior was changed into something more rigorous by a wave of young artists associated with the New English Art Club. Profoundly admiring of Vermeer and the seventeenth-century Dutch domestic genre, the style is limpid and sparsely ornamented. It was to have a wide influence on interior decoration in the twentieth century through the rarefied elegancies of the 'Georgian' movement.

William Rothenstein's deceptively simple views of his home in Hampstead demonstrate a decisive shift in the aesthetics of the artistic interior. He was influenced by the intimate scenes of everyday life in Dutch seventeenth-century painting, and by Vermeer in particular. Enigmatically titled, his *Mother and Child* (pl.210) is one of the portraits in which the room plays as important a part as the human figures. The plain panelling, spare furniture and absence of clutter look back to the London interiors in early eighteenth-century 'conversation piece' paintings of the 1740s and 1750s. Rothenstein's wife and their elder son, John, who was born in 1901, are in the first-floor sitting room of 26 Church Row, to which they had moved in November 1902. The minimal furnishings and ornaments consist of a plain eighteenth-century chair and, carefully placed on the mantelshelf, two books (surely introduced for the note of red which they bring to this otherwise almost monochrome scheme), a seated Buddha and a ship model. Rothenstein loved the house, but admitted that eventually he found 'its very beauty a defect':

> At first I was happy about the house, with its panelled rooms, carved staircase
> and noble Queen Anne fireplaces. But I came to feel its very beauty to be a defect;
> it was all too perfect, too stylish; for I was aiming at something more elemental than
> a Queen Anne interior. I was painting wife and child, and wished to suggest every-
> wife and every-child; and Queen Anne got in the way, while for portraits the
> light was too diffused.[126]

Rothenstein was far-seeing; Hampstead is now somewhat self-consciously preserved, with a number of the artists' purpose-built houses surviving, albeit in different hands.

The time for the exotic studio milieu with its distinctive social role was nearly over. The centres of innovative energy altered. The activities of the Bloomsbury Group were barely over the horizon, with the social ambitions of artists undergoing a sea-change. Rothenstein's brother-in-law William Orpen set his nearly contemporary interior, *The Mirror* (pl.209), in his London lodgings: the cool, spare aesthetic is very similar, with the device of showing himself reflected in a concave mirror on the facing wall taken from Van Eyck's *Arnolfini Marriage*. The following year he set *Window in a London Street* on the first floor of 21 Fitzroy Street, where he had a basement studio. A reviewer commenting on the New English Art Club exhibition of 1901, where the picture had its first airing, remarked:

> Mr Orpen … rings the changes on a very familiar theme. The theme is of grey-
> green walls hung with engravings – an admirable taste, no doubt – of a highly
> polished card table with flower vases or other knick-knacks to relieve the general air
> of drabness, and of one or more figures … In one of his works, 'A Window in a
> London street', the high room containing the familiar figure in blue, the inevitable
> greenish walls and the shining card table, has one dark corner, the darkness of which

210. W. Rothenstein, *Mother and Child,*
oil painting, signed and dated 1903
(Tate, London)

*speaks of its own veritable mystery. Then through the large window with the domed
top one is shown the over-the-way line of houses. They are plain houses, grey, with
the greyness of London city; the sky, too, is harmoniously grey. But, putting aside the
clever manipulation of shadows and the sense of indoor atmosphere, the picture posses
the true inwardness, not so much of London, as of a particular part of London –
the Fitzroy-square neighbourhood which has gentility for its shell.*[127]

Much of the description in the review is familiar territory, the 'grey-green',
wall colour, the polished mahogany and the engravings. The distinctive decorative
milieu of the Victorian art world was swept away with surprising rapidity.

Afterword

A SUMMARY AND THREE CASE HISTORIES

In spite of the widespread abhorrence of Victorian architecture that persisted, against passionate representations by such enthusiasts as John Betjeman, well into the second half of the twentieth century, a good number of architecturally distinguished artists' houses survive, adding originality and eclecticism to London's urban panorama. At the close of the nineteenth century there were hundreds of artists' studios and houses in London but the taste for the magnificent architectural statements that had produced Leighton's Arab Hall and palatial mansions for Millais and Alma-Tadema was running out. In 1895 Burne-Jones remarked to his assistant T.M. Rooke, 'What possible enthusiasm or interest could one get up about a house by Aitchison … There couldn't be any gain in making public property of it and to have all those splendid things from the East built up in such a way couldn't please me, could it?'[1] Burne-Jones had a distinctly austere notion of the appropriate working studio, but he was not alone in questioning the need for the opulent studio-house.[2]

Among those artists' houses still standing, frequently unmarked and unnoticed, few are now inhabited by artists. By modern standards they are large, although they were seen as suitably modest when they were built. The social revolution which brought them into being continued its inexorable progress onwards and upwards, and they are now for the most part far too expensive for practising artists. Architecturally they relieve the urban landscape with asymmetry and scale. Their story in the twentieth century veers between survival on the brink and some deplorable losses. To Whistler's despair, his beautiful White House, for example, had been quickly altered by his successor, the critic Harry Quilter. James Whitall, a visiting American, made the pilgrimage to see it when he was trying his luck at a literary career in London in 1914. Having heard that Chelsea was the bohemian quarter of London, he was disappointed that it was now inhabited by 'the smart and rich'. He found for himself a 'discreet Queen Anne house in Cheyne Row', close to Oscar Wilde's 'dreary abode', Edwin Austin Abbey's 'commonplace dwelling' and Henry James's last residence in Carlyle Mansions on the Embankment. Whistler's house was occupied by a fellow American, Annabel Douglas. He knocked, and the shiny black front door opened onto what seemed to be a maze of staircases. 'The studio at the top [of the house] was now a spacious brocaded drawing room', but 'It was a fantastically inconvenient house … every room reached by a staircase that led nowhere else. It was as though Godwin had wanted to pester Whistler with stair-climbing.'[3] By the mid-twentieth century the house had been irretrievably compromised by alterations and it was demolished – not without protest – in 1965, a year of shame in terms of preserving artists' houses.

While many studios and houses in Tite Street survive and some of the studios are still occupied by professional artists, Chelsea's artistic heritage was so comprehensively erased by the mid-twentieth century that it took action at a municipal level to remedy the situation. In the 1950s Chelsea Borough Council initiated a programme of studio-building in order to keep a significant presence of working artists in the area which was, on its own terms, successful, but it failed to stem the transformation of most of the Victorian purpose-built studios into glamorous – and outrageously expensive – private houses.[4] The inexcusable demolition in 1957 of The Grange, Burne-Jones's house in Fulham, destroyed not only a significant site in Victorian art history, but the dwelling of the eighteenth-century novelist Samuel Richardson.

In Kensington the most devastating loss was Holland House, all but destroyed by fire after a bombing raid in the Second World War. Colin Hunter's Melbury

Road house was also destroyed. The first of the Holland Park studio houses, Val Prinsep's in Holland Park Road, was converted into flats. These old, often dilapidated buildings were not in tune with post-war Utopianism and the mood in the 1950s and 1960s posed a real threat. The expiry of the leases in Melbury Road in 1963 put the houses under pressure from development, resisted by the old London County Council. Before that, in 1960, Kensington Borough Council had protested at a preservation order proposed by the London County Council for Leighton House, and the Holland Park Estate opposed the similar order for numbers 6, 8, 9, 11, 15 and 17 Melbury Road (pls 211–13). As a news item in *The Times* revealed, councillors argued that 'the buildings were not of such architectural or historic merit as to warrant such a procedure'.[5] The Minister excepted number 6 when confirming the orders on the other Melbury Road properties, and so G.F. Watts's New Little Holland House, which had been bought by Parway Land and Investments Ltd in 1961, went in the same year as Whistler's White House, torn down to make room for Kingfisher House, an undistinguished block of flats. In spite of the failure to halt the demolition of Little Holland House, vigorous local protest saved most of the artists' houses and they have now become a much-valued tourist attraction.

Marcus Stone's studio was until recently actually occupied by a successful portrait painter. William Burges's Tower House was restored as a labour of love by the actor Richard Harris, having been vandalized in the early 1960s. The interior was recorded by the Greater London Council in 1967 in a bid to strengthen the case for preservation. When Harris bought the house in 1968 the terms of the lease stipulated that it should be for 'family use only', a pretty tall order given the eccentric nature of the interior decoration. It is really a showpiece – a show-stopper – and would surely send anyone forced to conduct ordinary family life there to distraction. At the time of writing it is cherished by Led Zeppelin guitarist Jimmy Page. Luke Fildes's house was turned into flats and has since been rescued and restored to a family house by the film-maker Michael Winner. However, farther afield, George Boughton's West House on Campden Hill, a much admired Aesthetic dwelling by Norman Shaw, was divided into flats and altered externally. In 1955 Arthur Lewis's Moray Lodge, scene of Victorian art world entertaining, was torn down to make way for Holland Park Comprehensive School.

James Rannie Swinton's large detached studio-mansion is still splendidly marooned at the corner of Warwick Square (number 33). Its size was against it in the modern world and it struggled to find a role. Isadora Duncan had a studio there, and in 1925 the distinguished Grosvenor School of Modern Art was founded there. Latterly it housed Milton Grundy's collection and philanthropic Warwick Arts Trust, before being put on the market in the present century for £11 million, still at that moment a considerable sum of money. Millais's similarly vast stately mansion is an ambassadorial residence and has proved to be almost impossible of access.[6]

Rossetti's Cheyne Walk house was rescued from a decayed state by a member of the Sainsbury family, closely supervised by that Ruskinian Arts and Crafts creation, the Society for the Preservation of Ancient Buildings. A rarity, George Price Boyce's West House, at 35 Glebe Place in Chelsea, was taken after his death by the Scottish colourists James Guthrie and E.A. Walton. It has been maintained by an artist-designer owner since the mid-twentieth century. Much photographed during the present owner's occupancy, the rooms still preserve a strong atmosphere of the Victorian studio:[7] the studio sitting room uncannily resembles the 1898 illustration to a long obituary of Boyce in the *Architectural Review*.[8] West House is heavily protected by listing and local preservation orders as it lies within the Cheyne Conservation Area. Sadly, C.R. Ashbee's Magpie and Stump in Cheyne Walk was not sufficiently protected, and followed White House and New Little Holland House just three years later, also to make way for flats, rounding out a decade of shameful destruction.

Hampstead has fared relatively well in retaining its artistic character, although inevitably there have been unfortunate demolitions during what in retrospect looks like an era of wanton destruction in the mid-twentieth century. At 39 Frognal the quaint tile-hung cottage commissioned by Kate Greenaway from Norman Shaw survives, identified by the blue plaque put there by the old London County Council in 1950. A French conceptual artist has taken it, intending to return it to its original purpose. Shaw's own house, at 6 Ellerdale Road (1874–6), where he lived until his death in 1912, was Grade I listed in 1950 and is, as of 2006, a convent and language institute run by the Sisters of St Marcellina. Shaw's second house for the Orientalist Edwin Long at 42 Netherhall Gardens (1888) is celebrated as having been the London home of Edward Elgar from 1912 to 1921. He named it Severn House and entertained there in the large music room. Historians have noted the influence of this striking Arts and Crafts house on architects in the bay area of San Francisco. It was demolished, in spite of its association with such a famous resident, in about 1937. Shaw's first Hampstead house for Long (he also designed Long's country house), Three Gables at 6 Fitzjohn's Avenue, was demolished to make way for the Tavistock Clinic in 1965.

William Morris's Red House in Kent is currently at the centre of discussions on presentation. The question that confronts all dwellings open to the public is whether it is better to strive for a continuum or a specific moment, frozen in time. Some of Morris's monumental built-in furniture is still *in situ*, including pieces with painted decoration by Morris, Rossetti and Burne-Jones, but other survivors from the original furnishings are now at Kelmscott Manor in Oxfordshire and the V&A. Many inhabitants have left their mark since Morris toiled at creating his Palace of Art. Acquisitions are being made of items associated with Morris's brief residence, but in order to entirely reinstate the Morris era, the V&A and Kelmscott Manor would have to be ruthlessly plundered and traces of subsequent occupants, by no means negligible persons, effaced.

Leighton's studio-house and Linley Sambourne's terraced house, both in Kensington and the latter substantially intact, are preserved as public museums, lone representatives of an experiment and an era. Sambourne's house survived as a Victorian artistic time-capsule through a mixture of inertia and expediency, to become the birthplace of the Victorian Society. It was bought from Sambourne's descendent, Anne, Lady Rosse, by the old Greater London Council, and is now owned and run by the Royal Borough of Kensington and Chelsea. Leighton House Museum was inadequately protected against the twentieth-century backlash which had such a dire effect on the posthumous reputations of Victorian artists, even though plans for its preservation as a memorial to the artist were put in hand immediately after his death (but not before it was stripped of its contents at auction). No buyer had been found for the house as the existence of only one bedroom was a problem (as it was with Watts's house and studio). In the event, the sale at Christie's of the collection and furniture alone fetched more than the package of house plus contents previously offered for sale. The house was acquired by the Council in 1925 from the Leighton House Association. There were no historical records – and no visual records of its fate since 1901 – to prompt a modern avatar, and when it was damaged by bombing in the Second World War it was boarded up and unused. Leighton's personality was entirely erased in the 1950s, when it was modernized with whitewash and modern narrow-strip flooring as a local arts amenity, but fortunately no actual destruction took place. Its survival in the 1960s was a 'skin-of-the-teeth' affair, but Kensington Borough Council was halted by a higher government authority from what would have been a disastrous architectural crime. A new curatorial direction under Stephen Jones in 1982 marked the start of the long struggle to reinstate Leighton himself in his prodigy house

Alma-Tadema's antique palace in St John's Wood, in many respects the equal in interest to Leighton House and among the most ambitious of them all, was allowed to descend into a ghostly wreck before its recent rescue operation. It, too, had been cleared at auction of all the fascinating furniture, antiquities and *objets d'art*. Discussed here along with Watts's studio-house and Ashbee's Chelsea house, the following case histories therefore represent two campaigns ending in failure and one long-awaited resurrection. The last, Ashbee's house is particularly pertinent owing to the involvement of the V&A and its partial success in rescuing the contents.

LITTLE HOLLAND HOUSE, 6 MELBURY ROAD, KENSINGTON

The 1961 London County Council proposal that preservation orders should be placed on Leighton's house and the Melbury Road houses of Watts, Marcus Stone, William Burges and Luke Fildes was intended to retain 'the nucleus of an area which was the home of many of the most celebrated artists of that time' (pl.211). The architect of the flats proposed by the developer, Parway Estates, on the site of red-brick studio-house built by Watts at 6 Melbury Road in 1876, challenged the LCC, saying that in his view 'Watts was not a man of such stature as to justify the retention of No. 6 as a memorial to him'.[9] Contrary to the LCC's vision, an idea prevailed at the time that such Victorian painters as Watts and Leighton would never regain the reputations they enjoyed in their own time, or indeed prove to be of any art-historical importance. Watt's Little Holland House was particularly ill adapted to domestic use, consisting as it did of a cluster of studios, two of them enormously large (pl.213). After the artist's death his widow let it to the Revd R.J. Walker, editor of the *Oxford and Cambridge Magazine*. Its fortunes thereafter can be followed in the classified property advertisements of *The Times*.

Little Holland House was still largely intact in 1919, but had been enlarged to include seven bedrooms, a ballroom and a covered badminton court in the garden. At some point it was given two entrances and divided into a number of awkward units forming not very practical flats. It was more or less unscathed during the Second World War, but much neglected and in need of expensive remodelling if it was to be returned to anything resembling its appearance in the artist's own time. Altogether it was in a very poor position to resist plans for redevelopment. Additionally, Watts's picture gallery, sculpture studio and house, Limnerslease, at Compton in Surrey, could be put forward as sufficient memorials to his life and work. In spite of opposition from all kinds of interested parties,

211. Melbury Road showing number 6, Little Holland House (National Monuments Record)

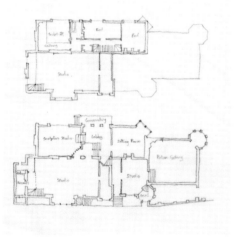

212. Ground plan of 6 Melbury Road (National Monuments Record)

213. Luke Fildes's house, Melbury Road (National Monuments Record)

including John Betjeman on behalf of the Victorian Society, it was demolished in 1965. Watts's Little Holland House was probably the hardest of these houses to defend against demolition. Apart from the stature of its former owner, not at that point in the fortunes of Victorian art much of an argument, it was perhaps the least distinguished of the Melbury Road studio-houses, but it formed part of an important architectural ensemble and should not have been the victim of such banal replacement.

The name Little Holland House is quaintly perpetuated in a small, pebble-dashed suburban Arts and Crafts house in Carshalton in Surrey. Lovingly built and furnished entirely by hand in 1902–4 by Frank Dickinson, an admirer of Ruskin and William Morris, it can be visited by arrangement.

ALMA-TADEMA'S HOUSE,
17 GROVE END ROAD, ST JOHN'S WOOD

The contents of Alma-Tadema's house were sold at the time of his death in 1913, and it quickly descended into multiple occupation; once empty of the sumptuous furnishings and roughly divided into flats, its richness began to seem tawdry. The studio was split into several floors. To between-wars taste the house appeared as a joke: John Betjeman's parents-in-law lived there, and Penelope Chetwode asked her fiancé to 'Tadema Towers', as he called it. Penelope's brother Roger called the impluvium 'the vomitorium'. The Chetwodes built a tennis court in the beautiful garden. In Penelope's sitting room was Tissot's replica of the windows of the Trafalgar Tavern at Greenwich which Alma-Tadema had moved to an upstairs room. She changed the window to an Art Deco design. The house was requisitioned by the army and suffered bomb damage in the Second World War; it was to decline much further, losing its decorative cladding and elegant approach. The house presented a formidable challenge in post-war austerity London: there was no question of restoration, and the solution in view of a severe housing shortage seemed to be a conversion into eleven flats. The building was managed by a post-war property-owning family until 1999, when a death prompted its sale. Meanwhile it had found its way on to the English Heritage 'Buildings at Risk' register.

The huge task of restoring the house for single-family occupation was begun in 2003. Alma-Tadema's studio has now returned to its former soaring dimensions; the exterior is finished with many of the original materials – terracotta, sandstone, stucco rendering in parts, slate, lead, zinc and copper. The marble colonnade in the garden has been restored.

Single-family covenants are the only way to recreate the integrity of the purpose-built studio-house, but they are quite a tall order. In a property market of massive wealth, number 17 (now renumbered 44) Grove End Road, like Burges's Tower House, has a niche, but such high-profile statements cannot survive very different fortunes in the property-owning classes.

THE MAGPIE AND STUMP,
37 CHEYNE WALK, CHELSEA

The Magpie and Stump in Chelsea, named after the public house which was demolished to make way for it, was the studio-house built by C.R.A. Ashbee for his mother and sisters after the break-up of his parents' marriage in 1893 (see p.111). In 1899, at numbers 38 and 39 next door, Ashbee designed two further tall, narrow houses, one with a studio for the artist Miss C.L. Christian (pl.214). The Arts and Crafts style of the house and the adjoining properties marked it out as intensely reticent in comparison with Godwin's many picturesque red-brick studio-houses nearby. An interior in this admired house was recorded in about 1900 (pl.88). Ashbee lived here briefly before his marriage, at which point he and his wife

214. F.C. VARLEY, 37–39 Cheyne Walk, watercolour, about 1899 (Royal Institute of British Architects)

Janet moved up the riverbank to 74 Cheyne Walk, also designed, with its next-door companion, by Ashbee himself (pl.87). These two houses were destroyed by enemy action in the Second World War, which makes the fate of the Magpie and Stump even more regrettable.

The house remained in possession of the Ashbee family until the death of old Mrs Ashbee in 1919. It housed family members and friends sporadically until 1924, when the lease was bought by Mr and Mrs Carpenter. When she was widowed Mrs Carpenter became a recluse and access to the house was difficult; only after her death were Ashbee's daughters able to discover what had become of the interior. The giant building and construction firm Wates had bought the property from the Cadogan Estate with the aged Mrs Carpenter still in residence, but when she died in November 1964, aged 96, the property became vacant. The leather wallpaper in the hall, with its raised pattern, and the copper light-fittings designed by Ashbee and installed when the house was built, were still *in situ*. There was still no electricity above the ground floor. Felicity Ashbee remarked: 'It was as though the clock had stopped. If only for this reason the house could be preserved as a museum piece.'[10]

The first threat to the house had appeared, by unfortunate coincidence, in 1963, the centenary year of Ashbee's birth. As the *Daily Telegraph* reported,

> *At the corner of the historic Cheyne Walk ... it is now proposed to build a 12-storey block of flats. This promises to mutilate the harmony of Nos. 37 to 39, a late Victorian group designed by C.R. Ashby [sic] which attracted international recognition when it was built.*

Numbers 38, occupied by George Malcolm, the conductor and harpsichordist, and 39 were already listed as being of historic and architectural interest, but number 37 was overlooked; the London County Council failed to recommend its inclusion. Fierce opposition to the plans came from the Chelsea Society, from Betjeman and the Victorian Society and from Shirley Bury of the V&A, expert on the period and curator of the Ashbee Centennial Exhibition in 1963. Although the height of the proposed block was lowered on appeal, the actual demolition was not opposed.

A Public Enquiry in 1965 failed to change the situation. In September 1966 the *Daily Telegraph* took up the case again, revealing that the Ministry of Housing had refused a preservation order for number 37.[11] As the reporter remarked, 'It is as a group that these unique Art Nouveau houses are most interesting'. The decision was seen as 'thoroughly bad'. But what is most curious is the reasoning behind this stance: although the property was vacant, many of the fixtures and fittings remained. In fact this told against the campaign, since adapting the property for modern living would inevitably result in their removal and a preservation order for the exterior alone was not thought worthwhile. On 11 November 1966 the *Chelsea News* reported: 'No hope now for No. 37'. The demolition involved other historic Chelsea sites – the pharmacy which had supplied Queen Victoria's perfume; the Blue Cockatoo café, raucous haunt since 1914 of the local artists; and the elegant Pier Hotel. As much as could be salvaged of the original fittings from the Magpie and Stump went to the V&A, the only result of Shirley Bury's vigorous campaign, but a good outcome nonetheless.

Public opinion has turned against the destruction mania of the 1960s and it will probably not be repeated, but money speaks. So long as art and tourism are valuable commodities and the prices for outstandingly original or unique properties remain staggeringly high, their relics will survive.

Cast of Characters

A

MAURICE BINGHAM ADAMS (1849–1933), architect and writer; joined the staff of *Building News* in 1872 and became editor in the same year. His articles for the *Building News* published under the title *Artists' Homes: a portfolio of drawings, including the houses and studios of several eminent painters, sculptors, etc.* in 1883 are a primary source for the subject of artists' houses and their decoration.

GEORGE AITCHISON, RA (1825–1910), President of the RIBA, Leighton's architect and leading Aesthetic Movement designer and decorator. He met Burges, Poynter and Leighton in Rome in 1853. His work on Leighton's studio-house lasted from 1864 until the artist's death in 1896.

HELEN ALLINGHAM, RWS (1848–1926), illustrator for *The Graphic* and watercolourist, married the poet William Allingham. She was a follower of Birket Foster in the rural idyll genre; Ruskin admired her work and linked her stylistically with Kate Greenaway.

SIR LAWRENCE ALMA-TADEMA, OM, RA (1836–1912), Dutch-born academic painter of scenes from ancient history, he came to London with his two daughters in 1870 after the death of his first wife. He married his English pupil, Laura Epps (1852–1909), in 1871; his daughter Anna was also his pupil and became an accomplished artist.

THOMAS ARMSTRONG (1835–1911), member of the 'Paris Gang' with Whistler, Poynter and Du Maurier. Collaborated with Leighton and Aitchison on a number of Aesthetic Movement decorative schemes.

CHARLES ROBERT ASHBEE (1863–1942), architect and pioneer of the Arts and Crafts Guild movement. He designed his family house in Cheyne Walk, Chelsea with interiors by his Guild of Handicraft.

B

GEORGE HENRY BOUGHTON, RA (1833–1905), historical and genre painter and owner of West House, an admired studio-house in Kensington designed by Richard Norman Shaw.

GEORGE PRICE BOYCE, RWS (1826–97), watercolour painter and friend and patron of Rossetti. Philip Webb built his studio house in Chelsea. His diaries (Surtees 1980) are a valuable source of information about the social life in Victorian artistic circles.

FORD MADOX BROWN (1821–93), friend of Rossetti and associate of the Pre-Raphaelite Brotherhood. He was involved from its foundation with William Morris's decorating firm, designing stained glass and furniture.

WILLIAM BURGES (1827–81), architect, designer, medievalist and collector, follower of A.W.N. Pugin. He met Leighton in Rome and designed candlesticks and vestments for Leighton's successful early work, *Cimabue's Madonna* (1853). He designed his own house in Melbury Road and filled it with mural decoration and painted furniture.

SIR EDWARD BURNE-JONES, ARA, 1st Bt (1833–98) met William Morris at Oxford in 1852. Follower of Rossetti and painter of romantic subjects from Arthurian legends; partner in the Morris decorating firm from its founding in 1861 to his death, designing stained glass and tapestries. In 1860 married Georgiana Macdonald (1840–1920), sister of Agnes Poynter; at her husband's request she became his biographer (*Memorials*, 1904). His son Philip, also an artist, succeeded to the baronetcy but died childless.

C

JULIA MARGARET CAMERON (née Pattle; 1815–79), one of the seven Pattle sisters, she married Charles Cameron in 1838 and took up photography in 1863, pioneering art photography and portraying many of her friends from the Little Holland House circle and the wider literary and artistic world. One of her sisters was Sara Prinsep, an important member of London's artistic circle in the 1860s.

JOSEPH COMYNS CARR (1849–1916), writer, art-critic and Deputy Director of the Grosvenor Gallery, he went on to found the New Gallery with his fellow director Charles Hallé. He married Alice Strettell, a theatrical costumier who designed for Ellen Terry, in 1873. His sister Kate was a painter and his brother Jonathan developed the artistic garden-suburb at Bedford Park. His memoirs provide many first-hand anecdotes of the late Victorian art world (Comyns Carr 1908 and 1914).

SIR HENRY COLE (1808–82), founding Secretary of the Department of Practical Art responsible for the Government Schools of Design, first Director of the

Museum of Manufactures (the South Kensington Museum, now the V&A). (See Bonython and Burton 2003.)

REVD MONCURE DANIEL CONWAY (1832–1907), American ethical preacher and anti-slavery campaigner, he became a writer on art and design and champion of the Pre-Raphaelites. His collected periodical writings, published as *Travels in South Kensington* (1884), give a detailed account of artistic architecture and design.

CLARENCE COOK (1828–1900), American art-critic and writer on furniture and decoration. His series of articles for *Scribner's Monthly* were collected in a volume called *The House Beautiful: Essays on Beds and Tables, Stools and Candlesticks* (1878) which went into several editions and rivalled Eastlake's *Hints on Household Taste* in popularity.

WALTER CRANE, RWS (1845–1915), leading Aesthetic Movement illustrator, interior decorator and designer of textiles, wallpapers, ceramics. Influenced by Burne-Jones for his painting and collaborated with Morris on the decorations for George Howard's house at Palace Green, 1 Holland Park for Alecco Ionides, and with Aitchison on Leighton's Arab Hall. Lectures by his sister Lucy on *Art and the Formation of Taste* were published in 1882.

D

WILLIAM FREND DE MORGAN (1839–1917), painter, potter and designer of stained glass, and associate of William Morris. In 1897 he married the painter Evelyn Pickering (1855–1919), niece of Watts's assistant J.R. Spencer Stanhope. He developed his peacock-blue tiles for Leighton's Arab Hall, incurring a substantial financial loss in the process.

CHRISTOPHER DRESSER (1834–1904), designer, writer and collector, Dresser was one of the most successful early graduates of the Schools of Design system of art education. He promoted design reform through his wallpaper, textile, metalwork and ceramic products. His Bond Street shop, the Art Furnishers' Alliance, was a pioneering attempt to retail the components of the artistic home.

GEORGE DU MAURIER (1834–96), illustrator, cartoonist and publicist of the Aesthetic Movement through his comic drawings for *Punch*. His popular novel *Trilby* (1894), featuring his friends as the 'Paris Gang' and chronicling the life of the Parisian artistic scene and the city's Latin Quarter, was dramatized and produced at the Haymarket Theatre in 1895 (Ormond 1969).

E

CHARLES LOCKE EASTLAKE (1836–1906), architect and journalist nephew of Sir Charles Lock Eastlake, the painter and Director of the National Gallery who virtually adopted him. His seminal publication for the reformed design home, *Hints on Household Taste* (1868) went into many editions and was so widely read in America that it gave birth to the 'Eastlake Style'.

SIR ROBERT EDIS (1839–1927), architect and writer, author of *Decoration and Furniture of Town Houses* (1881), with illustrations of his own aesthetically decorated rooms and many products by designers associated with the Aesthetic Movement. Friend of Godwin and Burges, with whom he visited Philip Webb's Red House in 1862. He was retained by the Duke of Westminster as architect to his Mayfair estate.

F

SIR SAMUEL LUKE FILDES, RA (1843–1927), illustrator, genre painter and successful royal portraitist, married the painter Fanny Woods, sister of Fildes's friend the painter of Venetian genre Henry Woods. His studio-house in Melbury Road was designed by Richard Norman Shaw (Fildes 1963).

MYLES BIRKET FOSTER, RWS (1825–99), watercolourist and illustrator, his Surrey house was the first domestic commission for Morris, Marshall, Faulkner & Co., with stained glass, painted tile panels and furniture from the Medieval Court at the 1862 International Exhibition in London, where the Morris firm made its debut (Reynolds 1984).

WILLIAM POWELL FRITH, RA (1819–1909), successful painter of panoramic scenes of Victorian life who satirized Aesthetic Movement artistic pretensions and dress in his painting *Private View Day at the Royal Academy* (1883). His daughter Cissie (Jane Ellen Panton) became a prolific writer on home making and decoration.

G

ERNEST GAMBART (1814–1902), picture dealer and printseller, Belgian by birth. Energetic and forceful, he brought French art to London and made the fortunes of a number of Victorian painters. He lived in St John's Wood and entertained lavishly (Maas 1975).

EDWARD WILLIAM GODWIN (1833–86), architect, designer and prolific writer on design and decoration. Friend and collaborator of Whistler, he designed the artist's White House in Chelsea. He lived with Ellen Terry after the collapse of her marriage to G.F. Watts and they had two children. Godwin's designs in the Anglo-Japanese style were marketed through the manufacturer William Watt. One of Godwin's last projects was interiors for Oscar Wilde's house in Tite Street, Chelsea.

KATE GREENAWAY, RWS (1846–1901), watercolourist and illustrator, inventor with Walter Crane of the Aesthetic children's book, embodying the nostalgic Aesthetic ideal of childhood. Like Crane's, her illustrations were widely influential on dress, house decoration and garden design. Her modest studio-house in Hampstead was designed by Richard Norman Shaw.

JOHN ATKINSON GRIMSHAW (1836–93), born in Leeds, son of a policeman, Grimshaw was entirely self-taught. Inspired by the success of Tissot's society pictures, he painted a series of interiors and garden scenes in the Aesthetic taste featuring his own houses in Leeds and Scarborough. In the 1880s he rented a studio in Chelsea.

H

MARY ELIZA HAWEIS (née Joy; 1848–98), writer on dress and interior decoration, and daughter of the painter Thomas Joy, assistant to W.P. Frith on his popular crowd scenes. She married the Revd H.W. Haweis, charismatic preacher and music historian. Her publications on dress and house decoration grew from her journalism which she took up from financial necessity. Her book *Beautiful Houses* gives detailed descriptions of a number of the most influential artistic scenarios of the 1870s and 1880s. After Rossetti's death she took his Cheyne Walk house in 1884 and presided over Aesthetic soirées for the artistic and literary *beau monde*.

SIR HUBERT VON HERKOMER, RA, RWS, CVO (1849–1914) studied under Luke Fildes and was influenced by Frederick Walker, and became a successful painter of social genre and portraits. His house at Bushey, Hertfordshire, was the only English architectural commission by the American Henry H. Richardson; it was filled with elaborate wood-carvings by Herkomer's father and brother. He established an art school as an adjunct to the house.

JOHN CALLCOTT HORSLEY, RA (1817–1903), ruralist and painter of historical genre and an early patron of Richard Norman Shaw, who made alterations to his house at Cranbrook in Kent.

GEORGE HOWARD (became 9th Earl of Carlisle in 1889), HRWS (1843–1911). Amateur landscape painter and watercolourist and friend of Leighton. Grosvenor Gallery exhibitor and owner of a grand studio-house at 1 Palace Green designed by Philip Webb and decorated by Morris and Burne-Jones (Surtees 1988).

WILLIAM HOLMAN HUNT, OM, ARSA, RWS (1827–1910), founding member of the Pre-Raphaelite Brotherhood and Grosvenor Gallery exhibitor. He visited the Holy Land in search of authentic backgrounds for his religious works. Collector of Old Master paintings and curiosities. Married Fanny Waugh in 1865 (died 1866) and after her death married her younger sister Edith illegally in Switzerland, resulting in their social ostracism.

I

ALEXANDER CONSTANTINE IONIDES (1810–90), Aesthetic Movement collector and patron of G.F. Watts, who painted the Ionides family over five generations. Married Euterpe (née Sgouta; 1816–92). The Ionides family belonged to the close-knit wealthy banking and trading community of Phanariot Greeks in London. Their businesses were in Finsbury Circus and their marriages were largely within the group, although a cousin, Helen Ionides married J. McNeill Whistler's brother William. Whistler was a favoured friend and admired artist within the group.

CONSTANTINE ALEXANDER IONIDES (1833–1900), son of Alexander Constantine and Euterpe, collector of Old Masters and modern French art and patron of Rossetti and Burne-Jones. He bequeathed his collection to the South Kensington Museum. His children were Aglaia Coronio (1834–1906), embroiderer,

bookbinder and confidante of William Morris and friend of Burne-Jones; Luke (1837–1924), who met Whistler in Paris and married Elfrida Bird in 1879; Alecco (Alexander: 1840–98), patron of Thomas Jeckyll and Morris & Co.; and Chariclea (1844–1923), a musician who married Edward Dannreuther, pianist and admirer of Wagner.

J

THOMAS JECKYLL (1827–81), architect and designer, and brilliant exponent of the Anglo-Japanese style in metalwork. Designed a billiard room for Constantine Alexander Ionides at 1 Holland Park in 1870 and a dining room for F.R. Leyland at 49 Prince's Gate. This room was altered by Whistler and became the notorious 'Peacock Room', high profile Aesthetic statement and work of art. This desecration, as he saw, it hastened Jeckyll's final illness.

LOUISE JOPLING, RBA (1843–1933), portrait painter, married secondly in 1874 Joseph Jopling a fellow artist. They had a studio in Chelsea designed by Burges. She was a friend of Whistler and Millais painted her portrait (NPG). Her reminiscences are full of gossip about the artistic circles of her time.

L

SIR EDWIN LANDSEER, RA (1802–73), sporting and animal painter and royal portraitist. Landseer moved to rural St John's Wood, starting the flourishing artists' colony that developed there in the second half of the nineteenth century.

LILLIE LANGTRY (Emilie Charlotte, née Le Breton; 1853–1929), actress and famous beauty, who was competed for as a model by Watts, Millais and Poynter when she first arrived in London. She was a friend of Oscar Wilde.

SIR FREDERIC LEIGHTON, RA, PRA, 1st Bt (1830–96), supremely accomplished painter, sculptor and draughtsman; Leighton was one of the most prominent figures in the Victorian art world. He was elevated to the peerage as Baron Leighton of Stretton in 1896. His house in Holland Park Road (begun 1864), one of the early examples of the purpose-built studio, is now a museum to the artist and his work.

GEORGE DUNLOP LESLIE, RA (1835–1921), painter of 'Regency' genre interior scenes based on his homes in St John's Wood and Wallingford on the Thames. Member of the St John's Wood Clique with, among

others, decorative painter H. Stacy Marks, historical genre painter G.A. Storey and art photographer D. Wynfield, all contributors to aspects of the Aesthetic style.

ARTHUR LEWIS (1824–1901), a wealthy haberdasher who derived his substantial fortune from the family firm of Lewis & Allenby, silk mercers by appointment to Queen Victoria. He lived from 1862 at Moray Lodge in Kensington, which he turned into an artistic and theatrical rendezvous. He married the actress Kate Terry, sister of Ellen. The entertainments at Moray Lodge provided a link between the art world and W.S. Gilbert and Arthur Sullivan, whose comic operetta *Patience* satirized artistic circles.

JOHN FREDERICK LEWIS, RA, RWS (1805–76), artist-traveller whose watercolours based on his residency in Cairo inspired the exotic decoration of many studios and smoking rooms. On his return from the Near East he lived in St John's Wood.

FREDERICK RICHARDS LEYLAND (1831–92), millionaire business tycoon and owner of the Leyland Steamship Line. Collector and patron of Rossetti, Whistler and Burne-Jones, he was the owner of the famous 'Peacock Room' painted by Whistler in his artistic mansion at 49 Princes Gate. His daughter Florence married Val Prinsep (q.v.).

ARTHUR LASENBY LIBERTY (1843–1917), friend and protégé of Arthur Lewis and founder in 1876 of Liberty's, Oriental Warehouse and emporium for art fabrics, furniture, metalwork and dress, in Regent Street.

SIR COUTTS LINDSAY, Bt, RI (1824–1913), painter and decorative artist and founder of the Grosvenor Gallery in New Bond Street, 1877. He married Blanche Fitzroy (1844–1912), also a painter; she was a member of the wealthy Rothschild family and an active partner in the Grosvenor Gallery enterprise, using her considerable social skills to make it a success (Surtees 1993).

M

CHARLES RENNIE MACKINTOSH (1868–1928), architect, designer and painter, he designed the Glasgow School of Art in 1897. His Glasgow flat and subsequent commissions for decoration moved the Aesthetic concept of living space as a total work of art into full-blown Art Nouveau on the Continental model.

SIR JOHN EVERETT MILLAIS, RA, PRA, 1st Bt (1829–96), an artistic prodigy who at the height of his success was the highest-earning artist of the Victorian period. A founding member of the Pre-Raphaelite Brotherhood, his later career was based on genre, history painting and storytelling subjects as well as his lucrative portrait practice. He married Euphemia (Effie) Gray, formerly the wife of John Ruskin, and built a magnificent studio-house at 2 Palace Gate in Kensington.

ALBERT JOSEPH MOORE, ARWS (1841–93), painter and decorative artist, his classically inspired subjects include artistic textiles and ceramics of the kind collected by artists. His most Aesthetic work, *Pomegranates* (pl.46), shows his taste as a designer and decorator, although he never made his studio anything other than a working environment.

WILLIAM MORRIS (1834–96), designer of stained glass, wallpapers and textiles, embroideries, furniture and carpets and proprietor of 'the Firm', Morris, Marshall, Faulkner & Company, founded in 1861. His Red House at Bexleyheath in Kent, designed by his partner Philip Webb, was the prototype 'Palace of Art' and an important influence on artistic domestic building style. His other artist-partners in the Morris firm were Rossetti, Ford Madox Brown and Burne-Jones.

P

JANE ELLEN PANTON (née Frith; 1848–1923), daughter of the painter W.P. Frith and writer of household instruction manuals on house management and decoration. On her marriage to a Dorset brewer, James Albert Panton, she moved to the country and from financial necessity contributed an advice column to the *Ladies Pictorial*, which developed into her first book, *From Kitchen to Garret* (1887).

SIR EDWARD POYNTER, PRA, 1st Bt (1836–1919), member of Du Maurier's 'Paris Gang' (he is Lorimer in *Trilby*), married Agnes Macdonald (1843–1906), sister of Georgiana Burne-Jones, Alice Kipling (mother of Rudyard) and Louisa Baldwin (mother of Stanley, future Prime Minister).

SARA PRINSEP (née Pattle; 1816–87), like Julia Margaret Cameron and Virginia, Countess Somers, was one of the seven Pattle sisters, renowned for their beauty and unusual social and artistic talents. She married in 1835 (Henry) Thoby Prinsep (1792–1878). It was through Virginia that Sara met G.F. Watts, the presiding genius of the social circle centred on the Prinseps' home, Little Holland House, which included most of the literary and artistic luminaries of the day (Dakers 1999).

VALENTINE CAMERON PRINSEP, ARA (1836–1904), son of Thoby Prinsep and Sara Pattle, was a member of the 'Paris Gang' with Whistler, Poynter and Du Maurier (he is Taffy in Du Maurier's *Trilby*). He was a close friend and next-door neighbour of Leighton. His studio-house, one of the earliest, was designed by Philip Webb and influenced George and Rosalind Howard in their choice of architect and style. Through his marriage in 1884 to Florence, daughter of Frederick Leyland, Liverpool collector and shipping magnate, patron of Whistler and owner of the 'Peacock Room', Prinsep became a wealthy man.

R

WALFORD GRAHAM ROBERTSON, RP, RBA, ROI (1867–1948), portrait painter and follower of Whistler and Albert Moore, with whom he studied as a young man. His memoir, *Time Was* (1931), contains anecdotes of Moore's life and art and his studio life.

DANTE GABRIEL ROSSETTI (1828–82), painter and designer of stained glass, was a founding member of the Pre-Raphaelite Brotherhood and partner in Morris, Marshall, Faulkner & Co. After the demise of the Brotherhood, in 1857 Rossetti brought together a band of younger artists, who would become associated with the Aesthetic Movement, in his scheme for the mural decoration of the Oxford Union Society Debating Hall. Among them were Morris, Burne-Jones, Val Prinsep and Spencer Stanhope. Rossetti's late Venetian-style paintings were Aesthetic statements without moral or narrative intentions. He parted from the Morris firm acrimoniously in 1876. His seventeenth-century house on the riverside in Chelsea was the centre of a Bohemian artistic coterie, including his neighbour, Whistler (q.v.).

JOHN RUSKIN (1819–1900), famous Victorian writer, was the most widely read critic of the age; his influence is a recurring thread in the development of artistic taste in architecture and decoration (Hilton 1985). He was the first husband of Effie Millais (née Gray); their marriage was dissolved.

S

EDWARD LINLEY SAMBOURNE (1844–1910), Punch cartoonist responsible for a series of caricatures ridiculing the vagaries of fashion, including the cult of 'artistic' dress. His house in Kensington, with top-floor studio, survives as a museum, with furniture and decoration intact. The diaries of his wife, Marion (Nicholson 1988), are an important source for the social life of the Kensington artistic circle, including Leighton, Fildes and Marcus Stone.

MACKAY HUGH BAILLIE SCOTT (1865–1945), architect and designer, was involved with the late experiment in artistic design for the Grand Duke of Hesse in the Grand Ducal palace at Darmsdadt (1898). By this time eclectic, free-form artistic decorating taste had evolved into a more highly controlled statement of the Art Nouveau style.

JOHN POLLARD SEDDON (1827–1909), architect, was a member of the long-established Seddon dynasty of furniture-makers and designers. He was associated with William Morris and William Burges in the Mediaeval Court at the 1862 London International Exhibition; his brother Thomas, a landscape painter, was a friend of artists in the Pre-Raphaelite circle. J.P. Seddon designed a small group of studio-houses in Chelsea.

RICHARD NORMAN SHAW, RA (1831–1912), architect and designer of furniture, cast-iron, stained glass and embroideries. Successor to Philip Webb in G.E. Street's office, he was a pioneer of the 'Old English' or Queen Anne style for domestic building and architect of choice for a number of painters. He designed the London houses of Marcus Stone, Luke Fildes, Frank Holl, Edwin Long and Kate Greenaway, as well as his own in Hampstead, and a number of the artistic residences in Bedford Park. His later career took him from artistic circles into public building and urban development.

MARIE SPARTALI (1844–1927), artist daughter of Michael Spartali, Greek Consul-General in London, was related to the Ionides family. She was a serious painter and a pupil of Ford Madox Brown, determined to rise above the amateur status to which many women were condemned. She exhibited at the Grosvenor Gallery and modelled for Rossetti, Burne-Jones, Prinsep and Julia Margaret Cameron. She married American journalist William Stillman. Along with her cousins Marie Zambaco and Aglaia Coronio, she was known as one of the 'Three Graces' so admired in artistic circles (Elliot 2006).

JOHN RODDAM SPENCER STANHOPE (1829–1908), painter protégé of G.F. Watts, Spencer Stanhope was one of the artists associated with the decoration of the Oxford Union Debating Hall in 1857. His country house was an early work by Philip Webb

MARCUS STONE, RA (1840–1901), illustrator and painter of nostalgic Regency genre and portraits, his purpose-built studio-house in Melbury Road was designed by Richard Norman Shaw. The house and garden formed the backdrop to sentimental scenes of courtship in Regency costume.

GEORGE EDMUND STREET (1824–81), architect whose practice, first in Oxford and then in London, nurtured an important generation of artistic architects, including Philip Webb and Richard Norman Shaw. His Reformed Gothic red-brick domestic architecture was significant in pointing the way for the Queen Anne style preferred by so many artist and Aesthete patrons.

JAMES RANNIE SWINTON (1816–88), Scottish-born portrait painter with a successful career painting fashionable beauties. He commissioned one of the earliest London purpose-built studio houses having made an aristocratic marriage.

T

BRUCE JAMES TALBERT (1838–81), architect and prolific commercial designer of artistic furniture, metalwork, ceramics, textiles and wallpapers, was popular with Aesthetic decorators. His three publications, *Gothic Forms Applied to Furniture, Metal Work and Decoration for Domestic Purposes* (1868), *Examples of Ancient & Modern Furniture, Metal Work,*

Tapestries, Decorations, &c. (1876) and the posthumously published *Fashionable Furniture* (1881), gave his ideas wide currency.

DAME ELLEN ALICE TERRY (1847–1928), actress, married G.F. Watts at St Barnabas Church, Kensington, when she was still a week short of her 17th birthday. After less than a year she returned to her family. Her relationship with E.W. Godwin produced two children and lasted until 1874, when she returned to the stage and to a distinguished partnership with Henry Irving at the Lyceum Theatre. She retained her artistic friendships, and her taste in house decoration and furniture was permanently set by her association with Godwin. Her sister Kate, also an actress, married the wealthy draper Arthur Lewis (q.v.).

JAMES-JACQUES-JOSEPH TISSOT (1836–1902), Parisian painter of modern life subjects, many of which were set in the garden of his villa in St John's Wood. After the death of his mistress he returned to Paris, which became the backdrop for his scenes of fashionable life.

V

CHARLES FRANCIS ANNESLEY VOYSEY (1857–1941), architect and designer, was articled to J.P. Seddon and was involved in the initial stages of the development of Bedford Park.

W

FREDERICK WALKER (1840–75), landscape watercolourist and historical painter, used his technical mastery of watercolour to paint scenes of Pre-Raphaelite detail and intensity. He was a member of the St John's Wood Clique and used his London garden in Bayswater as a backdrop; he also painted on the Thames round Wallingford.

GEORGE FREDERIC WATTS, OM, RA (1817–1904), one of the Victorian great masters, was called without irony 'England's Michelangelo'. He was the pivotal figure in the artistic circle round Holland House in Kensington and lived for more than twenty years with the Prinseps at Little Holland House. He married, in 1864, the young Ellen Terry, and secondly in 1886, Mary Seton Fraser Tytler (1849–1938), artist and ceramicist, who became his biographer. His purpose-built studio was in the artists' colony that developed in Melbury Road and

also housed Burges, Marcus Stone, Luke Fildes and the Thornycroft family of sculptors.

PHILIP WEBB (1831–1915), architect and designer, met William Morris in G.E. Street's Oxford architectural practice. Their association was lifelong, with Webb designing furniture, metalwork, glass and textiles for the Morris decorating firm. Webb designed Morris's pioneering Red House, a 'Palace of Art' that inspired many artists' studio-houses, and was also responsible for the London houses for Val Prinsep, George and Rosalind Howard and G.P. Boyce. He devised the decorative scheme for the Green Dining Room at the South Kensington Museum, precursor of many artistic schemes.

JAMES ABBOTT MCNEILL WHISTLER (1834–1903), American-born artist widely credited with stimulating the early interest in Japanese art among his artist friends, he was responsible for the 'Peacock Room' in F.R. Leyland's London house. His Chelsea house was designed by E.W. Godwin and they collaborated on a striking decorative scheme for the 1878 Paris International exhibition. His entertaining was a notable feature of artistic social life.

Z

MARIE ZAMBACO (1843–1914), model and sculptor cousin of the Ionides family; conducted a very public affair with Burne-Jones in 1866, resulting in his attempted suicide. Family tradition has it that Burne-Jones included portraits of the Greek 'Three Graces', Marie Zambaco, Marie Spartali and Aglaia Coronio in *The Mill*, his large painting for Constantine Alexander Ionides (see pl.111).

Notes

Chapter One

PRINCES OF BOHEMIA

1 Quoted in Brennan 1987, p.108.
2 For the history of the building, see *Survey of London* 1975, p.44; for a detailed description of the architecture and interior, see Musson 2001, pp.95–118.
3 *Furniture Gazette*, vol.5 (1876), p.76.
4 William Ewart's involvement with the South Kensington Museum is discussed in Burton 1999, pp.16ff.
5 The full title of the of the exhibition was 'The Great Exhibition of the Works of Industry of all Nations, 1851', and it was immediately identified with the building that housed it, the 'Crystal Palace', a popular and permanent pseudonym for a great ground-breaking architectural innovation.
6 Burton 1999, p.109.
7 See Morris 1986.
8 Ruskin 1851.
9 Hilton 2000, p. 465.
10 Dearden 1967, p. 132.
11 The stages of building Leighton House are detailed in Robbins and Suleman 2005.
12 Quoted in Gaunt 1975d, p.233.
13 Walter Armstrong, *The Art Annual*, 1884–5, published by the *Art Journal* (London, 1885).
14 'Particulars, Plans and Conditions of Sale', Palace Gate, 1897; see Musson 2001, pp.102–3.
15 *The Art Annual*, 1884–5, p.30.
16 *Sir John Everett Millais, 1st Bt, in his studio*, photograph by Rupert Potter, National Portrait Gallery, London.
17 Linder 1966, p.10, entry for February 1882.
18 Langtry [1925] 1978, pp.36–7.
19 Dumas 1882.
20 The chairs were bought from Millais's posthumous sale at Christie's by Holman-Hunt; see Holman-Hunt 1984, p.206.
21 For the cultural context of the purpose-built studio-house, see Girouard 1977.
22 *Punch* (February 5, 1876), p.33.
23 Laver 1946, p.71.
24 See, for example many stories in the *Art Journal*, the *Athenaeum*, and the *Illustrated London News*. A strictly utilitarian picture of artists and their working environment is presented in Robinson 1892. *The Strand Magazine* published a series of illustrated interviews in the 1890s, including accounts of Luke Fildes and Lawrence Alma-Tadema. These publications are fully discussed in Maas 1984.
25 Reporting on artists expanded with the introduction of popular publications on artistic domestic decoration. C.L. Eastlake's *Hints on Household Taste*, first published in book form in 1868, and Mrs Haweis's *Art of Decoration* (1882) started out as articles in periodicals.
26 The book, consisting of a collection of articles written for *The Queen* (1880–1), was published in 1882.
27 See Leonée Ormond, 'The Aesthetic Movement', in Ormond 1969, pp.243–307.
28 *Punch* (14 April 1877), p.162.
29 Whistler 1890, p.241.
30 Linder 1966, p.97.
31 The memoirs came out in two publications, with much of the second being a rehash of the first. Comyns Carr 1908 and 1914.
32 Girouard 1972.
33 Quoted in Comyns Carr 1908, p.74.
34 The fictional treatment of 'The Artist Versus Society' is examined in Jeffares 1979, chap.3.
35 Hyams 1957, pp.208–9.
36 For *Trilby* and the identification of the characters, see Ormond 1969, pp.431–62. Du Maurier had to give up his successful career as a *Punch* cartoonist when his sight failed.
37 Two of them play important roles in this study: Lawrence Alma-Tadema and James-Jacques-Joseph Tissot.
38 Tissot is an example of a Parisian succeeding in London, in spite of the ambivalence of the London critics.
39 Quoted in Gunn 1964, p.88.
40 See Simon 1996; Campbell 1999, pp.267–93.
41 Disraeli 1870, vol.3, pp.122–3.
42 See Baldwin 1960, p.178. Poynter's baronetcy was awarded in 1902.
43 There are several publications dealing with this family saga: see Baldwin 1960; Taylor 1987; Flanders 2001; the latter is the most detailed.
44 See Codell 2003. The bibliography of primary sources gives an idea of artists' biographical coverage in the period under discussion.
45 Franklin Gould 2004.
46 Wentworth 1984.
47 Fitzgerald 1975; see also Cassavetti 1989.
48 Dimbleby 2004.
49 Burne-Jones 1906, vol.1, p.111; see also Williams 1996, pp.1–12.
50 Holman-Hunt 1969.

51 Fredeman 2002–, vol.2, p.290, note 1.

52 A comment by Ruskin in his criticism of the work for *The Times*: Cook and Wedderburn 1903–12, vol.12, pp.333–5.

53 'The Grosvenor Gallery (Second Notice)', *Daily Telegraph* (10 May 1879), p.3.

54 The position of Victorian painters is investigated in detail in Gillett 1990.

55 *The Spectator* (23 November 1872), pp.1454–6, 1486–7.

56 Henry James, 'The Picture Season in London', *Galaxy* (August, 1877), quoted in Sweeney 1956, p.136.

57 Henry James 1877 in Sweeney 1956, p.137.

58 Smalley 1890, vol.2.

59 Du Maurier 1951, p.33, quoted in Hacking 2000, p.21.

60 Warwick 1929, p.80.

61 St Helier 1909.

62 Arnold 1869.

63 See Sachko MacLeod 1996.

64 See Bailey 1996; Leonée Ormond 1994.

65 For an account of the revolution in technique and the place of the watercolour societies in the Victorian art world, see Wilcox 1992, pp.41–52.

66 *Court Suburb Magazine* (1868), quoted in *Survey of London* 1986.

67 Clarke 1881. Also in the immediate vincinity was Richard Ansdell, animal painter; E.W. Cooke, marine painter; John Bell, sculptor; and Alfred Elmore, genre painter. Towards the end of the century J. Comyns Carr, the critic and director of the Grosvenor Gallery, lived in this neighbourhood.

68 See Maas 1975; Surtees 1980, p.38.

69 For a description of Keene's living arrangements, see Christie's n.d., p.14.

70 Dante Gabriel Rossetti, *Lizzie Siddal at Chatham Place* (Marillier 1899, p.58).

71 Surtees 1973, p.146.

72 Surtees 1980, p.25.

73 Burne-Jones 1906, vol.1, p.129.

74 Doughty and Wahl 1965–7, vol.2, no.363, p.392.

75 Fennell 1978, p.68.

76 For a study of these collectors, see Sachko Macleod 1996.

77 For the Grosvenor Gallery project, see Surtees 1993, chaps 26 and 27.

78 See Bryant 2004, cats 54, 55.

79 Henry James 1877 in Sweeney 1956, p.139.

80 The Grosvenor's interior was described in detail for the *Illustrated London News* (5 May, 1877), p.419.

81 Jopling 1925, p.114.

82 Casteras and Denney 1996.

83 The Cosmopolitan Club came into existence earlier than the Hogarth Club. The meeting place was in Charles Street in rooms once occupied by G.F. Watts; although there were a number of artist members, the Cosmopolites were more literary and political than the Hogarth Club members.

84 For a discussion of Webb's involvement with the Hogarth Club, see Kirk 2005, pp.17–18.

85 For the Arts Club, see Denvir 1989; for the Chelsea Arts Club, see Cross 1991.

86 Du Maurier [1937] 2004, p.216.

87 Stephens 1884: see Maas 1984.

88 Jopling 1925, p.228.

89 Jopling 1925, p.71.

90 Doughty and Wahl 1965–7, vol.2, p.425.

91 Surtees 1981 and 1980.

92 See Hacking 2000.

93 Baring 1922, p.55.

94 The party was in February 1878, at Townshend House; see Collier 1946, p.31.

95 For a full description of the commission, see Kisluk-Grosheide 1994, pp.151–81.

96 Comyns Carr 1914, p.28.

97 The cartoon featured in *Punch*, vol. 77 (November 1879), p.198.

98 For the connections between the Sassoons and the Thornycrofts, see Moorcroft Wilson 1998, pp.7–27.

99 Stevenson 1889, chap.7, p.71. The studio described by Stevenson was based on the Chelsea house of a wood-carver, John Turner, who lived in Radnor Street and let rooms to Fanny Osbourne (Stevenson's wife-to-be) and her children in the summer of 1878.

100 Hind 1896.

Chapter Two

THE VICTORIAN ARTIST'S HOUSE

1 Quoted from a letter written by Edward Burne-Jones to Frances Graham, daughter of his most valuable patron, William Graham. Frances married Sir John Horner in 1883. See Horner 1933, pp.127–8.

2 See Jeffares 1979.

3 Baldry 1904, p.102.

4 Quoted in Fleming 1998, p.249. Holman Hunt's letter is in the Huntington Library.

5 Morris 1986.

6 Morris 1986, pp.94–106.

7 See Ormond 1975.

8 See Haweis 1881, pp.55, 368–9.

9 Panton 1890, p.12.

10 Social implications and connections are explored in Dakers 1999. The studio-houses on the Holland estate, particularly Leighton's, are examined in detail in Lamb 1987. Individual case studies are noted under the discussion of the particular house.

11 This is particularly well demonstrated in McLeod 1996.

12 The successive works on the interior of 49 Prince's Gate are described in the *Survey of London*, vol.45: *Knightsbridge* (London, 2000), pp.198–204.

13 *Punch* (26 August 1876).

14 *The Daily News* (11 April 1881), p.3.

15 *Funny Folks* (13 April 1881), p.123. I would like to thank my colleague and Dresser scholar David A. Taylor for this reference.

16 The importance of the Art Movement to aspirational middle-class sense of identity is examined in Girouard 1977.

17 Dresser 1873, p.85.

18 Cook 1878, p.61.

19 The chance discovery by David A. Taylor of a lampoon entitled *The Dadocracy*, in the *Washington Post* for 1881, led to the emergence of this rich vein of satire; see Taylor 2005, pp.112–17. The examples of dado-mockery cited here I owe to him.

20 Opening paragraph of a review published in *Bell's Life in London and Sporting Chronicle* (5 February 1881), p.5. Messrs Bancroft and Hare were managers of the Prince of Wales Theatre. I would like to thank David A. Taylor for bringing this interesting contemporary view of artistic taste to my attention.

21 *The Observer* (6 February 1881), supplement, p.1.

22 From a letter in the Yale University Library, quoted in Ormond 1969, pp.278–9.

23 Godwin 1881b, p. 379

24 *Punch* on 21 November 1881.

25 Martin 1889, pp.17–18. The book was illustrated by Joseph Pennell, friend and first biographer of Whistler.

26 Thoron 1936, p.148.

27 Hitchcock 1958, p.211.

28 Quoted in Physick and Darby 1973, p.61.

29 Muthesius 1979 edn, p.164.

30 Muthesius 1979 edn.

31 Pevsner 1936.

32 Robertson 1931, p.57.

33 Robertson 1931, p.58.

34 For an account of their collaboration see Robbins and Suleman 2005.

35 Conway 1882, p.220.

36 Bendix 1995.

37 See *Country Life* (30 August 1973).

38 For a description of the house, see *Country Life* (30 August 1973).

39 Wilson 1998, pp. 30–51.

40 Sassoon 1938.

41 Dunn 1984, pp.26–7.

42 Meynell 1882, pp.184–8.

43 Haweis 1881, p.3.

44 Mary Eliza Haweis's book on interior decoration promoted the idea of furnishing with a mixture of old and new. She was the daughter of Thomas Joy, a minor painter of modern genre who assisted William Powell Frith with his vast – and hugely popular – crowd scenes. Frith's own daughter Cissie wrote decorating advice under her married name of Mrs Panton.

45 *The Studio* (1894–5), p.76.

46 See Banham 1989.

47 Crane 1907, p.156.

48 *Tailor and Cutter Magazine* (18 November 1897).

49 Millais 1899, vol.2, p.354.

50 The series was so popular that Nash continued to repeat his scenes in watercolour well into the 1870s.

51 MacCarthy 2003, p.125.

52 MacCarthy 2003, p.186.

53 Marsh 1999, p.333.

54 Robbins and Suleman 2005, p.67.

55 Nicholson 1988, pp.65–8.

56 Fitzgerald 1975, p.223.

57 Cherry 1993, p.98.

58 For a detailed analysis see Cherry 1993.

59 Burne-Jones 1904, vol.1, p.230.

60 Burne-Jones 1904, vol.1, p.218.

61 Burne-Jones 1904, vol.1, pp.235–6.

62 For useful account of artistic dress see Newton 1974. For an exhibition dealing with the same topic, see Bennington and Wilson 1996.

63 Bryson and Troxell 1976, pp.3–4.

64 The jewellery given to Jane by Rossetti is now in the V&A, including the chain, and a Burmese bracelet similar to the one worn here.

65 To his sister, Alice, 10 March 1869, in Lubbock 1920, p.17.

66 Thoron 1936, p.130.

67 Frith 1888, pp.432–3.

68 Taylor 1924, p.217.

69 Ritchie 1919, p.3.

70 Panton 1908, pp.9–10.

71 Jonathan Carr was the elder brother of Grosvenor Gallery director Joseph Comyns Carr. For Bedford Park, see Bolsterli 1977.

72 Conway 1882, p.218.

73 Conway 1882, p.223.

74 For Grimshaw's life and work, see Robertson 1996.

75 Marks 1896, p.178. J.G. Marks, brother of Henry Stacy Marks, was Walker's brother-in-law.

76 See Knight 1986, p.136.

77 Muthesius believed that in Baillie Scott's work 'all the coolness and naked rationality which distinguishes the Anglo-Saxon south seems to have vanished. We seem already to have stepped into the world of fantasy and romance of the ancient bardic poetry …'. He regarded Baillie Scott as having 'discovered an entirely personal means of expression'. Muthesius 1904, p.47.

78 Haigh 2004.

79 From an article entitled 'Artistic Houses' by J.S. Gibson, FRIBA, *The Studio* (September 1893).

80 The interior of The Magpie and Stump is analyzed in detail in Crawford 1985, pp.297–306.

81 Anon. 1895, pp.66–74; *Kunst und Kunsthandwerk* (Vienna, 1901), vol.4, p.464; *Moderne Bauformen* (Stuttgart), vol.2, p.75.

Chapter Three

AMATEURS AND AESTHETES

1 Longford 1991, p.14.

2 Storey 1929, p.64.

3 Trethewey 2002.

4 Frith 1888, p.174.

5 See Gillett 1990, pp.18ff.

6 See Roberts 1987, pp.146–62.

7 The catalogue of the Victorian watercolours in the Royal Collection (Millar 1995) is particularly illuminating on this topic.

8 This was suggested by Dakers 1999, p.135; for a life of Kate, see Hawkesley 2006.

9 Stirling 1924, p.105. Spencer Stanhope was an asthmatic and London did not suit him. He eventually lived in Florence.

10 Myers 1883, p.213.

11 See Merrill 1998.

12 Surtees 1988, pp.50ff.

13 *The Studio*, vol.15 (October, 1898), p.3.

14 Bailey 1927, vol.1, p.289.

15 Escott 1886, p.165.

16 Their network of aristocratic social life and artistic patronage is fully explored in Abdy and Gere 1984; Dakers 1993.

17 For an account of the Lehmann-Benzon circle, see Dakers 1999, pp.133–7.

18 For the collecting activities of Mr and Mrs Eustace Smith, see Wilcox 1993, pp.43–57.

19 Conway 1882, pp. 163–4.

20 The two letters referring specifically to the frieze are nos 12640 and 12612A in the Leighton archive.

21 Juxon 1983.

22 The letters were bequeathed to the British Museum; see Christian 1988. For the Burne-Jones panel, see Cooper 2003, pp.165–6.

23 Girouard 1977, p.11.

24 Canziani 1939, pp.66–7.

25 Canziani 1939, p.66.

26 Canziani 1939, p.78.

27 Du Maurier 1951, p.31.

28 *The Lady's Realm*, 1905: Coleridge 1972, p.257.

28 Shonfield 1987.

30 Zusanna Schonfield, 'Miss Marshall and the Cimabue Browns', *Costume*, no.13 (1979), entry for 11 May 1883; for Jeanette's views on artistic dress, see Schonfield 1987, pp.117–21.

31 Barrington 1906, vol.2, p.25.

32 Warwick 1929, p.72.

Chapter Four

THE HOUSES AND THEIR OWNERS

1   This artistic colony is explored in detail in Dakers 1999.
2   For a recent major biography of Watts, see Gould 2004.
3   Ritchie 1919, p.3.
4   Fitzpatrick 1923, p.18. Earl Somers was the owner before F.R. Leyland of 49 Princes's Gate, eventual site of Whistler's Peacock Room.
5   Quoted in Hill 1973, p.161.
6   For a full analysis of the portrait and Virginia Dalrymple's dress, see Bills and Bryant 2008, pp.182–4.
7   Fitzpatrick 1923, pp.14–15. Lady Henry's husband, Lord Henry Somerset, was a younger son of the Duke of Beaufort.
8   Stirling 1924, p.219.
9   Little Holland House inspired him to illustrate an album, published in facsimile in 1981; see Christian 1981.
10 Burne-Jones 1904, vol.1, p.183.
11 Laver 1946, p.66.
12 Maurice B. Adams's articles for *Building News* were published under the title 'Artists' Homes' in 1883.
13 Chesterton & Sons, Kensington High Street, sale catalogue, 3 July 1919.
14 Maurice B. Adams, 'Artist's Homes, No. 8', *Building News* (29 October 1880).
15 *Building News* (30 November 1866), pp.799–800.
16 The creation of Leighton House and its collections is detailed in the guidebook to the house, Robbins and Suleman 2005.
17 This purchasing seems to be confirmed by Anne Anderson's ongoing research into matching the decorative accessories in Leighton's paintings with lots in the posthumous sale catalogue.
18 Barrington 1906, vol.2, p.218.
19 Christie, Manson and Woods, London, 16 July 1896.
20 As well as an account of the development of the house and studio, the guidebook to Leighton House Museum includes a summary of the categories in the catalogue.
21 The Dresser connection is explored in Campbell 1999, p.281. By the date of the additions to Leighton's house, Dresser had published *The Art of Decorative Design* (1862), *Principles of Decorative Design* (1873), and *Studies in Design* (1874–6), all of which could have been known to Leighton and his architect, George Aitchison.
22 Evelyn De Morgan in Stirling 1922, p.204.

23 Shannon 1933, pp.64–5.
24 Conway 1882, p.196.
25 Quoted in Redman 1952.
26 See Nicholson 1988 for a full account of the house and the family. See also Robbins et al. 2003.
27 Sambourne made drawings for his earliest employer, an engineering firm, to use on their Paris 1867 exhibition stand, and he may have had the opportunity to visit the show himself. Personal communication from Shirley Nicholson, and Nicholson 2003, p.19.
28 Haweis 1882.
29 Crane 1907.
30 The portraits of Frith, Grant, Maclise, David Roberts, Clarkson Stanfield and Faed were all sold at Christie's, 2 February 1978 (see Richard Ormond in *Christie's Review of the Season*, 1978).
31 Hardwick 1990, pp.5–7.
32 Feret 1900, vol.2, p.68.
33 Waterhouse 1981, pp.473–7.
34 Holman-Hunt 1984, pp.206–25.
35 For a detailed discussion of the artistic community in Holland Park, see Dakers 1999.
36 Holman-Hunt 1960, pp.29ff.
37 Haweis 1882, p.19.
38 Godwin 1881a, pp.213–14. Godwin's writings on artists' houses, Aestheticism and artistic dress are collected in a single volume (Kinchin and Stirton 2005).
39 The house is very fully described in Fildes 1963.
40 It is the very first house to be discussed by Hermann Muthesius in his study of *The English House* published in 1904, a Continental view of all that was singular in English domestic buildings from 1860.
41 For a definitive modern biography, see MacCarthy 1994.
42 Plans were made by Webb and a tender was drawn up for additions to the house to accommodate the Burne-Joneses in 1864.
43 Doughty and Wahl 1965–7, vol.2, p.436.
44 Doughty and Wahl 1965–7, vol.1, no.254, p.312.
45 Kirk 2005, p.24.
46 Minto 1902, vol.2, p.61.
47 Burne-Jones 1904, vol.1; the Red House days are recalled on pp.208ff.
48 Mackail 1899, vol.1, p.143.
49 Kelvin 1987, vol.2, p.227.
50 For the details of the founding and organization of Morris & Co., see Harvey and Press 1991.
51 For the prospectus in full,

see Harvey and Press 1991, p.42.
52 This passage from Mackail's biography of Morris was quoted in the Morris and Company catalogues for many years. In fact it was the firm's adjustable-back reclining chair designed by Webb that was actually based on a traditional Sussex chair made by a carpenter in Herstmonceaux.
53 Conway 1882, p.150.
54 Crane 1911.
55 Quoted in Covert 2000, p.21.
56 Mackail 1899, vol.1, p.162.
57 Doughty and Wahl 1965–7, vol.3, no.1137, p.957.
58 The auctioneer's catalogue to the sale of contents afer Rossetti's death reveals many items of figured green velvet (T.G. Wharton, Martin & Co., Auctioneer, 5–7 July 1882, at 16 Cheyne Walk, Chelsea).
59 From a typescript in the author's possession.
60 Mackail 1899, vol.1, p.371.
61 Morris 1882, pp.107–10.
62 Mackail 1899, vol.1, p.372.
63 Hall-Caine 1882, pp.47–8.
64 Macleod 1996.
65 The sale catalogue of the contents of Rossetti's house after his death is a poignant mixture of his old paintings and curiosities among lengths of drugget and iron bedsteads.
66 Bendix 1995, pp.194, 195, figs.70, 71.
67 Weinberg 2004.
68 Herbert Horne, *Botticelli: Painter of Florence* (London, 1908), p. xvii, quoted in Weinberg 2004, p.20.
69 For a description of Rossetti's animals and their various fates, see Marsh 1999, pp.267–8.
70 Hall-Caine 1882, pp. 46–7.
71 Hall-Caine 1882, p.47.
72 Doughty and Wahl 1965–7, vol.2, p.599.
73 Hall-Caine 1882, p.47.
74 Marillier 1899, pp.121–2.
75 Comyns Carr 1914, p.47.
76 Rogers 1993, no.69, p.134.
77 Dunn 1984, p.14.
78 Rossetti made a number of versions of the *Pandora*, including an oil in 1871. The first chalk drawing of 1869 belonged to T. Eustace Smith, patron of Leighton and Thomas Armstrong, whose wife created an artistic salon in their house in Prince's Gate. The Eustace Smiths were near neighbours of Frederick Leyland, Whistler's patron, in whose house Whistler created the notorious Peacock Room.

79 'Sale of house contents on the premises', Debenham, Tewson, Farmer & Bridgewater, 18 June 1877.

80 See Kirk 2005, p.76.

81 Glasgow University Library, w.516; quoted in Anderson and Koval 1994, p.143.

82 Conway 1882, pp.183–4.

83 Pennell 1921, opp. p.152.

84 From an unpublished transcript in the Library of Congress, Washington, DC, quoted in Bendix 1995, pp.153–4.

85 Godwin 1876.

86 Soros 1999, p.226.

87 Library of Congress, Washington, DC, Pennell Collection.

88 Jopling 1925, p.71.

89 Burne-Jones 1904, vol.1, p.205.

90 Horner 1933, p.8.

91 Burne-Jones 1904, vol.2, p.3.

92 Storey 1929, p.59.

93 Robertson 1931, pp.73–4.

94 *The Paintings, Graphic and Decorative Work of Sir Edward Burne-Jones*, exh. cat., Arts Council of Great Britain (London, 1975), no.350.

95 Feret 1900, vol.2, p.296.

96 Burne-Jones 1904, vol.2, p.137.

97 Robertson 1931, p.76.

98 Eyre 1913, p. 181. See also Hillier 1964, pp.490–5.

99 Eyre 1913, p.258.

100 Dollman 1899.

101 Swanson 1990, p.162, no.134, illus. p.334.

102 Treuherz 1996.

103 Conway 1882, p.193.

104 'Mr Alma-Tadema's House', in Haweis 1882, p.25. See also Meynell 1882, pp.184–8.

105 Haweis 1882, pp.29–30.

106 The extent of the textile collection can be appreciated in the posthumous sale catalogue, Hampton & Sons, London, 9–16 June 1913.

107 Bornand 1977, p.46. This is borne out by the quantity of Japanese objects in the posthumous sale catalogue of Alma-Tadema's collection.

108 Anon. 1883, pp.33–7, 65–8.

109 Doughty and Wahl 1965–7, vol.2, pp.526–7. One of the other of the *japonisme* paintings of this date was set in the magnificent conservatory in the Paris house. The young woman is Japanese, in national dress, holding up a blue-and-white porcelain vase and a dark square vase in her other hand. She is shown surrounded by tropical plants with large fleshy leaves.

110 *The Illustrated London News*, vol.72, no.2028 (11 May 1878), p.435.

111 Brydon 1874.

112 Galinou 1989, pp.120–3.

113 *The Spectator* (31 May 1879).

114 Zimmern 1886.

115 See Kisluk-Grosheide 1994, pp.151–81.

116 Alice Meynell, *Art Journal* (1883), p.345.

117 *British Contemporary Artists*, 1899.

118 The diary entry is dated Monday 6 March 1893, see Collier 1946, p.220–1.

119 Hampton's, London, 9–16 June 1913.

120 George Dunlop Leslie, *Home Sweet Home* (1878), ex RA 1878; Sotheby's, 15 June 1982, lot 91.

121 Du Maurier's life in Hampstead and his ambivalent views about living there are fully described in Ormond 1969, chaps 6 and 9.

122 Quoted in White 1901, p.83.

123 The organization of the studio-house has been studied in detail by Louise Campbell in Campbell 2003, pp.1–22.

124 The house is described in detail and illustrated inside and out in Saint 1976, pp.176–84, pls 140–4.

125 Phipps-Jackson 1883, pp.71–5.

126 Rothenstein 1932, p.32.

127 Review in *The Speaker* (30 November 1901), quoted in Arnold 1981, pp.104–5.

AFTERWORD

1 Lago 1981, p.102.

2 'Artists' Studios: As they were and as they are', parts I and II, *Magazine of Art* (1901).

3 Whitall 1936, pp.20–1.

4 For an account of the twentieth-century Chelsea studios, see Croot 2005.

5 *The Times*, 10 April 1961, p.19.

6 When he was writing his study of the house, Jeremy Musson tried repeatedly to see inside, without success. See Musson 2001, pp.95–118.

7 See, for example, the article in *House and Garden* (December, 1994), pp.104–13.

8 *Architectural Review*, vol.III (1898), pp.151–60.

9 The situation of Watts's house and the other Melbury Road houses in discussed in detail in Dakers 1999, pp.274–7.

10 *Chelsea Post* (22 January 1965).

11 *Daily Telegraph* (7 September 1966).

Bibliography

A

JANE ABDY and CHARLOTTE GERE,
The Souls (London, 1984)

MAURICE B. ADAMS, 'Artists' Homes',
Building News, published in book form
(London, 1883)

RONALD ANDERSON and ANNE KOVAL,
James McNeill Whistler, Beyond the Myth
(London, 1994)

Anon., 'The Works of Lawrence
Alma-Tadema, RA,', *The Art Journal*,
1883, pp.33–7, 65–8

Anon., 'The new "Magpie and Stump",
a successful experiment in domestic
architecture', *The Studio*, vol. 5 (1895),
pp.66–74

WALTER ARMSTRONG, 'Sir John E Millais,
Bart., His Life and Work', *The Art Annual*
(1884–5), published by *The Art Journal*
(London, 1885)

BRUCE ARNOLD, *Orpen: Mirror to an Age*
(London, 1981)

MATTHEW ARNOLD, *Culture and Anarchy*
(London, 1869)

ELIZABETH ASLIN, *The Aesthetic Movement:
Prelude to Art Nouveau* (London, 1969)

B

JOHN BAILEY (ed.), *The Diaries of
Lady Frederick Cavendish*, 2 vols
(London, 1927)

KATE BAILEY, 'Leighton – Public and
Private Lives: Celebrity and the
gentleman artist', in *Lord Leighton and
Leighton House*, published by *Apollo*
(London, 1996)

A.L. BALDRY, *Hubert von Herkomer:
A study and a biography* (Londaon, 1904)

A.W. BALDWIN, *The Macdonald Sisters*
(London, 1960)

JOANNA BANHAM, 'Walter Crane and the
Decoration of the artistic Interior', in
*Walter Crane 1845–1915: Artist, Designer,
Socialist* (exh. cat., Whitworth Art Gallery,
University of Manchester, 1989)

MAURICE BARING, *The Puppet Show
of Memory* (London, 1922)

MRS RUSSELL BARRINGTON,
*The Life, Letters and Work of Frederic,
Baron Leighton* (London, 1906)

DEANNA MAROHN BENDIX,
*Diabolical Designs: Paintings, Interiors
and Exhibitions of James McNeill Whistler*
(Washington, DC, 1995)

JONATHAN BENNINGTON and SOPHIA
WILSON (eds), *Simply Stunning:
The Pre-Raphaelite Art of Dress*
(exh. cat., Cheltenham Art Gallery,
1996)

MARK BILLS and BARBARA BRYANT,
G.F. Watts: Victorian Visionary
(New Haven and London, 2008)

MARGARET JONES BOLSTERLI,
*The Early Community at Bedford Park:
The Pursuit of 'Corporate Happiness' in the
First Garden Suburb* (London, 1977)

ELIZABETH BONYTHON and
ANTHONY BURTON, *The Great Exhibitor:
The Life and Work of Henry Cole*
(London, 2003)

ODETTE BORNAND (ed.), *The Diary of
William Michael Rossetti 1870–1873*
(Oxford, 1977)

FLORA BRENNAN (trans.), *Puckler's Progress*
(London, 1987)

BARBARA BRYANT, *G.F. Watts Portraits:
Fame & Beauty in Victorian Society*
(exh. cat., National Portrait Gallery,
London, 2004)

J.M. BRYDON, 'Studio in the House of
James Tissot Esq.', *Building News*
(15 May 1874), pp.526–7

JOHN BRYSON and JANET CAMP TROXELL
(eds), *Dante Gabriel Rossetti and Jane
Morris: Their Correspondence* (Oxford, 1976)

GEORGIANA BURNE-JONES, *Memorials of
Edward Burne-Jones*, 2 vols (London, 1904)

ANTHONY BURTON, *Vision and Accident:
The Story of the Victoria and Albert Museum*
(London, 1999)

C

T. HALL CAINE, *Recollections of
Dante Gabriel Rossetti* (London, 1882)

LOUISE CAMPBELL, 'Decoration, Display,
Disguise: Leighton House Reconsidered',
in *Frederic Leighton: Antiquity, Renaissance,
Modernity*, eds T. Barringer and
E. Prettejohn (New Haven and London,
1999)

LOUISE CAMPBELL, 'Questions of Identity:
Women, Architecture and the Aesthetic
Movement', in *Women's Places: Architecture
and Design 1860–1960*, eds Brenda Martin
and Penny Sparke (London, 2003), pp.1–22

ESTELLA CANZIANI, *Round and About
Three Palace Green* (London, 1939)

J. COMYNS CARR, *Some Eminent Victorians:
Personal recollections in the world of art
and letters* (London, 1908)

J. COMYNS CARR, *Coasting Bohemia*
(London, 1914)

EILEEN CASSAVETTTI, 'The Fatal Meeting
and the Fruitful Passion', in *The Antique
Collector*, vol.60, no.3 (March 1989),
pp.34–45

SUSAN CASTERAS and COLLEEN DENNEY
(eds), *The Grosvenor Gallery: A Palace of
Art in Victorian England* (New Haven,
1996)

DEBORAH CHERRY, *Painting Women:
Victorian Women Artists* (London, 1993)

JOHN CHRISTIAN, *Burne-Jones* (exh. cat.,
Arts Council of Great Britain, London,
1975)

JOHN CHRISTIAN (ed.), *Little Holland House
Album* (privately printed, North Berwick,
1981)

JOHN CHRISTIAN (ed.), *Letters to Katie*
(London, 1988)

CHRISTIE'S, LONDON, *Charles Keene:
'The Artist's Artist' 1823–1891* (London,
n.d.)

W.S. CLARKE, *Suburban Homes of London*
(London, 1881)

JULIE F. CODELL, *The Victorian Artist:
Artists' Lifewritings in Britain, c.1870–1910*
(Cambridge, 2003)

DEBORAH COHEN, *Household Gods:
The British and their Possessions*
(New Haven and London, 2006)

COLERIDGE, LADY GEORGINA (intro.),
*The Lady's Realm. A Selection from the
Monthly Issues: November 1904 to April 1905*
(London, 1972)

E.F.C. COLLIER (ed.), *A Victorian Diarist:
Extracts from the Journals of Mary,
Lady Monkswell* (London, 1946)

MONCURE DANIEL CONWAY, *Travels in
South Kensington, with notes on decorative art
and architecture in England* (London, 1882)

CLARENCE COOK, *The House Beautiful:
Essays on Beds and Tables, Stools and
Candlesticks* (New York, 1878)

E.T. COOK and A. WEDDERBURN,
The Works of John Ruskin, 39 vols
(London, 1903–12)

SUZANNE FAGENCE COOPER,
*Pre-Raphaelite Art in the Victoria and
Albert Museum* (London, 2003)

JAMES COVERT, *A Victorian Marriage:
Mandell and Louise Creighton*
(London, 2000)

WALTER CRANE, *An Artist's Reminiscences*
(London, 1907)

WALTER CRANE, 'The English Revival in
Decorative Art', *William Morris to Whistler*
(London, 1911)

WAYNE CRAVEN, *Gilded Mansions,
Grand Architecture and High Society*
(New York, 2008)

ALAN CRAWFORD, *C.R. Ashbee: Architect,
Designer and Romantic Socialist*
(New Haven and London, 1985)

PATRICIA E.C. CROOT (ed.), *A History
of the County of Middlesex*, vol.12
(London, 2005)

TOM CROSS, *Artists and Bohemians:
100 years of the Chelsea Arts Club*
(London, 1991)

D

CAROLINE DAKERS, *Clouds:
Biography of a Country House*
(New Haven and London, 1993)

CAROLINE DAKERS, *The Holland Park Circle:
Artists and Victorian Society*
(New Haven and London, 1999)

GAIL S. DAVIDSON, FLORAMAE
MCCARRON CATES and CHARLOTTE
GERE, *House Proud: Nineteenth-century
Watercolor Interiors from the Thaw Collection*
(exh. cat., Cooper-Hewitt, National Design
Museum, New York, 2008)

JAMES DEARDEN (ed.), *The Professor:
Arthur Severn's Memoir of John Ruskin*
(London, 1967)

BERNARD DENVIR, *A Most Agreeable Society*
(London, 1989)

JOSCELINE DIMBLEBY, *A Profound Secret:
May Gaskell, her Daughter Amy and
Edward Burne-Jones* (New York, 2004)

BENJAMIN DISRAELI, *Lothair*
(London, 1870)

FREDERICK DOLLMAN, 'Illustrated
Interviews, LXVIII: Sir Lawrence
Alma-Tadema', *Strand Magazine*
(18 December 1899), pp.602–14

OSWALD DOUGHTY and JOHN ROBERT
WAHL (eds), *Letters of Dante Gabriel
Rossetti*, 4 vols (Oxford, 1965–7)

CHRISTOPHER DRESSER, *Principles of
Decorative Design* (London, 1873)

F.G. DUMAS (ed.), *Illustrated Biographies
of Modern Artists*, vol.1 (London, 1882)

DAPHNE DU MAURIER, *The Du Mauriers*
(London, 1937)

DAPHNE DU MAURIER, *The Young George
du Maurier: A Selection of his Letters
1860–67* (London, 1951)

H. TREFFRY DUNN, *Recollections of
Dante Gabriel Rossetti & his Circle*,
ed. Rosalie Mander (Westerham, 1984)

E

C.L. EASTLAKE, *Hints on Household Taste*
(London, 1868)

DAVID B. ELLIOT, *A Pre-Raphaelite
Marriage: The Lives and Works of Marie
Spartali Stillman and William James
Stillman* (Woodbridge, 2006)

T.H. ESCOTT, *Society in London*
(London, 1886)

A. MONTGOMERY EYRE, *St John's Wood:
Its History, Its Houses, Its Haunts and
Its Celebrities* (London, 1913)

F

FRANCIS L. FENNELL JR, *The Rossetti-
Leyland Letters: The Correspondence of an
Artist and his Patron* (Athens, OH, 1978)

CHARLES JAMES FERET, *Fulham
Old and New* (London, 1900)

L.V. FILDES, *Luke Fildes RA:
Victorian Painter* (London, 1963)

PENELOPE FITZGERALD,
Edward Burne-Jones (London, 1975)

KATHLEEN FITZPATRICK,
Lady Henry Somerset (London, 1923)

JUDITH FLANDERS, *A Circle of Sisters*
(London, 2001)

G.H. FLEMING, *John Everett Millais:
A Biography* (London, 1998)

WILLIAM E. FREDEMAN (ed.),
*The Correspondence of Dante Gabriel
Rossetti*, 10 vols (Oxford, 2002–)

WILLIAM POWELL FRITH,
My Autobiography and Reminiscences
(London, 1888)

Furniture Gazette, vol.5 (London, 1876)

G

MIREILLE GALINOU, 'Green-finger
Painting', *Country Life* (13 July 1989)

WILLIAM GAUNT, *The Pre-Raphaelite
Tragedy* (London, [1942] 1975a)

WILLIAM GAUNT, *The Aesthetic Adventure*
(London, [1945] 1975b)

WILLIAM GAUNT, *Victorian Olympus*
(London, [1952] 1975c)

WILLIAM GAUNT, *Kensington and Chelsea*
(London, 1975d)

CHARLOTTE GERE, *Nineteenth-century
Decoration: The Art of the Interior*
(London, 1989)

CHARLOTTE GERE, *An Album of
Nineteenth-century Interiors: Watercolours
from Two Private Collections*
(The Frick Collection, New York, 1992)

CHARLOTTE GERE and MICHAEL
WHITEWAY, *Nineteenth-Century Design
from Pugin to Mackintosh* (London, 1993)

CHARLOTTE GERE and LESLEY HOSKINS,
*The House Beautiful: Oscar Wilde and the
Aesthetic Interior* (London, 2000)

CHARLOTTE GERE and ALAN POWERS,
*A History of The Fine Art Society
1876–2001* (London, 2001)

PAULA GILLETT, *The Victorian Painter's
World* (Gloucester, 1990)

MARK GIROUARD, 'The Victorian Artists
at Home', part I, 'Chelsea's Bohemian
Studio Houses', *Country Life* (16 November
1972); part II, 'The Holland Park Houses',
Country Life (23 November 1972)

MARK GIROUARD, *Sweetness and Light:
The Queen Anne Movement, 1860–1900*
(Oxford, 1977)

E.W. GODWIN, 'My chambers and what
I did to them. Chapter 1: A.D. 1867',
Architect (1 July 1876), pp.4–5

E.W. GODWIN, 'William Burges ARA,
1827–1881', *The British Architect*
(29 April 1881a), pp.213–14

E.W. GODWIN, 'Theatrical Notes',
The British Architect (29 July 1881b)

VERONICA FRANKLIN GOULD, *G.F. Watts:
The Last Great Victorian* (New Haven and
London, 2004)

PETER GUNN, *Vernon Lee: Violet Paget
1856–1935* (London, 1964)

H

JULIET HACKING, *Princes of Victorian
Bohemia: Photographs by David Wilkie
Wynfield* (exh. cat., National Portrait
Gallery, London, 2000)

DIANE HAIGH, *Baillie Scott:
The Artistic House* (Chichester, 2004)

JOAN HARDWICK, *Immodest Violet:
The Life of Violet Hunt* (London, 1990)

CHARLES HARVEY and JON PRESS,
*William Morris: Design and Enterprise in
Victorian Britain* (Manchester, 1991)

MRS (MARY ELIZA) HAWEIS,
The Art of Decoration (London, 1881)

MRS (MARY ELIZA) HAWEIS,
Beautiful Houses (London, 1882)

LUCINDA HAWKESLEY, *Katey: The Life
and Loves of Dickens's Artist Daughter*
(London and New York, 2006)

BRIAN HILL, *Julia Margaret Cameron:
A Victorian Portrait* (London, 1973)

BEVIS HILLIER, 'The St John's Wood
Clique', *Apollo*, vol.79 (June 1964),
pp.490–5

TIM HILTON, *John Ruskin*, 2 vols
(London, 1985, 2000)

LEWIS HIND, 'How Famous Painters Work.
Peeps into their studios', *The Windsor
Magazine* (1896)

HENRY-RUSSELL HITCHCOCK, *Architecture:
Nineteenth and Twentieth Centuries*,
Pelican History of Art (London, 1958)

DIANA HOLMAN-HUNT, *My Grandmothers
and I* (London, 1960)

DIANA HOLMAN-HUNT, *My Grandfather,
his Wives and Loves* (London, 1969)

DIANA HOLMAN-HUNT, 'The Holman
Hunt Collection: A Personal Recollection',
in *Pre-Raphaelite Papers*, ed. Leslie Parris
(London, 1984)

FRANCES HORNER, *Time Remembered*
(London, 1933)

EDWARD HYAMS (trans. and intro.),
Taine's Notes on England (London, 1957)

J

BO JEFFARES, *The Artist in Nineteenth-
Century English Fiction* (Gerrards Cross,
1979)

LOUISE JOPLING, *Twenty Years of My Life,
1867–1887* (London, 1925)

JOHN JUXON, *Lewis and Lewis: The Life
and Times of a Victorian Solicitor*
(London, 1983)

K

N. KELVIN (ed.), *The Collected Letters of
William Morris*, vol.2 (Princeton, 1987)

JULIET KINCHIN and PAUL STIRTON,
*Is Mr Ruskin Living Too Long?
Selected Writings of E.W. Godwin on
Victorian Architecture, Design and Culture*
(Oxford, 2005)

SHEILA KIRK, *Philip Webb: Pioneer of
Arts & Crafts Architecture* (Chichester, 2005)

DANIELLE O. KISLUK-GROSHEIDE,
'The Marquand Mansion', *Metropolitan
Museum Journal*, no. 29 (1994)

V. KNIGHT, *The Works of the Corporation
of London* (London, 1986)

L

MARY LAGO (ed.), *Burne-Jones Talking*
(London, 1981)

JOSEPH F. LAMB, 'Lions in their Dens:
Lord Leighton and Late Victorian Studio
Life', unpublished dissertation, University
of California, Santa Barbara, 1987

LILLIE LANGTRY, *The Days I Knew*
(London, [1925] 1978)

JAMES LAVER, *Taste and Fashion*
(London, 1946)

LESLIE LINDER (ed.), *The Journal of
Beatrix Potter* (London, 1966)

ELIZABETH LONGFORD (ed.), *Darling Loosy:
Letters to Princess Louise 1856–1939*
(London, 1991)

PERCY LUBBOCK (ed.), *The Letters of
Henry James*, 2 vols (New York, 1920)

M

JEREMY MAAS, *Gambart: Prince of the
Victorian Art World* (London, 1975)

JEREMY MAAS, *The Victorian Art World
in Photographs* (London, 1984)

FIONA MACCARTHY, *William Morris:
A Life for Our Time* (London, 1994)

J.W. MACKAIL, *The Life of William Morris*,
2 vols (London, 1899)

DIANNE SACHKO MACLEOD, *Art and the
Victorian Middle Class: Money and the
Making of Cultural Identity*
(Cambridge, 1996)

H.C. MARILLIER, *Dante Gabriel Rossetti:
An Illustrated Memorial of His Art and Life*
(London, 1899)

JOHN GEORGE MARKS, *Life and Letters of
Frederick Walker, ARA* (London, 1896)

JAN MARSH, *Dante Gabriel Rossetti,
Painter and Poet* (London, 1999)

BENJAMIN ELLIS MARTIN, *Old Chelsea*
(London, 1889)

LINDA MERRILL, *The Peacock Room:
A Cultural Biography* (New Haven and
London, 1998)

WILFRED MEYNELL, 'Artist's Homes:
Mr Alma-Tadema's at North Gate,
Regent's Park', *Magazine of Art*, vol. 5
(1882), pp.184–8

J.G. MILLAIS, *The Life and Letters of
Sir John Everett Millais* (London, 1899)

DELIA MILLAR, *Victorian Watercolours and
Drawings in the Collection of Her Majesty
The Queen* (London, 1995)

W. MINTO (ed.), *Autobiographical Notes
of the Life of William Bell Scott*, 2 vols
(London, 1902)

BARBARA MORRIS, *Inspiration for Design:
The Influence of the Victoria and Albert
Museum* (London, 1986)

WILLIAM MORRIS, 'The Beauty of Life',
in *Hopes and Fears for Art* (London, 1882)

JEREMY MUSSON, 'Has a Paint Pot
Done All This? The Studio-House of
Sir John Everett Millais, Bt.', in *John
Everett Millais: Beyond the Pre-Raphaelite
Brotherhood*, ed. Debra N. Mancoff,
Yale Studies in British Art (New Haven
and London, 2001)

HERMANN MUTHESIUS, *Das Englishe Haus*
(1904, *The English House*), trans. Janet
Seligman (London, 1979)

FREDERICK MYERS, 'Rossetti and the
Religion of Beauty', *Cornhill Magazine*,
no. 42 (1883), p.213

N

JUDITH NEISWANDER, *The Cosmopolitan
Interior: Liberalism and the Victorian Home,
1870–1914* (New Haven and London,
2008)

STELLA MARY NEWTON, *Health, Art
and Reason: Dress Reformers of the
19th Century* (London, 1974)

SHIRLEY NICHOLSON, *A Victorian Household*
(London, 1988)

O

LEONÉE ORMOND, *George du Maurier*
(London, 1969)

LEONÉE ORMOND, 'A Leighton Memorial:
Frederic Leighton and the South London
Art Gallery', in *Art for the People: Culture
in the Slums of Late Victorian Britain*,
ed. Giles Waterfield (exh. cat.,
Dulwich Picture Gallery, London, 1994)

RICHARD ORMOND, *Leighton's Frescoes*,
Victoria and Albert Museum Brochure 6
(London, 1975)

P

MRS (JANE ELLEN) PANTON,
Homes of Taste: Economical Hints
(London, 1890)

MRS (JANE ELLEN) PANTON,
Leaves from a Life (London, 1908)

LINDA PARRY, *William Morris Textiles*
(London, 1983)

LINDA PARRY (ed.), *William Morris*
(exh. cat., Victoria and Albert Museum,
London, 1996)

ELIZABETH and JOSEPH PENNELL,
The Whistler Journal (Philadelphia, 1921)

NIKOLAUS PEVSNER, *Pioneers of the
Modern Movement from William Morris to
Walter Gropius* (London, 1936)

M. PHIPPS-JACKSON, 'Cairo in London:
Carl Haag's Studio', *Art Journal*
(March 1883), pp.71–5

JOHN PHYSICK, *The Victoria and Albert
Museum: The History of its Building*
(London, 1982)

JOHN PHYSICK and MICHAEL DARBY,
*Marble Halls: Drawings and Models for
Victorian Secular Buildings* (exh. cat.,
Victoria and Albert Museum, London,
1973)

R

ALVIN REDMAN (ed.), *The Wit and Humour
of Oscar Wilde* (New York, 1952)

JAN REYNOLDS, *Myles Birket Foster*
(London, 1984)

ANNE THACKERAY RITCHIE, *Alfred,
Lord Tennyson and his Friends*
(London, 1893)

ANNE THACKERAY RITCHIE, *From Friend
to Friend* (London, 1919)

DANIEL ROBBINS, REENA SULEMAN and
PAMELA HUNTER, *Linley Sambourne
House, 18, Stafford Terrace, Kensington*,
RBKC Libraries and Arts Service
(London, 2003)

DANIEL ROBBINS and REENA SULEMAN,
Leighton House Museum, RBKC Museums
and Arts Service (London, 2005)

JANE ROBERTS, *Royal Artists from
Mary Queen of Scots to the Present Day*
(London, 1987)

ALEXANDER ROBERTSON,
Atkinson Grimshaw (London, 1996)

WALFORD GRAHAM ROBERTSON,
Time Was (London, 1931)

RALPH W. ROBINSON, *Members and
Associates of the Royal Academy of Arts,
1891, photographed in their studios*
(London, 1892)

MALCOLM ROGERS, *Master Drawings
from the National Portrait Gallery*
(London, 1993)

WILLIAM ROTHENSTEIN, *Men and Memories* (London, 1932)

JOHN RUSKIN, *The Stones of Venice* (London, 1851)

S

LADY ST HELIER, *Memories of Fifty Years* (London, 1909)

ANDREW SAINT, *Richard Norman Shaw* (New Haven and London, 1976)

SIEGFRIED SASSOON, *The Old Century: Weald of Youth* (London, 1938)

KITTY SHANNON, *For My Children* (London, 1933)

ZUZANNA SHONFIELD, *The Precariously Privileged: A Professional Family in Victorian London* (Oxford, 1987)

ROBIN SIMON (ed.), 'Frederic, Lord Leighton, 1830–1896 and Leighton House: A Centenary Celebration', *Apollo* (London, 1996)

GEORGE SMALLEY *London Letters*, 2 vols (London, 1890)

SUSAN WEBER SOROS, *The Secular Furniture of E.W. Godwin* (New Haven and London, 1999)

F.G. STEPHENS, *Artists at Home* (London, 1884)

ROBERT LOUIS STEVENSON, *The Wrong Box* (London, 1889)

A.M.W. STIRLING, *William De Morgan and his Wife* (London, 1922)

A.M.W. STIRLING, *Life's Little Day: Some tales and other reminiscences* (London, 1924)

GLADYS STOREY, *All Sorts of People* (London, 1929)

VIRGINIA SURTEES, 'A Conversation Piece at Blackfriars', *Apollo*, vol. 97 (February 1973)

VIRGINIA SURTEES (ed.), *The Diaries of George Price Boyce* (Norwich, 1980)

VIRGINIA SURTEES (ed.), *The Diary of Ford Madox Brown* (New Haven and London, 1981)

VIRGINIA SURTEES, *The Artist and the Autocrat: George and Rosalind Howard, Earl and Countess of Carlisle* (Salisbury, 1988)

VIRGINIA SURTEES, *Coutts Lindsay 1824–1913* (Norwich, 1993)

Survey of London, vol.38: *The Museums Area of South Kensington and Westminster* (London, 1975)

Survey of London, vol.42: *Southern Kensington: Kensington Square to Earl's Court* (London, 1986)

Survey of London, vol.45: *Knightsbridge* (London, 2000)

VERN SWANSON, *The Biography and Catalogue Raisonné of the Paintings of Sir Lawrence Alma-Tadema* (London, 1990)

JOHN L. SWEENEY (ed.), *The Painter's Eye* (London, 1956)

T

DAVID A. TAYLOR, 'The Dadocracy and other humorous reactions to "Aesthetic" interior decoration', in *Christopher Dresser in Context, Decorative Arts Society Journal* no. 29 (London, 2005)

INA TAYLOR, *Victorian Sisters* (London, 1987)

UNA TAYLOR, *Guests and Memories: Annals of a Seaside Villa* (Oxford, 1924)

WARD THORON (ed.), *The Letters of Mrs Henry Adams, 1865–1883* (Boston, 1936)

RACHEL TRETHEWEY, *Mistress of the Arts: The Passionate Life of Georgina, Duchess of Bedford* (London, 2002)

JULIAN TREUHERZ, 'Alma-Tadema, aesthete, architect and interior designer', in *Sir Lawrence Alma-Tadema*, ed. Edwin Becker (exh. cat., Van Gogh Museum, Amsterdam, and Walker Art Gallery, Liverpool, 1996)

RALEIGH TREVELYAN, *A Pre-Raphaelite Circle* (London, 1978)

W

CLIVE WAINWRIGHT, 'The Making of the South Kensington Museum', parts I–IV, *Journal of the History of Collections*, vol.14, no.1 (2002), pp.3–78

GILES WALKLEY, *Artists' Houses in London, 1764–1914* (Aldershot, 1994)

FRANCES, COUNTESS OF WARWICK, *Life's Ebb and Flow* (London, 1929)

ELLIS WATERHOUSE, 'Holman Hunt's "Giovanni Bellini" and the Pre-Raphaelites' own early Italian pictures', *Burlington Magazine*, vol.123, no.941 (August 1981), pp.473–7

GAIL S. WEINBERG, 'D.G. Rossetti's ownership of Botticelli's "Smeralda Brandini"', *Burlington Magazine*, vol.146, no.1210 (January 2004), pp.20–26

MICHAEL WENTWORTH, *James Tissot* (Oxford, 1984)

J. McNEILL WHISTLER, *The Gentle Art of Making Enemies* (New York, 1890)

JAMES WHITALL, *English Years* (London, 1936)

CAROLINE WHITE, *Sweet Hampstead* (London, 1901)

MICHAEL WHITEWAY (ed.), *Christopher Dresser: A Design Revolution* (exh. cat., Cooper-Hewitt, National Design Museum, New York, and Victoria and Albert Museum, London, 2004)

SCOTT WILCOX, 'Landscape in the Watercolor Societies', in *Victorian Landscape Watercolors: The Persistence of a British Tradition* (exh. cat., Yale Center for British Art, New Haven, Cleveland Museum of Art, OH, and Birmingham Museums and Art Gallery, 1992), pp.41–52

TIMOTHY WILCOX, 'The Aesthete Expunged', *Journal of the History of Collections*, vol.5, no.1 (1993), pp. 43–57

ISABELLE WILLIAMS, 'Re-thinking the Legend: Georgiana Burne-Jones and William Morris', *Review of the Pre-Raphaelite Society*, vol.4, no.1 (spring 1996), pp.1–12

JEAN MOORCROFT WILSON, *Siegfried Sassoon: The Making of a War Poet* (London, 1998)

Z

HELEN ZIMMERN, 'Alma-Tadema, His House and Studio', *Art Journal Special Number* (1886)

Picture Credits

© Annan Collection of Old Photographs: pl.45

Ashmolean Museum, University of Oxford, UK / Bridgeman: pl.137

Bateman's, Burwash, East Sussex, UK / National Trust Photographic Library /
    John Hammond / Bridgeman: pl.178

© Birmingham Museums and Art Gallery: pl.138

© Blackburn Museum and Art Gallery, Lancashire, UK / Bridgeman: pl.34

Bridgeman: pl.170

© Trustees of the British Museum: pls 20, 81, 82, 140

© Carlisle Art Gallery / Photo: Guy Pawle: pl.22

Photo © Christie's Images / Bridgeman: pl.200

Cincinnati Art Museum, Gift of Henry M. Goodyear, M.D.: pl.194

Cooper-Hewitt, National Design Museum, Smithsonian Institution, Thaw Collection,
    2007-27-72: pl.192

© Crown copyright. National Monuments Record: pls 13, 181, 182, 211, 212, 213

The De Morgan Centre, London / Bridgeman: pl.170

The Fine Art Society, London, UK / Bridgeman: pl.204

Fitzwilliam Museum, University of Cambridge, UK / Bridgeman: pl.147

By kind permission of the Trustees of the Geffrye Museum: pl.79

Photo by Erik Gould, Courtesy of the Museum of Art, Rhode Island School of Design,
    Providence, Rhode Island: pl.196

Guildhall Art Gallery, City of London / Bridgeman: pls 46, 84, 85, 141

Hampstead Museum / Burgh House: pl.205

Harris Museum and Art Gallery, Preston, Lancashire, UK / Bridgeman: pl.78

Kelmscott Manor, Oxfordshire, UK / Bridgeman: pl.68

Leeds Museums and Galleries (City Art Gallery) UK / Bridgeman: pl.63

Leighton House Museum, Royal Borough of Kensington and Chelsea: pls 5, 6, 47, 58, 101,
    102, 128, 130, 131, 135

Collection: Lord Lloyd Webber: pl.76

© Mallett Gallery, London / Bridgeman: pl.74

National Gallery of Art, Washington DC, USA / Bridgeman: pls 2, 201

Photo © National Gallery of Canada: pl.119

© National Portrait Gallery, London: pls 14, 15, 21, 24, 26, 89, 90, 91, 92, 121, 136, 161,
    172, 183

The Nelson-Atkins Museum of Art, Kansas City, Missouri. Bequest of Milton McGreevy,
    81-30 / 86: pl.191

Private Collection / Photo © Christie's Images / Bridgeman: frontispiece, pls 80, 195

Private Collection: pls 25, 96, 109, 117, 129, 162, 163, 166, 171, 189

Private Collection / © Mallett Gallery, London / Bridgeman: pls 33, 73

Private Collection / © Pope Family Trust / Bridgeman: pl.69

Private Collection / Photo © Bonhams, London / Bridgeman: pl.77

Private Collection / Bridgeman: pl.83

Rhode Island School of Design / Bridgeman: pl.199

© RIBA Library Drawings Collection: pls 7, 93, 97, 98, 99, 100, 132

© RIBA Library Photographs Collection: pl.214

© Royal Academy of Arts, London: pl.190

© Royal Academy of Arts, London / Photographer: John Hammond: pls 49, 193

© Royal Academy of Arts, London / Photographer: Prudence Cuming Associates Ltd:
    pls 50, 51, 52, 53, 206

Royal Borough of Kensington and Chelsea Libraries: pls 59, 118, 158, 165t

Russell-Cotes Art Gallery and Museum, Bournemouth, UK / Bridgeman: pl.112

© Tate, London 2008: pls 17, 19, 23, 169, 209, 210

Galleria degli Uffizi, Florence, Italy / Bridgeman: pl.10

© V&A Images: pls 18, 28, 29, 30, 31, 32, 35, 36, 37, 38, 39, 41, 48, 54, 55, 56, 62, 64, 66, 67,
    70, 75, 88, 94, 95, 104, 105, 106, 107, 108, 110, 111, 113, 114, 116, 125, 127, 133, 134, 142,
    144, 145, 148, 149, 151, 155, 156, 157, 159, 164, 168, 173, 175, 177, 179, 180, 186, 188,
    197, 198, 207

© Trustees of the Watts Gallery, Compton, Surrey, UK / Bridgeman: pls 120, 122, 124

Photo courtesy of Michael Whiteway: pl.87

Index   Numbers in italic refer to illustrations.